MAKING
AND
MASTERING
WOOD PLANES

David Finck

STERLING PUBLISHING CO., INC.
NEW YORK

Library of Congress Cataloging-in-Publication Data

Finck, David, 1961-

Making and mastering wood planes / David Finck.

p. cm.

ISBN 0-8069-6163-5

1. Planes (Hand tools) 2. Woodwork. I. Title

TT186. F544 2000

684'.082--dc21

10   9   8   7   6   5   4   3   2   1

Published by Sterling Publishing Co., Inc.

387 Park Avenue South, New York, NY 10016

© 2005 by David Finck

Distributed in Canada by Sterling Publishing

c/o Canadian Manda Group, 165 Dufferin Street

Toronto, Ontario, Canada M6K 3H6

Distributed in Great Britain by Chrysalis Books Group PLC

The Chrysalis Building, Bramley Road, London W10 6SP, England

Distributed in Australia by Capricorn Link (Australia) Pty. Ltd.

P.O. Box 704, Windsor, NSW 2756, Australia

Printed in China

Sterling ISBN 1-4027-2022-X

For information about custom editions, special sales, premium and corporate purchases, please contact Sterling Special Sales Department at 800-805-5489 or specialsales@sterlingpub.com.

Chris Swirnoff Design   •   Editor: Michael Cea

ACKNOWLEDGMENTS

There would be no book without James Krenov. The planes described and illustrated in the following pages were inspired by him. To him and all the teachers and students in the College of the Redwoods Fine Woodworking Program, my profoundest thanks. Most of what I know about planes and woodworking was learned there. I hope I've done justice to the subject of planes and Jim's spirit toward woodworking.

After leading numerous workshops on plane-making over the years, it is clear that I am deeply indebted to my students. I thank them all for the insights that come from questioning the "obvious" and demanding greater clarity of presentation.

I'd like to express my gratitude and love for the grandfather I never knew, my namesake. He started my father working with wood—and it is my father who then inspired me. And to Paula, my mother, who nurtured the artist in all her children, and then, as a business partner, nurtured my

career. Also to my sisters Amy and Tina, partners in childhood arts and crafts adventures, who always set the bar way over my head.

More thanks for the invaluable efforts of those who reviewed my manuscript: good friends David Esposito and Bojan Petek, Tina Casey (my sister), James Krenov, Marie Hoepfl (my wife), and especially Henry Finck (my father). Through their efforts this book was much improved.

To my wife, Marie, and two young daughters Ledah and Willa: It has been a long and rather lonely road. I have missed you! As I write these words, I look forward to more time spent with all of you and less time in front of a computer.

Finally, I dedicate this book to my father, Henry Finck. He has taught by example from my earliest years that a job worth doing is worth doing well. He has been a limitless source of knowledge and support, and an inspiration in so many ways. It is a debt that cannot be repaid. I can only hope to pass the gift along.

◈

Contents

CHAPTER FIVE

Planing Techniques ◆ 125

CHAPTER SIX

Planing Aids and Special Techniques ◆ 151

CHAPTER SEVEN

Scraping Techniques ◆ 167

Foreword

by James Krenov

The way that some of us work includes our emotions, our hopes, all the feelings that we have. In cabinetmaking, there are different ways of leaving one's spirit—or one's feeling about the material—in the completed object. All these processes involve an intimacy—a closeness to the wood, a closeness to the tools—and an awareness of what you're doing, of the possibilities and the limitations of the tools, and of your skills.

Certain tools that we use are classics; they have been around as long as woodworking —the chisel, the spokeshave, and certainly the plane are some. A long time ago, when I went to school, we had the classic European hand plane, which was made of pearwood with a lignum vitae sole. It had a long iron, a big, tall knob in the back, and a horn in the front. Now, it was a good plane, and people around me were using it and there was nothing that they found wrong with it. Certainly, if well cared for and properly used, they were, are, and will continue to be fine tools, just as a very fine-tuned metal plane can be. But I found the classical knob and horn plane very limiting, because you could only comfortably hold it in one way, and it wasn't very good for small work. So, just out of curiosity I made this small plane. That was about fifty years ago. Many readers and people working with wood are familiar with it; it sort of assumed my name, which is all wrong, because I didn't invent anything. I just changed the shape and size of a plane that was already made, used a shorter iron, and made the whole thing very comfortable and very versatile. You could hold it with two hands, you could hold it with one, you could do large-scale work, and you could do very fine details.

I think it's very important that you be patient and thorough. Let the first plane you make be a reasonable success. When we make something and we do not succeed, then we're not very likely to continue to make a second and a third. It's like making a guitar that has no tone, or a very bad tone. You put it up on a wall and you say, "Well, I made a guitar but it's not worth playing, so I don't think I'll make any more guitars; I'll buy one instead." Well, these very personal hand planes, as far as I know, can't be bought, and you probably shouldn't try. You should enjoy the making of them, and let some of that enjoyment give you energy to use them properly, and make a second and a third. Different sizes, different shapes.

Really, my simple message is that if you're going to approach woodworking with sensitivity and maybe refinement, planes are a good way to begin. They're a start to improving the rest of your tools that need improving. After all, the hand plane is the first part of the woodworker's aria. And what I'd like to see happen, through this book that David has written, is for you to make a plane or planes that will, in turn, make fine music.

Introduction

The distinctions between an object that is merely "crafted" and one that is *"finely crafted"* become apparent some time after the hum of the power tools has faded away. Think of power tools as apprentices that handle the drudgery that would otherwise sap the energies required for more refined work. For example, they excel at turning rough lumber into dimensioned stock. The magic happens at the workbench, though, with the use of hand tools. It comes down to wanting to go beyond the ordinary. Among all hand tools, few can take one farther than a good plane.

Swift strokes from a hand plane transform a machined surface to silky smoothness. Planes can join boards seamlessly and flatten any size surface. They polish end grain quickly and beautifully, trim boards to width and length, and can be used to fit the components in various joints, drawers, doors, and lids—all with a highly satisfying level of accuracy. Of course, power tools are commonly used for all these ordinary tasks, but with predictably ordinary results. Hand planes can elevate your efforts to a new level of craftsmanship.

There is another compelling side to hand planes. For many, woodworking is not about rushing to get things done. Perhaps you are drawn by the romance of working with wood. Maybe you have

Author David Finck

yet to even lift a plane or turn a plank. Your mind paints images of a lone craftsman planing heaps of gossamer-thin shavings, at one with the wood. Hold on to that vision, for it is surprisingly accessible.

But, likely as not, you have tried your hand at planing, and the romance has dwindled. Instead of shavings, frustrations have piled one atop another. You find sharpening plane irons to be tricky and time-consuming, and are uncertain if the blade is sharp enough. Setting the depth of cut is a tedious procedure that often produces inaccurate and unpredictable results, and the depth of cut is often altered when you can least afford it. It seems that the plane will make only thick shavings or none at all. Surfaces meant to be smooth have digs and ridges, and squaring an edge is all but impossible. The plane feels heavy and clumsy. And then, when everything is adjusted properly, the blade becomes dull after a few minutes' work. This means the entire procedure has to be started over again. Eventually the plane is placed back on the wall rack, where it collects dust with cruel irony.

But using hand planes does not have to be so frustrating. Shop-made wooden hand planes can revive that romantic vision. Few metal, factory-made planes can rival the performance of those made out of wood in your own shop. Wooden planes can accommodate extra-thick blades of superior tool steel that simplify sharpening and stay sharp longer. The blade is adjusted with a wedge-and-hammer system that is slop-free, extremely precise, and holds the setting tenaciously. The plane can have the smallest possible throat opening (the gap where shavings enter the body of the plane), greatly enhancing its performance on figured woods like curly or bird's-eye maple.

Additionally, these shop-made wooden planes are shaped for the comfort of your own hands. These simple shapes can be held several ways—which is very helpful for different planing tasks. In all, planing with a well-made wooden plane is a very pleasant experience.

With the information supplied in Chapter 4, it should take you a day and a half to make your first plane. With some practice, making a plane will take only a few hours. In short order, you can create a collection of planes impossible to duplicate with factory planes, on the basis of performance or cost. Specialized planes can also be made that expand your capability for work beyond ordinary tasks.

With the plane in hand, the obvious next step is learning to use it accurately and efficiently. Chapter 5 discusses proper techniques. However, experience also plays an important role. You will develop sensitivities which amount to an ongoing conversation between you, the plane, and the material being planed by monitoring the shavings flowing from the plane, listening for telltale sounds, and lightly brushing fingertips over the surface. It soon becomes second nature to respond to these cues. Sometimes this will mean simply tapping with the hammer to produce lacy shavings that will shoot through the plane. There are subtleties to attend to along the way: when to sharpen the blade iron and when to stop sharpening it; how much to arc the blade for polish-planing; setting the blade precisely; and what to listen for when tightening the wedge. These tuning and sharpen-

ing skills are discussed in Chapters 2 and 3. You also need to know when to use specific planes, and should have an arsenal of techniques to meet the various challenges that typically arise.

Don't expect to master it all overnight—it takes practice. It's like learning the guitar: at first it's a mystery and your fingertips ache from pressing the strings, but soon you learn a few chords and your fingertips toughen. Woody Guthrie said he could play any song using just three chords. Planing is like that too: learn the basics and you will be amazed by how much can be accomplished.

Odd as it may seem, a book on hand planes is incomplete if cabinet scrapers are neglected. Scrapers, which are discussed in Chapter 7, are part of the plane family. Although overshadowed by the hand plane, they have their own unique and important qualities. Chief among these is their ability to quickly smooth nearly *any* wood, no matter how wild the figure. Scrapers can take tissue-thin shavings and leave a surface ready for sanding with finest-grit sandpaper. Stock is removed more quickly than by hand-sanding, and with considerably less dust and more accuracy than when a portable sander is used. Thus, whether you are confronted by an entire tabletop of impossible-to-plane wood, or merely need to repair a small blemished area, scrapers are the solution to the problem.

In writing this book I offer up the information gleaned from my teachers, from my own endeavors, and from working with students, in as richly detailed a form as I can muster. I hope that makes the difference between things working out or not, or between things working very well or merely working. But there is a danger of over-burdening the reader with information to the point of distraction. I suggest that the different chapters be studied one at a time. Reread the sections you are unfamiliar with, try the techniques or procedures, and then read the text again to verify that everything has been done properly.

Without an experienced observer looking over your shoulder, you must be your own observer—a difficult task.

I have kept assumptions that the reader has an advanced knowledge of planes to a minimum, to help ensure the success of those with limited experience. In fact, the process of plane-making serves as an elegant framework for teaching many of the fundamentals of fine woodworking. It is also a vehicle for illuminating many of the little "tricks" that help yield clean and accurate work. To preserve the flow of the process, and prevent the more experienced among you from being bogged down, most of the ancillary information appears in boxes separate from the main text.

My sincerest hope is that the information that follows will be a bridge to a way of working that gives you great satisfaction, while positively influencing the quality of the work. With increased reliance on planes, you will also enjoy a quieter, safer, and cleaner shop. I do not mean to say that this approach is for everyone, but nearly anyone willing to try can have great success making and using planes. I hope to leave you brimming with the confidence to handle the numerous tasks that planes excel at and to get you started on amassing a collection of the finest planes available: the ones you make yourself!

David Finck

Ledah, age 3¹/₂, planing a cherry tabletop.

CHAPTER ONE

Tools and Materials for Making A Plane

This section can be broken down into two parts. The first contains lists of the basic tools used to make a wooden plane. Just the basic hand tools—those common to almost any woodworker's shop—are needed. However, elementary power tools are also very helpful for preparing the plane blank. Though it is quite possible to make a plane with fewer tools than those listed below, you may at times need assistance from a better outfitted woodworking friend. If you plan to purchase hand tools, refer to Chapter 2 for guidelines.

The second part contains information on selecting and/or making the plane components: the plane blank, the iron, and the chip breaker.

TOOLS

Hand Tools (1–1 to 1–4)

- Block plane
- Small hammer (2 or 3 ounces). Chapter 4 shows how to make one.
- Fine-tooth hobby razor or dovetail saw
- Marking and/or carving knife
- $1/2$-inch chisel
- 8- or 10-inch mill bastard or smooth file, preferably with one "safe" (free-of-teeth) edge
- File card with short metal bristles on one side and stiff plastic bristles on the other

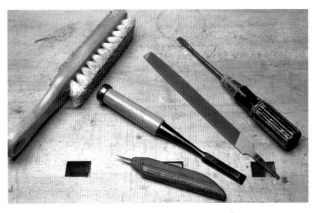

1–1. Hammer, block plane, and fine-tooth saw.

1–2. Shown here are a file card, knife, $1/2$-inch chisel, smooth file, and screwdriver.

- Slot-type screwdriver
- 6- or 12-inch combination square
- Pencil
- Straightedge (preferably 18 inches)
- Protractor
- Sharpening stones (800- and 6,000- or 8,000-grit water stones)
- Clamps (six to eight quick-action screw clamps, or something similar)
- Slow-speed grinder (hand-cranked or 800 to 1,800 rpm-powered)

1–3. Pencil, protractor, and 6-inch combination square, resting on an 18-inch straightedge.

1–4. 800- and 8,000-grit water stones with a nagura, a synthetic stone used to clean the surface of the 8,000-grit stone and create a slurry that speeds sharpening.

Optional Hand Tools

- Spokeshaves (flat- and curve-bottomed)
- Cabinet scraper and burnisher
- Lapping plate (glass or steel plate used with either diamond or Carborundum powders; it is used for flattening the iron)

Power Tools

- Jointer (four inches or larger). Refer to page 24.
- Planer. Refer to page 24.
- Band saw (14 inches or larger). Refer to pages 17 to 21.
- Drill press
- Router (with $5/16$-inch straight bit and template bushing) (1–5)

1–5. Router, straight bit, and template bushing.

SAFETY EQUIPMENT

- Eye and ear protection

MAKING A PLANE BLANK

Plane-Blank Material

Recommending wood for a plane blank is not as simple as mentioning oak, ash, hard maple, or beech. Any of these is *likely* to be a good choice, but there may be enough variation within any species to make one particular plank less desirable than another. Durability and stability are the basic criteria. Maple and beech are fairly consistent and often make good choices for a first plane. Carefully scrutinize your choice of oak or ash. Look at the end grain: closely packed growth rings may indicate denser wood with better wear qualities. Pecan, hickory, mulberry, and Osage orange are other domestic hardwoods that have been used successfully. Finally, choose wood that is free of defects like checks or knots. Both indicate a loss of strength and stability.

Walnut or cherry work well for larger planes, but are too light for smaller planes. These woods wear rapidly and will need a sole—a complete covering for the bottom of the plane—of a harder wood, if the plane will be used regularly. Alternatively, you may inlay a small wear plate, "an insert," just ahead of the throat opening, where most wear occurs (1–6). With that said, I *have* come across walnut and cherry planks that had exceptional density. They would have made fine planes of any size.

1–6. Foreground: maple plane with an iron-bark insert. Background: round-bottom maple plane with a coco-bolo sole.

I do not encourage the use of woods associated with ecological degradation, but if you already have a stash, tropical hardwoods do make beautiful planes. These hardwoods include so-called "rosewoods" (not always of the genus *Dalbergia*), bubinga, coco bolo (a true rosewood), goncalo alves, and others. Many of the recently available "alternative" woods—lesser-known rain-forest species—are also good picks. Typically these choices share such

1–7. Resawn plane blank (hard maple) showing cheeks and midsection.

desirable features as high density, durability, fine grain, and an inherent waxiness that lends added slickness to the plane bottoms. Experiment with different species. If the density is there, usually the plane will wear well; if it doesn't, a retrofitted insert resuscitates the plane.

The method for making planes described in this book will influence material selection. Planes made via this method are a glued-up assemblage. In a nutshell, a block of wood is sawn into three sections, yielding two thin cheeks and a thick midsection (1–7). The midsection is partitioned, yielding front and back blocks with angled ramps. The back block is routed for a clearance slot for the cap screw, and a cross-pin is made and installed, as discussed in the following pages. Finally, all the components are reglued. A well-made plane may look as if it were carved from a solid block of wood.

For a unified look, then, it is better to make the plane from a thick chunk of wood (1–8). This may present a difficulty since most planes shaped beyond a simple rectangle require stock thicker than two inches, which can be difficult to come by.

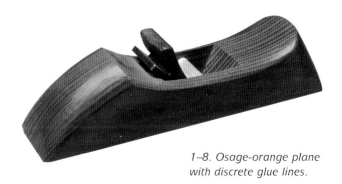

1–8. Osage-orange plane with discrete glue lines.

Some better-stocked lumberyards or hardwood dealers carry 2$\frac{1}{2}$- or 3-inch-thick, rough-sawn stock (often indicated as 10/4 or 12/4), which is ideal. You may find 3 x 3 x 30-inch "furniture squares" intended for table legs. Structurally, laminating a plane blank from readily obtainable 1-inch (4/4) stock is a perfectly viable alternative and likely yields the most stable blank.

The firewood pile may be a good source of wood if you have the patience for both finding a suitable piece of wood and then drying it. Consider visiting a sawmill for another source of green wood. Sawmills usually have four-inch-square, or larger, stock for stacking piles of lumber. You may also be able to intercept a very nice billet of wood considered too short for use in the sawmill. Take care not to become a nuisance at a sawmill. Most are set up only for wholesaling tractor-trailer-sized loads of wood. A polite inquiry never hurts, though.

Preparing a Plane Blank

The information in this section describes how to prepare a plane blank from *dry*, 2$\frac{1}{2}$-inch stock. The section Alternative Plane Blanks on pages 26 and 27 contains information on preparing a plane blank from firewood chunks; this includes how to handle green wood and laminate a plane blank.

Plane Length

Chapter 4 offers suggestions for lengths and widths of various types of plane. A multi-purpose 12-inch-long jack plane with a 1$\frac{3}{4}$-inch-wide iron is a good beginning plane to make. When determining the size of the plane blank, add 1 inch to the 12-inch length of the plane. This extra inch will ultimately be trimmed to remove dowel-positioning pins located at the ends. Some jointers and planers "snipe" (remove an excessive amount of wood at the beginning and/or end of the cut). If this condition cannot be corrected, add the amount sniped to the length of the plane blank (typically two to three inches per end). Once you can plane confi-

dently, additions for snipe can be left off because the blank can be cleaned up readily by hand. Crosscut the plank to length using a handsaw, radial arm saw, chop saw, or carpenter's circular saw (1–9 and 1–10).

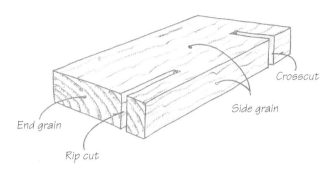

1–9. A crosscut is made perpendicular to the grain of the wood. A rip cut is made with the grain.

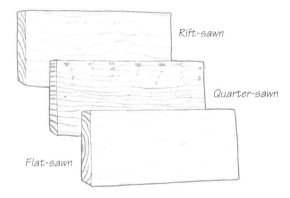

1–10. Flat-sawn, quarter-sawn, and rift-sawn grain patterns. The orientation of the growth rings, with respect to the face (the widest surface) of the board, determines the type of cut that was made. Flat-sawn wood has been sawn approximately tangent to the growth rings. Quarter-sawn wood has been sawn perpendicular to the growth rings. Rift-sawn wood displays growth rings at approximately 45 degrees to the wide face of the board.

Plane Width

A rough block is sawn oversized and then resawn into the three basic parts of the plane blank. After the wood has "settled"—that is, is given a period of time to allow internal tensions to equalize—the rough-sawn parts are milled to final dimensions. To determine the minimum necessary width of the rough blank, add the following: the width of the plane iron (typically $1^1/4$ to 2 inches) plus $3/16$ inch, yielding the width of the midsection. Add $7/16$ inch for each cheek, for a total of $7/8$ inch. Then add *twice* the width of the saw kerf (the width of the saw cut, determined by the thickness of the blade plus the set of the teeth), which usually totals $1/8$ to $1/4$ inch. Finally, add an additional $1/8$ inch for squaring up the blank (1–11).

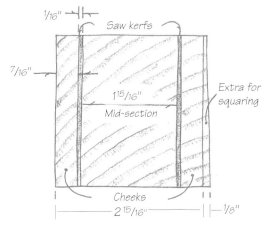

1–11. *An end view of a rough-sawn plane blank showing the cheeks and saw kerfs and its dimensions. The midsection is sized for a $1^3/4$-inch-wide plane iron.*

For example, if you are resawing with a band saw and the plane will have a $1^3/4$-inch-wide iron, figure the final width of the blank as follows:

Midsection: $1^3/4$ + $3/16$ inch = $1^{15}/16$ inches
Cheeks (2): $7/16$ inch x 2 = $7/8$ inch
Saw kerfs (2): $1/16$ inch x 2 = $1/8$ inch
Extra for squaring up = $1/8$ inch
Total: = $3^1/16$ inches

If resawing with a table saw, measure the thickness of the saw kerf and substitute that figure.

Resawing the Plane Blank

I highly recommend the band saw for resawing the plane blank (1–12). For many woodworkers, the band saw is relegated to curved work, even though band saws truly excel at straight-line ripping. They have important advantages over the table saw, typ-

1–12. *A band saw is a useful tool for making planes.*

ically the tool chosen for ripping. Band saws are safer. There is no opportunity for dangerous kickback, because the force of the cut pushes the wood down onto the table rather than back toward the operator. Band saws are more economical because the thinner saw kerf saves wood with every cut. They also have the capacity to saw considerably thicker stock: 6 inches or more for the typical small-shop band saw, versus $3^1/2$ inches or less for the typical 10-inch table saw.

The performance of a band saw suffers more dramatically than that of a table saw, though, if it is not set up and maintained properly. Tires must be trued, crowned, and kept clean. Using a sharp blade of the right type and tensioning the blade

Continued on page 23

Band-Saw Pointers

Use sharp ¹/₂-inch-wide, 4 teeth-per-inch (TPI) wood-cutting blades. Hook-tooth blades cut faster and rougher, and skip-tooth blades cut smoother and more slowly. Skip/hook-tooth blades (sometimes called "furniture bands") are a hybrid that I prefer, combining adequate speed with a smooth cut (1–13).

1–13. Evaluating blade-weld alignment.

Critically examine the blade weld. The sides should be smooth and free of lumps. Check that the blade was properly aligned when welded by gauging the back edge of the blade with a six-inch straightedge; it should present a straight line (1–13). Faulty welds are fairly common and seriously undermine the performance of the saw. The blade may bump and shudder each time it contacts the thrust guide. A lump in the weld may prevent the side-mounted guides from being spaced closely enough to support the blade adequately. Keep blades and tires free of gummy deposits and sawdust. Scrub them off with the metal bristles of a file card at the first sign of buildup.

Set the upper and lower saw guides precisely. Arrange them as close as possible to the blade without rubbing it. The side-mounted guides are positioned just behind the gullets (the arcing gaps separating each tooth) of the blade (1–14). The guides on the back of the band saw, the thrust guides, contact the blade as soon as sawing commences.

Tensioning the blade correctly dramatically improves the quality of cut. Unplug the saw and remove

1–14. Properly adjusted guides on a band saw.

the upper wheel cover. Tension the blade while slowly rotating the wheel by hand to stretch the blade evenly. Occasionally twang the free section of the blade (the portion unencumbered by guides) and note the increase in pitch. It goes from a rattle to a very low but discernible tone and proceeds to climb in pitch with increases in tension. Best results usually come with the blade tensioned to a clear, musical tone. Spin the wheel a turn or two to see if the blade is tracking in the center of the tire, adjust the blade if necessary, and reinstall the wheel cover.

If the wheels have been trued and crowned and the saw is running smoothly, the tension can be fine-tuned with the saw running. Bring the upper guide post down low to the table to provide maximum protection from the blade. Loosen the upper and lower guides so that they are well away from the blade. Turn on the saw and observe the blade, assisted by bright lighting and a white background. If the tension is correct, the blade will appear sharply in focus with no trace of flutter. The blade looks blurry if it's vibrating.

Try altering the blade tension in very small increments while the saw is running. Be careful! Keep well away from the blade while making the adjustments and pay attention to where the blade is tracking. As the tension is increased, the blade creeps forward on the tire, and as it

Band-Saw Pointers (continued)

is decreased, the blade creeps back. Carefully alter the tracking adjustment while tensioning the blade to keep it in the center of the tire. Scrutinize the blade after each adjustment.

When the flutter is gone, stop the saw, note the position of the pointer on the tension scale (if the saw has one) for future reference, and twang the blade once again to get an idea of the amount of tension on the blade. If the saw is less than an industial-quality machine, consider relieving the blade tension when it is not in use to save wear on the bearings and castings. As a pertinent aside, remember, when a blade breaks or hops off the wheel, a loud bang ensues from the release of spring tension on the upper wheel (provided by the blade and the spring on the upper wheel assembly). When this happens, cut the power immediately. Then step back and wait for both wheels to coast to a stop.

BAND-SAW CHECKUP

Properly trued and crowned tires and a saw free from excessive vibration critically impact the saw's performance. These points are easy to check, as described below. Corrective measures are not difficult, but go beyond the scope of this book. For more information on tuning band saws, refer to Mark Duginske's *Band Saw Handbook*.

Trueness and Crown

Every point where the blade contacts the perimeter of the tires must be the same distance from the axis of the wheels. If not, the tire is "out of true" and the blade will undergo changes in tension, resulting in potentially excessive vibration.

"Crown" is the convex arc across the width of the tire. Lacking sufficient crown, the blade will not track properly, wandering on the face of the tire, even hopping off completely.

Checking Tire Trueness

Unplug the saw and remove the wheel covers and the blade. Use the guide post, the table, or some other convenient part of the saw to steady a stick, and hold its end about $1/32$ inch from the surface of the tire, where the blade would normally ride. Spin the wheel slowly by hand and observe the gap between the tire and stick (1–15). If the width of the gap holds steady, the wheel is true; if it fluctuates, the tire is out of true. Check both tires.

Checking Tire Crown

Place a six-inch ruler on edge, across the width of the tire. Rocking the ruler end to end should reveal a nicely rounded arc. With the ruler centered on the high point of this arc, there should be about $1/16$ inch of space between the edges of the tire and the edge of the ruler (1–16).

1–15. Checking the circumference of a band-saw tire for trueness.

1–16. Evaluating the amount of tire crown.

VIBRATION

Excessive vibration results in rough and wandering cuts. To check for vibration, with the saw running, lay a small wrench near the edge of the table. It should remain there quietly without moving. Any rattling or motion betrays excessive vibration. By systematically isolating portions of the drive system, vibration sources can be isolated and rectified.

A band saw in top shape will still cut poorly when used improperly. Particular attention must be paid to the "drift angle" and the fence. Each is discussed below.

DRIFT

Rip-sawing requires the use of a fence to guide the cut, or the wavering cuts that ensue will waste a significant amount of wood. A band-saw fence must be adjustable in two modes: laterally, to accommodate different width cuts, and angularly, to account for "drift." The first is obvious enough, but what is "drift"?

It is a mistake to assume that a fence on a band saw can simply be oriented perpendicular to the front edge of the table to get proper rip cuts. That is rarely the case. Instead, if you freehand-saw a straight line parallel to the edge of a board, invariably the edge of the board will trend off of perpendicular. That is the "drift angle," and the fence must be clamped at that angle to ensure accuracy when resawing. If not, the board may either be dragged away from the fence as you saw, resulting in a tapered cut, or squeezed against the fence, causing the blade to distort and give a bad cut. The thicker the wood being sawn, the more pronounced the effect.

Determining Drift Angle

Prepare a piece of wood about 2 inches wide and about 18 inches long, one face and one long edge jointed flat and square to each other. Ideally, this stock should be the same species and thickness as the piece for the plane blank. The more critical the cut, the more closely the test piece should resemble the actual workpiece.

Assuming that the fence will be placed to the left of the blade, set an adjustable bevel gauge at about 100 degrees and clamp the blade so it is easily movable, but not floppy. Place the board on the table, jointed facedown and with the jointed edge on your right. Begin sawing, slow and steady, about ⅛ inch from the right edge.

The goal is to produce a cut that is parallel to the jointed edge. Often, you will waggle a bit until you hit upon the drift angle, allowing you to saw without wavering. When sawing on track for a few inches, stop and hold the stock down firmly to the table. Register the beam of the bevel gauge off the front edge of the table and bring the blade up against the jointed edge of the stock to gauge the drift angle (1–17). Set the bevel gauge aside without jostling it and complete the cut. Lock in the adjustment of the bevel gauge. If this is a frequently used type of saw blade, record the angle on the table or

1–17. Capturing the "drift angle" with a bevel gauge.

another handy surface for future reference. Be advised, however, that for critical sawing tasks it is always wise to determine drift angle for the particular blade and wood being used.

Most commercially available band-saw fences found on smaller saws are not readily adjustable for drift angle. This fact alone probably accounts for most woodworkers' disdain for ripping with the band saw, perhaps having used such a fence with predictably atrocious results. A simple remedy is to make your own fence that can be clamped on the table at the proper drift angle.

Making a Band-Saw Fence

First consider the saw table. The fence will be clamped at the front and back of the table. Is the edge of the table wide enough to clamp to? If not, consider bolting on 1 x 1½-inch rails of oak or hard maple for convenient, secure clamping. Drill and tap holes for ¼-inch bolts. Don't hesitate here if metalwork is out of your province; cast iron is easy to work. Make the holes in the rails oversized, allowing room to adjust the top of the rail perfectly flush to the tabletop.

The fence should be as long as the table is deep (including clamping rails if applicable). Using ¾-inch particleboard or high-quality plywood, such as Baltic birch, cut two pieces 3 inches wide and glue and screw them together to form a right angle (1-18). Reinforce these pieces by attaching three squares in a similar manner. Place the end squares sufficiently inboard to be out of the continued on next page

Rip-Sawing with a Band Saw *(continued)*

way of the clamps used for securing the fence to the table. Face one surface with plastic laminate for a slick, difficult-to-wear surface. Make sure the face of the fence is flat and check the fence for square (1–19). Shim the bottom with masking tape along one edge to adjust it if it is out of square.

Using a Band-Saw Fence

Whenever possible, clamp the fence to the left of the blade. This allows unrestricted access to the stock being sawn and the ability to move around the saw while maintaining contact with the stock and fence. Finishing the cut by *pulling* the stock from the back side is very helpful when sawing long stock or thin pieces that would otherwise require a push stick to complete the cut. Be certain the fence is square to the table and the table is square to the blade. The stock must also have

one face and edge squared and straightened, for referencing to the table and fence.

The teeth of the blade are alternately "set," or bent, to the left and right. Bring a tooth of the blade with the left hand "set" down on top of the rule at the proper measurement. Move the fence so that it's near the end of the ruler; then place the fence at the drift angle by using the bevel gauge referenced off the front of the table. Hold the ruler firmly to the table and slide the fence into contact while maintaining the drift angle—a degree or two of error is insignificant.

Apply clamps front and back. Quick-action screw clamps of the Jorgenson "pony" type can be manipulated so that they clamp without moving the fence. Place the fixed half of the clamp head on the fence, apply firm pressure down onto the table, slide the movable

half into contact from below, and tighten the clamp. Check the drift angle again and make alterations to both the drift angle and the width of cut by loosening either the front or back clamp and pivoting the fence. This procedure sounds laborious, but the entire process is done in seconds.

To make the rip cut, keep gentle pressure against the fence *in front of the blade*. When your fingers get three inches from the blade, shift the pressure against the fence to *behind* the blade and either use a push stick or pull the stock through from behind to complete the cut.

Sawing at the proper feed rate enhances the quality of cut. Sawing too quickly causes the blade to flutter, resulting in a rippled "washboard" surface. Sawing too slowly is simply inefficient and may cause you to tire and lose concentration. Avoid stopping and starting within a cut. If you must stop, maintain light pressure against the fence while shifting your hands.

1–18. A shop-made band-saw fence.

1–19. Checking the fence for square.

"Run-Out"

"Run-out" describes the angle at which the wood fibers intersect a particular surface of a board. It is a critical concept to grasp for machining and hand-planing, because it directly affects the quality of cut. If the fibers are parallel to the surface in question, then there is no run-out. If the fibers form an angle with that surface, then there is run-out (1–20). When there is no run-out it does not matter which end of the board you start machining from. If the board does have run-out, then it matters very much (1–21). The more run-out, or steeper the angle of the wood fibers to the surface in question, the more

it matters, because the likelihood for damage increases if the board is machined in the wrong direction.

In the classic example, the fur of a dog is smoothed when stroked from head to tail. Pet it from tail to head and the fur stands up and fights your hand. Likewise, if you plane or machine in the wrong direction, that is, "against the grain," wood fibers are torn off, marring the surface. This is called "tear-out."

Sometimes determining run-out is easy. At other times, it is more difficult. Look at the **adjoining** surface to figure the surface you are interested in. Note the difference between the wood fibers and the

grain pattern (the readily apparent contrasts of color in the wood). Sometimes, the fibers run counter to the larger grain pattern. If you see angled fibers, draw a bold diagonal line in the same direction on the surface you are looking at and on the opposite surface to indicate the presence and direction of run-out in that board (1–22). The second mark will save time and mistakes if the first is obliterated in subsequent machining.

1–22. Grain run-out direction of the bottom is marked with a diagonal line on the plane blank's side.

If you are not sure there is run-out, chances are it is minimal. Take a light pass over the jointer and look for tear-out; this will appear as rough patches when the board is observed at a low angle toward strong light. These rough spots are also easily felt with a gentle stroke of the fingertips over the length of the surface. Tear-out can also be heard as it occurs: there will be a sharp cracking sound instead of the sound of the board being smoothly cut. If the surface has been machined smoothly, draw the diagonal mark on the adjoining surface to indicate run-out direction. If there was tear-out, feed the board in the opposite direction; if the tear-out is removed, mark the board appropriately.

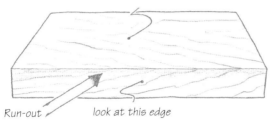

1–20. Determining grain run-out.

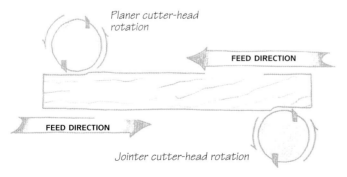

1–21. Run-out determines proper orientation of board feed when using a jointer or a planer to machine a board.

Continued from page 17

precisely are critical. Also, vibration must be kept to a minimum, and the blade guides properly set. If you have met with frustration attempting straight-line rip cuts on a band saw, doubtless the saw needs attention. Likewise, your technique may be off as well. Time invested in both goes well rewarded.

Selecting the Plane's Bottom

Choose a surface to become the bottom of the plane blank. Avoid any defects or areas of swirling or reversing grain that may machine poorly by placing these on the sides or top. I have noted no discernible difference in the performance of planes whether the growth rings (viewed from the end of the blank) are oriented perpendicular, parallel, or diagonally to the bottom.

Milling the Blank

With a jointer, flatten the bottom and joint one side square to it. Draw the reference marks shown in 1–23 to identify the squared edge and face. In the future, you'll know at a glance that these surfaces have been squared up. Also mark a sideways "V" on the end of the blank to graphically key the parts of the plane for easy assembly after resawing (1–24). Set the band saw for a $^7/_{16}$-inch cut and saw one

1–25. Ripping the first cheek of the plane blank.

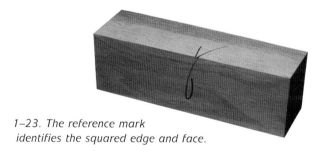

1–23. The reference mark identifies the squared edge and face.

1–24. The sideways "V" keys the plane blank for easy reassembly after resawing.

cheek (1–25). Adjust the fence to cut out the midsection ($1^{15}/_{16}$ inches for a $1^3/_4$-inch-wide iron) and saw it. If you prefer, the iron itself may be used as a spacer between the fence and blade. Then eyeball the additional $^3/_{16}$ inch, to set the fence. Reset the fence to $^7/_{16}$ inch using the first cheek as a spacer. Cut the second cheek. If the saw produces a lumpy surface, after each cut joint the side of the blank which will be against the fence for the next cut.

An alternative method requiring only one fence setting starts with an accurately sized and squared blank. The fence is set to the thickness of a cheek. Cut one cheek, rotate the blank end for end, and cut the other. Be sure that the midsection does not end up too narrow. To check, make shallow test kerfs for both cheeks at one end of the blank. The space between the kerfs delineates the midsection. Compare it to the plane iron's width.

If you are confident that the wood is dry, it is still a good idea to let the blank settle overnight to release internal tension. Allow air to circulate freely around each part. If the wood is not fully seasoned, tape the blank back together in its original arrangement and separated with $^1/_8$-inch spacers. Leave the blank for anywhere from a couple of days to a couple of weeks or months to dry. Drying time

The Logic of Truing Boards Using a Jointer and Planer

Usually the proper sequence for use of these machines is first the jointer, and then the planer. The jointer can true a face of a board, making it straight and free of twist. It can then true another surface at a right angle to the first. These are called "reference surfaces." They determine the accuracy of the completely milled stock. Always place the bowed side of a board down so it rests on its ends and can be milled without rocking as it passes over the jointer knives. If you are careful *not* to press out the bow, by keeping pressure at the ends rather than in the middle, the jointer will do its job. If the board is springy enough and you press it flat while making the cut, the surface will be smoothed, but not trued; it will simply return to its original bowed shape. The flattened face is held firmly against the fence for the next cut, to square and true the adjacent surface to the first.

Send a board through the planer with a trued surface down. The cutter heads above the board will produce a parallel surface, one that is as equally as flat and straight as the first. When the second jointed surface is run through the planer facedown, the result is a squared board; each surface is at 90 degrees to the adjacent ones. Bear in mind, if a board is much wider than it is thick, such as 1 inch by 4 inches or greater, the second narrow edge should not be trued with a planer, as it may be unstable while running through the machine. Instead, true it by ripping with a table saw or band saw, keeping the reference edge against the fence. Finish up the edge with a light pass on the jointer. The planer is generally *not* useful for truing a reference surface, because the powerful feed rollers temporarily flatten the board as it passes by the cutters, only to resume its original shape; as with an improperly used jointer, the board is smoothed but not necessarily trued.

---

depends on the species, how wet the wood was when resawn, and the ambient relative humidity of the shop. Giving the wood time to equilibrate and dry helps ensure flat stock after final dimensioning and, ultimately, a more stable plane body.

Orienting the Plane Blank

Determine the front end of the plane by considering the run-out direction. First, utilizing the "V" on the end of the blank, assemble the cheeks and midsection to their original relationship. The wood fibers of the plane body should slope downward from front to back, to reduce friction between the plane and the wood and guard against chipping the bottom of the plane while it is in use (1–26). Draw a cabinetmaker's triangle on the top to indicate the front and back (1–27). Think of it as an arrow with the tip pointing forward to indicate the front. Draw the points at the base of the triangle so that they meet the outer edges of the blank. When the blank

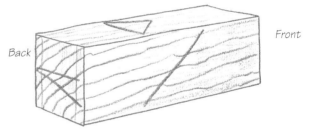

1–26. The diagonal mark on the plane blank shows grain run-out direction on the bottom of the plane.

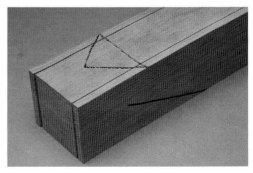

1–27. A cabinetmaker's triangle has been drawn on top of the plane blank.

Cabinetmaker's Triangle

This marking system is simple and useful. Whether building something as straightforward as a plane or as complicated as a large hutch, it is critically important as the work progresses, and during final assembly, to know which pieces should be positioned up, down, inside, outside, back, and front. What could be more frustrating than carefully dovetailing a corner only to find later that a drawer front has been fitted to a back, or some other part has been glued upside down or backwards?

When working in a vertical format— for example, on a cabinet with a top, bottom, and sides—think of the triangle as an arrow pointing up. The opposite sides, or the top and bottom, are placed together in proper orientation and the triangle is drawn across the parts with a tip of the triangle always pointing up (1–28). One convention must be established: the marks are always on the back edge. For horizontally oriented pieces like a box or drawer, think of the triangle as an arrow pointing to the front with the convention that the marks will always be on the top or the bottom edge; choose whichever one is more convenient and be consistent throughout. With more complicated scenarios, such as keeping track of parts for five drawers, each part of the triangle can be numbered. The first drawer would have all ones, the second all twos, and so on.

Should you get confused while becoming familiar with this system, simply reassemble the triangles. All the markings visible on the same plane and opposite parts create a complete triangle that points the same way when the pieces are oriented correctly. You will know instantly if that fateful cut will be made in the right place or not. As you gain familiarity, a quick glance at any one marking indicates exactly how that piece is oriented in the whole structure, showing whether it is an inside or outside surface, up or down, left or right, or front or back.

1–28. A cabinetmaker's triangle used to mark a frame, or the edges of a cabinet or box.

is disassembled, the triangle is a foolproof guide to proper reassembly for glue-up and other intermediate operations.

Final Milling

With the cheeks and midsection together in proper relation, mark the direction of run-out with a bold diagonal line across the bottom of the blank, to show at a glance the correct way to feed each part as you thickness them. If the cheeks and midsection stayed perfectly flat, mill each to their final thickness with the planer. The cheeks should be $5/16$ to $3/8$ inch thick. The midsection should be $1/16$ to $1/8$ inch wider than the plane iron being used. If not, smooth and flatten one side of each cheek with the jointer. Use push blocks for safety. Flatten the opposite side with the planer, thicknessing the cheeks to final dimension. Mill the midsection to its final thickness. Check that the sides of the cheeks and midsection have remained square to the bottom. Square the bottoms to the side if needed. The plane blank is ready to become a plane.

Beware of milling pieces shorter than 12 inches. They may lodge in the planer or tip into the mouth of the jointer, with potentially disastrous results. For short planes, crosscut the pieces after they have been milled safely from longer stock.

Wedge and Cross-Pin Preparation

The wedge locks the plane iron in place through repeated taps with a light hammer and is subjected to primarily compressive forces. Nearly any hard wood will serve well. Use the same type as the plane body, or a wood with complementary coloration. The blank should be 6 to 8 inches long, the same width as the plane iron, and 3/4 inch thick. The sides must be parallel and square to one face; the other face may be left rough, as it will be sawn away during shaping.

The cross-pin should also be of hard wood, but pay particular attention to grain direction. The stock should exhibit little or no run-out; otherwise, the finished cross-pin may be vulnerable to splitting caused by the forces developed by the wedge bearing against it. As with the wedge, choose wood that either complements or is the same species as the plane body. Dimension it 1/2 inch square x 8 to 12 inches long.

Alternative Plane Blanks

◦ Firewood

Firewood chunks that entirely avoid the pith may yield fine plane stock (1–29). Select a promising piece and trim off the ends until they are free of checks. Establish a trued face, two to three inches wide, with the jointer. Follow this simple method to safely saw a face square to the one that was just jointed: Cut a carrier from a scrap of 3/4-inch-thick particleboard or plywood that is longer and wider than the chunk being resawn. Attach the carrier to the flat firewood chunk with two 2-inch drywall

1–29. This chunk of sound ash may yield a good plane blank.

screws spaced 1/2 inch in from each end, well out of the path of the eventual cut. Position the wood so that no portion of the chunk overhangs one long edge of the carrier (1–30). That edge contacts the fence, guiding the cut on the band saw, yielding a face 90 degrees to the initial flattened surface (1–31).

Next, remove the carrier. Seal the ends with a coating of glue or paint to retard moisture loss. Once the ends are dry, follow the basic instructions for resawing the blank, but add an extra 1/8 inch to all the thicknesses to allow for shrinkage and warping. Do not leave wet sawdust or wood in contact

1–30. A firewood chunk screwed to a carrier. Its down side has been flattened on a jointer.

1–31. The band-sawn ash ready for milling off the carrier.

with the machines or they will start rusting within hours.

Next, use rubber bands to reattach the pieces as they were before resawing, adding 1/8-inch spacers at the ends and the middle. Put the bundle in an unheated garage or some other location that is well ventilated, that is, is not too dry and not too hot. Leave it there for a few months; then bring it inside to season in the shop for several months. Final-dimension the blank when it is well seasoned.

• **Laminating Thinner Stock**
Building up a plane blank by laminating thinner stock is an acceptable solution. Size and glue the laminations so that they will be perpendicular to the plane blank bottom. For one-inch-thick stock, resaw both cheeks from one piece, leaving only the midsection to be laminated. With thicker stock, the entire width can be laminated and then the plane blank resawn as described above. Orient run-out in the same direction for each piece to avoid tear-out problems while machining the blank. Also, observe the orientation of the growth rings on the end grain of each laminate. Try to keep their general direction consistent. This is done to minimize stresses occurring from changes in relative humidity, which may cause the completed plane to warp.

Make the laminates the same width so that they

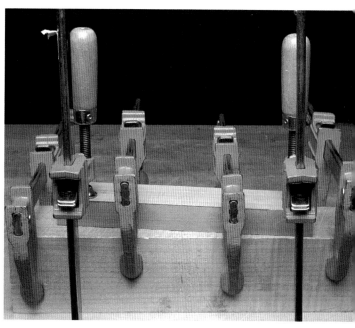

1–32. Gluing set-up for a laminated blank (to avoid gluing it in place, remove the top caul once the other clamps are in place).

may be aligned during glue-up by clamping them to the bench top (1–32). (Plastic or wax paper prevents the blank from getting glued to the bench or clamping block.) Stagger the clamps while gluing and use cauls to keep from marring the surfaces. Use a water-resistant yellow glue.

PLANE IRONS

A good plane iron will be easy to tune up and sharpen, and will hold a keen edge for a long time (1–33), amounting to more time spent planing and less time spent sharpening. Irons that are easy to sharpen can be easily found. Those that are easy to tune are less common. Irons that hold a keen edge for a long time are rarer still.

A part of assessing a particular plane iron relies on your knowledge of how to sharpen and tune the iron and the function of the chip breaker. Sharpening irons is discussed on pages 51 to 67 and chip breakers are discussed below. In the following sections I examine some sources for plane irons.

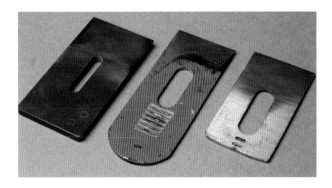

1–33. Various plane irons. Left, specialty iron for wooden planes; middle, Kunz block-plane iron; right, Stanley block-plane iron cut down for wooden planes.

Standard Replacement Irons for Metal Planes

These represent the easiest type of blade to find, while generally being affordable and consistent in quality. They should be easy to tune up and sharpen. Expect relatively poor edge retention. It is necessary to cut down on the length of the iron so that it does not interfere with the hand while planing (this goes for block-plane irons as well as the larger bench-plane irons). You will also need to make your own chip breaker (see below for a discussion on chip breakers and how to make them). In all, this type of iron is an option for those on a budget or those who want to get an iron from the local hardware store.

Flea Markets

Plane irons can be found at flea markets, jumbled in boxes with assorted rust-crusted tools or still united with ancient, battered wooden planes. Avoid severely rusted and pitted blades; they considerably lengthen the tune-up procedure. The quality of the steel is unpredictable, ranging from very good to poor; this can only be determined with use. Some old plane irons lack a slot for attaching a chip breaker. This means either foregoing a chip breaker (a possibility) or having a slot milled, which is added work or expense. The irons on many older

planes taper in thickness, but that poses no difficulty. Again, the iron will likely need to be cut down in length. If you find an iron in good shape or have time to spare, this approach may prove suitable.

Specialty Irons

I currently produce high-quality plane irons, in limited quantities, especially for the type of plane described in this book. Check my web site for availability (www.davidfinck.com).

Shop-Made Irons

Making plane irons is actually not as daunting as the uninitiated might suspect, although the guidance of a machinist, knife maker, or blacksmith helps greatly. Purchase tool steel from an industrial supply house. Consider using $3/16$-inch-thick O-1 stock in the appropriate width—anywhere from one to two inches suits a variety of needs. *The Making of Tools,* by Alexander G. Weygers, is a good source of information for heat-treating the irons.

CHIP BREAKERS

The chip breaker is a separate piece of mild steel, profiled to a knife edge and clamped to the back of the plane iron with a screw (1–34). The knife edge of the chip breaker is set just back from the cutting edge of the iron. When planing off very thick shavings during rapid stock removal ("hogging"), any grain reversal in the board would have you momen-

1–34. A chip breaker mounted on an iron, and one detached.

tarily planing against the grain, with the risk that a shaving might split down into the surface. This will tear out small chunks of wood in the process, leaving a roughened surface (tear-out). The chip breaker functions by bending the shaving back, breaking it off before much damage is done (1–35).

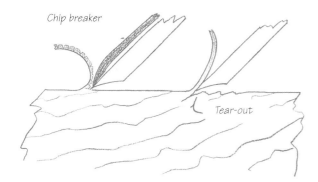

1–35. A chip breaker folds back the shaving. A plane iron used alone may cause tear-out.

For use with the planes described in this book, though, the chip breaker performs a different function. Most often, the shavings being made are so fine that the blade is not extending deeply enough into the wood to cause significant damage. Here, the chip breaker is brought up very close to the cutting edge—$1/64$ to $1/32$ inch—acting to stiffen and pre-tension the edge and helping to eliminate any tendency to chatter. At the very least, the chip breaker adds mass, a welcome addition to most wooden planes.

Planes do function without chip breakers. Molding planes, block planes, and shoulder planes come immediately to mind. Molding planes are most often intended for planing straight-grained softwoods, block planes for end-grain and light trimming jobs, and shoulder planes for end-grain and across-the-grain planing; all these tasks run minimal risk of tear-out damage. A wooden bench plane without a chip breaker may function just fine for many situations. I have tried such planes, with good results, but I still like my planes with chip breakers best.

Evaluating a Chip Breaker

There are two critical points to consider when evaluating a chip breaker: its profile and the point of contact between its knife edge and the back of the plane iron. If these areas do need correcting, refer to Making a Chip Breaker on the following page.

1. *The Profile.* The tip of the chip breaker must come to a knifelike edge and swoop back from its point of contact with the iron in a shallow arc (1–36). Shavings can then pass smoothly over the chip breaker and exit the plane body without jamming. This is of particular importance for very fine shavings; their flimsiness causes them to crumple and jam on any obstruction.

2. *The Chip-Breaker and Plane-Iron Fit.* The point of contact between the knife edge of the chip breaker and the back of the plane iron must be a seamless line (1–37). Again, this is of most importance for very fine shavings because they will jam in the slightest opening. With the chip breaker in place on the iron, point the cutting edge of the assembly at a bright light, peer through the space

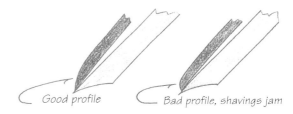

1–36. Correct and incorrect chip-breaker profiles.

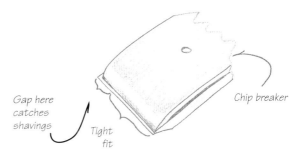

1–37. Checking the seam between the chip breaker and the iron.

between the back of the iron and the bend in the chip breaker, and look for daylight along the tip of the chip breaker. You should see none. Light seen in the middle or out at the ends identifies gaps and potential problems with jammed shavings (1–38).

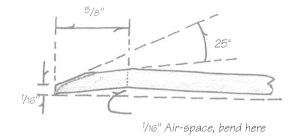

1–39. Chip-breaker details.

1–38. Checking for gaps between the tip of the chip breaker and iron.

Making a Chip Breaker

Use $1/8$-inch mild steel for irons that are approximately $3/16$ inch thick. For thinner irons, use $3/32$-inch-thick stock. The chip breaker should be the exact width of the iron. You may find bar stock (a flat bar of metal) that is the correct width. Cut the stock to length, about $1/2$ inch shorter than the iron. Have a machine shop shear the stock to size if it is obtained in sheet form. The end that will become the tip should be squared off.

Bending a Chip Breaker

A slight bend is made in the chip breaker to help ensure a tight seam where the tip of the chip breaker meets the back of the iron. If there is a burr at this end, orient it on what will become the outside of the chip breaker, so when the tip is shaped the burr is obliterated. Draw a line on the underside of the chip breaker that is $5/8$ inch from the tip and square to the sides (1–39). Clamp the chip breaker very tightly in a metalworking vise, placing the line you drew even with the top of the vise jaw. Bend the chip breaker slightly, to produce a $1/16$-inch space when the chip breaker is laid on a flat surface. I use the tool illustrated in 1–40 to make the bend. Any stout, slotted block of wood that's the approximate width of the chip breaker or wider would suffice.

1–40. A shop-made tool used to make a bend in the chip breaker.

Drilling and Tapping for the Cap Screw

The cap screw holds the chip breaker to the iron. First locate the hole. Mark a lengthwise centerline on the outside of the chip breaker (the side with the rounded tip). Lay the plane iron on top of the chip breaker (its convex side), aligning the tips of both. Stencil the forward extent of the slot in the plane iron on the chip breaker. Center-punch the position of the hole on the centerline, allowing 3/16-inch clearance between the outer diameter of the hole for the cap screw and the front of the plane-iron slot.

Authentic cap screws are difficult to come by. They are short screws with extra-wide heads. Fine-threaded ones are even tougher to find (they are desirable because they minimize the risk of stripping threads in the rather thin chip-breaker stock). An excellent alternative is a 1/4- to 5/16-inch fine-threaded roundhead machine screw in conjunction with a fender washer no wider than 5/8 inch in diameter. The washer eliminates the tendency for the screw to skew the iron relative to the chip breaker as it is tightened down.

Select the appropriate drill for the size screw at hand and chuck it in a drill press. Bring the drill into position down on the chip breaker. If the drill press sports a quill lock, clamp the chip breaker in position with the drill bit. Clamp a board right up against the long edge of the chip breaker. This prevents the chip breaker from spinning during drilling, especially when the drill bit exits the stock (1–41). Please note that the correct way to drill the

hole is with the concave side of the chip breaker down; this way, the chip breaker is being drilled at the correct angle, so that the head of the screw will rest flat on the plane iron when the components are assembled.

It's important to tap the threads at the correct angle for the same reason. When tapping thin material by hand, it is easy to wander off course. A simple jig will keep you right on target. Use a scrap of wood that's about 3/4 inch thinner than the length of the tap. Position and drill a hole that's the same diameter as the tap, as shown in 1–42. Locate a dry-wall screw, which acts as both a stop and a hold-down; the chip breaker should wedge underneath the curve of the screw head.

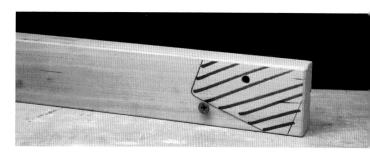

1–42. A chip-breaker tapping jig.

Next, mount the jig in a vise. Chuck the tap into a handle and insert it through the jig hole so that the point protrudes on the side with the stop. Position the chip breaker on the jig as shown in 1–43. Tap the threads, remembering to lubricate them with oil and to back out the tap a half-turn for every two revolutions forward.

Shaping the Knife Edge

All the work can be done with a sharp mill-bastard file, but a quicker way is with a stationary belt or disc sander. Using very coarse sandpaper (36- to 60-grit), grind a 25-degree bevel, but leave the end blunt, with a 1/16-inch-wide flat (1-39). Switch to medium paper (100- to 150-grit). Grind the bevel freehand to a smooth arc, bringing the end to almost, but not quite, a knife edge. This measure is

1–41. Drilling a hole in a chip breaker for the cap screw.

1–43. The chip-breaker tapping jig in use.

taken to preserve squareness. Finish the sanding with 220-grit paper and take the arc to a knife edge.

As you create the arc, do not exceed a 35- to 40-degree angle at the tip or a bullnose will be created that's sufficient to cause a shaving jam. (A bullnose is a blunt roundover rather than a gradually arcing one.) Development of a slight burr on the bottom surface indicates the formation of a knife edge. To grind safely, make a holder by screwing the chip breaker to a stick of wood (1–44). If you have a

buffer, gently polish the arc, which simultaneously removes the burr from the underside. Alternatively, stroke the arc on 320-grit and then 400-grit sandpaper backed by a flat surface. Polishing the arc on an 800- and then an 8,000-grit stone will remove the burr.

Final Fitting

True the underside of the tip of the chip breaker, crafting a tight fit between it and the plane iron. Using a board as shown in 1–45, clamp a strip of 100- to 150-grit sandpaper about 18 inches long to a flat surface, exposing about $^1/_4$ inch of the sandpaper. The best type is resin-bonded, cloth-backed aluminum oxide such as that used for sanding belts. Butt the tip of the chip breaker up to the clamping board and rest the heel directly on the table. This arrangement slightly undercuts the chip breaker, ensuring that the tip contacts the iron when assembled instead of some point slightly behind the tip, which would create a small shaving-catching gap (1–46). Make three or four unidirectional strokes, keeping the pressure centered right in the middle of the tip. Look at what has been sanded and see if

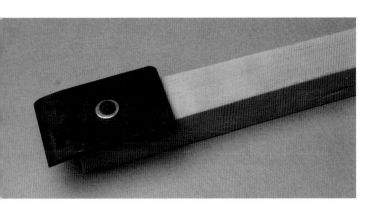

1–44. The chip breaker mounted on the holder, ready for grinding.

1–45. Truing the bottom of the chip breaker on sandpaper.

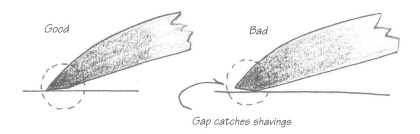

Good

Bad

Gap catches shavings

1–46. Properly and improperly undercut chip breakers.

there is a flat going from corner to corner. If not, try a few more unidirectional strokes and check again. Do not pump back and forth or a hump will surely be created. Brush away the accumulated grit every three or four strokes.

Check for a tight fit, as described earlier, with the mating plane iron. The plane iron must be properly flattened first (see Chapter 3). If you see daylight at the corners, the chip breaker is arced on the bottom and no amount of truing as described will amend that. You must cut away the hump, creating the slightest hollow in the center, without touching the corners. This is easily done using a mill-bastard file that is narrower than the chip breaker. Lay the file on a table and the chip breaker on the file, tip to tip. Stroke back toward the tang. Do not allow the file to cut into the corners of the chip breaker and keep pressure on the tip so that no material is removed from the opposite end. Repeat until a barely discernible hollow is formed; check this against the plane iron. Return to the truing process. Now the corners will rest firmly on the sandpaper without rocking. Check after each stroke until flatness is restored.

A burr will have formed at the tip on the rounded side. Stroke this off on your finest-grit water stone, gently working both the flat and the rounded sides alternately. Keep in mind when stroking the rounded side not to finish at greater than a 40-degree angle, or you will produce a small dam right at the tip capable of catching shavings. The chip breaker is complete save for any cosmetic improvements that might be undertaken.

CHAPTER TWO

Tuning and Using Hand Tools

Before beginning to make a plane, take the time to evaluate the condition of the tools used in the process and "tune" them, which simply means putting them in good working order. These tools include the combination square, straightedges, block planes, and spokeshaves. The procedures used to put them in working order are easy and make a world of difference when it comes to doing careful, accurate work. The material in this chapter also includes pointers on how to use these tools properly.

COMBINATION SQUARE

From their most obvious task of checking boards for square to a host of other vital chores, squares are a fundamental tool. They are indispensable for machine setup and joinery layout and work great as smaller straightedges. I find combination squares (2–1) to be far more useful than the wide-bladed, wooden-handled try squares usually associated with fine woodworking. Beyond their usefulness for all the above tasks, combination squares can also be used to gauge depths and, when the sliding beam is used as a depth stop for the ruler, can make repeated layouts or measurements. They also measure and lay out 45-degree angles.

2–1. Combination square.

The shavings made with wooden planes on a workaday basis typically range from .001 to .004 inch thick. If the square is off to that degree, or your technique obscures a proper reading, chances are the capabilities of the planes won't be fully utilized. Machinist-grade tools from reputable manufacturers are undoubtedly ready to use off the shelf. Inexpensive hardware-store-variety or flea-market squares usually need work.

Because they have removable rulers, combination squares can be tuned up relatively easily. The gradations on the ruler of a cheap square are usually embossed, deforming the edge and interfering with accurate readings. Smooth and straighten the edge as follows: Clamp a strip of 150-grit resin-bond sandpaper, at least twice the length of the blade, to a flat surface (jointer or table-saw bed). True a board that's the same length as the sandpaper, about 3 inches wide, and $^1/_4$ inch thinner than the width of your square's blade. Place the board on the abrasive so that a $^1/_2$-inch section of abrasive is revealed. The edge of the board acts as a fence, maintaining a square relationship between the face of the rule and the edge to be sanded (2–2).

Grasp the ruler in the center, keep light pressure against the edge of the board, and sand the edge smooth and true with long, deliberate strokes. *Never* sand back and forth. Make one stroke, examine the ruler, and repeat. Working stroke by stroke, you'll arrive expeditiously at your goal. Sand back and forth with abandon and the goal may never be achieved. Every three or four strokes, clean the sandpaper with a stiff brush, removing all debris. Start and stop the stroke with the ruler fully on the sandpaper; if it runs off the end, it will develop a hollow in the edge. Strive to maintain (or create) flatness by concentrating pressure in the center of the ruler; otherwise, the tendency is to remove more material from the ends, creating a hump in the middle.

Check for straightness against a reliable straight-edge or reference surface, using a strong source of light on your back. Use 220-grit sandpaper to fine-tune and finish the edge.

Next, scrutinize the body of the square. Two of its faces form a right angle. The face of the longer leg must be true and free of imperfections, such as seams left from the manufacturing process. Lumps or bumps ruin the reliability of the measurements. Inaccuracies can be sanded away in the manner just described. Sand the absolute minimum amount and beware of tapering the face and altering its square relationship to the ruler.

Assemble the square, tighten down the ruler, and check for squareness as follows: Joint the edge of a 1 x 8-inch board (12 inches or longer) dead flat. A light-colored wood such as pine or maple will show the following marks clearly. Halfway along the length, draw a line square to the edge with a very sharp, hard pencil. Rotate the handle so that the same edge of the ruler that drew the line is now on

2–2. *Truing the edge of a combination square's ruler.*

the other side of the line. Compare the ruler to the line. If they are parallel, then all is well; if they are not, an adjustment is necessary.

To make an adjustment, remove the ruler and observe the slot in the beam with a bright light. Two raised bars on the bottom of the slot support the ruler; lowering one in relation to the other angles the ruler when it is reinstalled. Effect the adjustment with a flat needle file. Go slowly. One stroke can make a significant change. Keep the bars flat, or dipped toward the center of the handle, so that when the ruler is secured it will contact the outer edge of bar. If there are no bars, it may be possible to make adjustments by tapering the face of the handle that is referenced off the edge of the board by careful sanding.

Using a Square

Consistent technique and a bit of savvy produce reliable readings. Checking a board for square implies the presence of a reference surface: one face or edge (usually a face) of the board that is flat and free from wind (a twisted planar surface). Check the reference surface for imperfections like raised lines left by nicks in jointer or planer blades. Correct or avoid any such defects when gauging. The reference face is the foundation of the measurements; problems here inevitably lead to a cascade of problems elsewhere.

The face of the ruler belonging to the square should generally be held perpendicular to whatever surface is being gauged. Rulers (or straightedges) 12 inches or longer are often curved to some extent along the length of their face. Any such curvature comes into play as soon as the blade is tipped off of

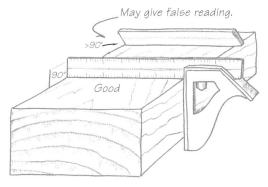

May give false reading.

>90°

90°

Good

2–3. Tipping the blade of a square when gauging a surface may give a false reading if the blade is at all curved.

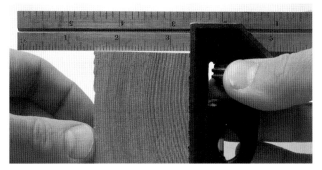

2–4. Taking a reading with a square. The beam of the square is flat on the reference surface, while the blade indicates the condition of the surface being gauged.

perpendicular, rendering a false reading (2–3). Place the body of the square firmly against the reference surface, with the ruler not quite touching the surface being gauged; then bring the ruler into light contact. Avoid the natural tendency to allow the ruler to lay flat on the surface being checked; that entirely defeats the purpose of the measurement. The *full length* of the body of the square must remain in firm contact with the reference face. Sight against a bright light source. A tapering band of light between the ruler and target surface indicates that they are out of square (2–4).

STRAIGHTEDGE

An 18-inch straightedge is very useful for general woodworking and for checking the bottoms of longer wooden planes for flatness. Precision-ground flat stock, 2 inches wide and $3/32$ inch thick, makes a good straightedge. (This type of stock

is available from industrial supply houses.) As with squares, keep the face of the straightedge perpendicular to the target surface, and always sight toward a bright light.

BLOCK PLANE

For the plane you will make, a small metal block plane (2–5) is essential for creating a perfectly flat ramp on which to firmly bed the plane iron. The plane must be tuned for accurate performance. There are many styles and makes of block plane, most of which are serviceable once some key items have been attended to.

The first task is to properly "tension" the plane. Tension is the amount of pressure used to lock the blade in place. This is of critical importance: not enough pressure and the plane will not hold the adjustment; too much and the plane will not only be difficult to adjust, but the body may distort and render the plane incapable of making fine shavings. In nearly all cases, pressure is provided by a screw. Better planes use a screw in conjunction with a cam, which captures the blade (2–6). Once the screw is properly set, it need never be read-

2–5. Block plane.

2–6. (below). Block plane with cap iron removed, showing the tensioning screw within the slot of the plane iron.

2–7. *A block plane disassembled and the adjustable throat plate removed.*

justed. To release the blade, just loosen the cam. Lesser-quality planes rely on a screw working directly on the cap iron to capture the blade. With these, correct pressure must be determined each time the blade is removed and replaced. When the depth of cut is adjusted, the blade should stay clamped. It often takes two or three tries to adjust the blade perfectly; to release and clamp the blade each time the setting is altered would remove all precision from this task.

Applying Proper Tension to the Blade

First lubricate all moving parts. With the blade and cap iron in place, and the cam—if the plane has one—thrown to the tightening side, entirely release the pressure on the tensioning screw. Slowly tighten the tensioning screw; as it begins to engage, stop tightening and wiggle the back end of the blade from side to side. Continue incremental tightening while alternately wiggling the blade. The proper amount of tension has been reached when the blade can no longer be moved with modest effort. Experience shows that this minimum amount of pressure is sufficient to lock the blade securely, while allowing for easy and accurate adjustments. Consistency is important: when the feel of adjusting the plane remains constant, it's easier to perform that task quickly and confidently.

Assessing the Bottom

When the plane is properly tensioned, you are ready to check the bottom—the "sole." You will be taking shavings only a few thousandths of an inch thick; if irregularities in the bottom of the plane

approach that dimension, the plane will not function properly. Before proceeding, note if the plane has an adjustable throat opening. This is a movable plate on the bottom of the plane that forms the front edge of the opening (the "throat") for the blade. A thumbscrew locks the plate in place. If the plane has this arrangement, remove the thumbscrew and the plate (2–7) and make sure the grooves the plate rests on are free of any debris. Then reassemble the thumbscrew and plate.

Check the condition of the bottom along its width and length with a straightedge (2–8). Do this whether the plane is right out of the box, has been in use for years, or was just picked up at the flea market. The plane will frequently be hollowed along its length. The straightedge will contact the ends, but there will be a discernible gap at the center. A hump just behind the throat opening is also a common finding. Neither configuration is acceptable. When planing, the blade may start to take a shaving, but then the hump or the bow will lift the blade off the wood and interrupt the shaving. When the blade is reset for a heavier cut, the same thing happens. When the plane is reset for a still heavier cut, a thick shaving will be plowed off. The result is an all-or-

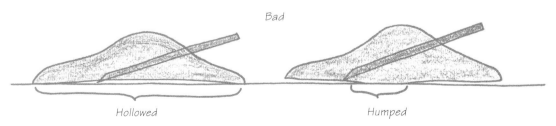

Bad

Hollowed   *Humped*

2–8. *The straightedges used on these two block planes indicate that the bottoms are curved.*

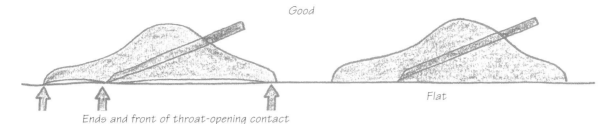

Good

Flat

Ends and front of throat-opening contact

2–9. A straightedge indicates two acceptable conditions for a plane bottom.

nothing situation: either no shaving or an unacceptably thick one. Accurate planing is not possible.

Indented areas leading into the throat opening are another common finding. They will not prevent the plane from taking a fine shaving, but the indentation in the front, in effect, creates a larger-than-apparent throat opening.

There are two acceptable conditions for the bottom. It can either be dead flat, or (when gauged with a straightedge) there can be points of contact at the front edge of the plane, the area immediately in front of the throat opening, and at the rear of the plane (2–9). The latter configuration is arguably more favorable, in that friction while planing is reduced since the plane bottom has less contact area. Flatness across the width of the plane is also crucial. If the plane is humped in the center, the blade will have more exposure at the corners, increasing the likelihood of digs. A hollow down the center exposes more of the blade at the center, creating difficulties when planing narrow surfaces (as in edge-joining).

Flattening the Bottom

If the plane bottom needs attention, the inaccuracies can be carefully sanded out. This may sound daunting, but cast iron sands fairly easily and the work goes quickly. Clamp a two-foot-long strip of three- to six-inch-wide 100-grit resin-bond sandpaper to the bed of a flat machine table (check it for flatness!). Again, unidirectional strokes are the key to success. *Be sure the plane is properly tensioned with the blade in place but retracted.*

Grasp the plane as shown in 2–10, rather than as you might naturally hold it while planing, to avoid

sanding a wind into the plane bottom. Subtle changes in hand pressure have a dramatic and potentially unwanted effect. Center the plane with the center of your body, concentrate the pressure on the center of the plane, and stroke firmly. Do not allow the plane to go beyond the end of the sandpaper and do not lift it up at the end of the stroke while it is still in forward motion. Instead, stop the plane while it is still in full contact with the sandpaper. Brush off the sanding debris after each stroke. After two strokes, observe the bottom of the plane. There should be a readily apparent scratch pattern from the sanding that is helpful in gauging your progress (2–11), but do not rely on this alone; also use your straightedge, checking the length and width of the plane. You are done when the bottom

2–10. Gripping the plane for flattening the bottom.

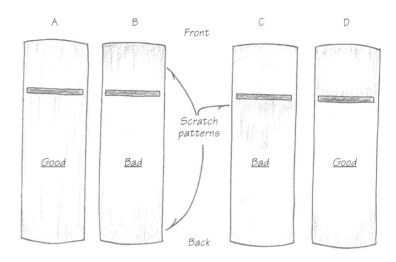

2–11. Sanding the bottom of the plane reveals its condition.
A: Flat runs from one end of the bottom to the other.
B: A hollow on the bottom.
C: A hump behind the throat opening.
D: The ends and point in front of the throat opening are planar; the other portions are hollowed.

conforms to one of the acceptable conditions described above.

One problem that requires special attention when truing a plane bottom is the appearance of a slight (sometimes not-so-slight) arc along either its width or length. The tendency is to rock on that arc with each stroke, making it very difficult to flatten out unless you change your approach. The idea is to sand out the hump or high spot without touching the areas that are already low (2–12). If the arc is lengthwise, use a piece of sandpaper at least two inches narrower than the length of the plane. Turn the plane sideways to the sandpaper and take one or two strokes, sanding the middle, where the high spot is. You must guard against forming a widthwise arc in the bottom while doing this. Make each stroke count and concentrate on your goal. Check with the straightedge. Stop when the center hump has been removed, leaving the bottom slightly hollowed.

Now, return to lengthwise sanding. The plane will rest on its ends and will not rock with each sanding stroke. A crisscross scratch pattern will appear on the bottom, visible on the ends at first, and lengthening toward the center with each stroke. Continue until lengthwise scratches go from end to end. Do not be concerned if some widthwise scratches are still evident in the center.

If the problem is a widthwise arc, then rip a length of sandpaper that is about $1/2$ inch narrower than the width of the plane. Sand lengthwise down the center of the plane. Sand the center of the plane, where the high spot is, without touching the side edges of the plane. As in the previous example, continue sanding until a widthwise reading with the straightedge reveals that the hump is gone and the center is now slightly cupped. Return to the normal truing procedure, check with the straight-edge after every other stroke, and stop when the bottom reads dead flat across.

Be highly critical of your efforts. If a bump or gap is suspected where it should not be, get a brighter light and be sure. Unless the bottom is properly flattened, frustration will be experienced when planing. Once you are happy with the results, the only thing standing between you and beautiful shavings is the sharpness of the blade and your ability to properly adjust it in the plane.

Lengthwise Arc   Widthwise Arc

Sandpaper   Sandpaper

Sand here only   Sand here only

2–12. End and side views of planes showing arc and where to concentrate sanding.

SPOKESHAVE

The type of spokeshave I find most convenient and useful is the No. 151 pattern, available with a flat or curved bottom (2–13). In plane-making, this tool is good for shaping the body. The flat-bottom type is used for convex and gently radiused concave surfaces. The round-bottom one shapes tighter concave surfaces. The tool will slide more easily and leave a better finish if the bottom is polished. Take the same approach used for the block plane to smooth the flat-bottom spokeshave. Stroke in an arc to polish the round-bottom one. Finish up with the water stones to polish the surfaces. The round-bottom spokeshave may be gently buffed.

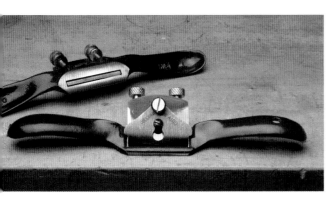

2–13. Number 151 spokeshaves.

Chattering is a common difficulty with spokeshaves. This arises from combining too heavy a cut with a dull blade, and exerting force too high on the tool. (See Chapter 3 for information on sharpening.) Here is how to properly adjust the depth of cut: First, make sure that the cap iron is gripping the blade correctly. The small screw that passes through the blade acts as a pivot. Let's call it the "pivot screw." The larger, knurled screw—the "cap screw"—presses against the end of the blade, causing the cap iron to pivot on the pivot screw and press tightly against the tip of the blade. Do not tighten the pivot screw down onto the blade; the head of the screw must be about $1/8$ inch above the blade to do its job (2–14). The two knurled screws

that register with slots in the blade are the "blade-adjusting screws."

Once the spokeshave blade has been sharpened, assemble the tool and apply slight clamping pressure with the cap screw—just enough to hold all the components together, but without hindering the motion of the blade-adjusting screws. Work the screws in tandem to retract the blade fully; then bring the blade forward until the edge just peeks out beyond the bottom. Now, try cutting a shaving. Ideally, none should yet come forth.

Next, gradually bring the edge out further until it just begins to slice the finest shaving. Try the center of the blade and the outer edges too. If the shavings are thicker on one side than the other, work the blade-adjusting screws individually to compensate. If you retracted the blade at all, always finish by rotating the blade-adjusting screws forward until the lip of the screw comes up against the slot in the blade, to fully support it. Tighten the cap screw to lock the adjustments in place. To remove the blade for resharpening, simply loosen the cap screw and lift off the cap iron and blade. It is unnecessary to alter the pivot-screw setting.

Start off with very fine shavings. As you gain experience, it becomes easier to take controlled heavy shavings for rapid stock removal. The spokeshave may be pushed or pulled, but it is important to focus your energy as low on the tool as possible to prevent chatter.

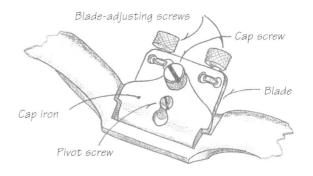

2–14. The parts on a No. 151 pattern spokeshave.

CHAPTER THREE

Sharpening Techniques

It is impossible to overstate the importance of sharp blades for efficient, reliable, and just plain pleasurable use of hand planes (3–1). "Sharp" is a nebulous term, though, and open to interpretation. What a person deems "sharp" may not be sharp *enough*, rendering the finest plane less useful than a cruder version equipped with a properly sharpened blade. This extends to other basic cutting tools as well: chisels, spokeshaves, and knives.

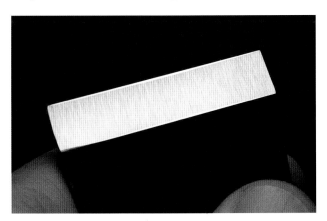

3–1. A well-sharpened iron.

But attaining sharpness is the conclusion of the saga; the sharpening method used is the crux of the matter. It is easy to get bogged down if sharpening is time-consuming, troublesome, or inconsistent.

The method and tools must work effectively every time with ease, speed, and certainty. If problems arise, as they occasionally do, you need reliable guideposts to get back on track. Sharpening need not be onerous, nor is it particularly difficult. Admittedly, it is a slow process at first, but even the occasional hobbyist, set on the right course, can see improvement with every effort.

PRESHARPENING PROCEDURES: PREPARING THE GRINDER, HONING STONES, AND WORKSTATION

Grinder

For the purposes of this book, "grinding" means metal removal with an abrasive wheel assisted by a tool rest. The typical 3,600-rpm electric grinder is adequate when fitted with the proper wheel and tool rest and used with caution. However, things go much better with a good-quality 1,800-rpm grinder. Have you ever noticed the blade you were grinding turning blue at the edge? That indicates overheating. You have "drawn the temper" of the blade, meaning the metal has been softened. The blade will no longer hold an edge adequately. The only remedy is to retemper the blade or carefully grind back beyond all the discolored metal. A slower-speed grinder diminishes the risk of overheating the blade, but care still must be taken.

Another viable option is a good-quality hand-cranked grinder (3–2). The battered antique type of grinder found frequently at flea markets is often inadequate. Unfortunately, I know of no source that currently sells new, good-quality hand-cranked grinders.

3–2. A good-quality hand-cranked grinder mounted on a board for setup in a vise at a metalworking area.

A good grinder should handle six- to seven-inch wheels, have a high gear ratio—about 20:1, or 20 revolutions for one crank of the wheel—and a stout clamp, or preferably bolts, for table attachment. The knack of cranking steadily while grinding accurately may prove difficult at first, but is not too hard to master. Excellent control, simplicity, relative quiet, and freedom from electricity are the advantages of hand-grinding.

Grinder Placement

Proper orientation of the grinder is critical for good results. All too often grinders are set up backed against a wall or other obstruction, limiting your stance to directly in front of the wheel(s). In fact, the best place to park yourself is to the *side* of the wheel. Situate the grinder with that in mind. Your body's front and centerline should be aligned with, or even slightly *behind*, the axis of wheel rotation. From this vantage the edge of the blade in relationship to the face of the wheel can be seen precisely—that is, it can be determined whether it is flat on the wheel or slightly angled one way or the other. If you are in front of the wheel, that all-important relationship cannot be viewed directly. You must rely on secondary clues such as the relationship of the blade to the tool rest or the edge of the wheel, neither of which is reliable. Even if the cutting edge is only slightly angled off the face of the wheel, grinding will be done with a corner of the wheel, making it easy to grind waves and dips but difficult to achieve the objective: a perfectly straight or slightly arced cutting edge.

Wheel and Tool Rest

Just as important as the choice of grinder are the wheel and tool rest it is fitted with. The wheel should be composed of "friable-bond" aluminum oxide. "Friable bond" means that the particles of abrasive are sloughed off the wheel as it is being used, constantly exposing fresh abrasive. The result is cooler and faster grinding. The coarser the grit the better, because coarser grits also result in cooler, faster grinding. Sixty-grit abrasive is as coarse an abrasive as I have found, but use 36-grit if it is available. The diameter of the wheel, while affecting the degree of hollow grind, is not critical: a diameter of five to seven inches is a reasonable range. Avoid the gray Carborundum wheels found on most grinders. They glaze quickly, cut slowly, and heat up fast. If you must use one, try one with 36-grit abrasive and use a very light touch—more soon on technique.

Tool Rest

A wide, stable tool rest that adjusts easily can be the difference between smooth, accurate results or a flawed grinding job. Accuracy is essential, to minimize time spent honing. The stock tool rest found on most grinders fails all the above criteria. The shop-made tool rest illustrated in 3–3 and 3–4 is easily made and serves well.

Preparing the Grinding Wheel

As with all grinding operations, use eye protection. Wear a good dust mask when preparing the grinding wheel. All of the following operations produce clouds of irritating dust. To work well, the circumference of the wheel surface (let's call it the "face") must be straight across its width, free of glazing, and true about its axis of rotation. Check the width of the face with a straightedge. If the face is hol-

lowed or domed, there will be considerable difficulty grinding a proper edge on the iron because only the corners or a small portion of the wheel will make contact.

To shape the wheel, I prefer using a 1-inch-square x 3-inch-long dressing stick of Carborundum among the several options available. Its relatively broad surface straightens the face quickly and easily. Turn on the grinder, support the dresser stick with the tool rest, and with small side-to-side motions press an end of the stick firmly into the revolving wheel. Both the wheel and the dresser abrade fairly rapidly. While straightening the face, also try to keep the end of the dresser stick flat and straight too (it will round if you pivot it while using it). Check your progress occasionally, with the wheel at a standstill. For a hand-cranked wheel, spin it as fast as can be comfortably maintained, remember-

Making a Tool Rest

Determine the height of the tool rest so that the blade will contact the grinding wheel at about the height of the wheel's axle when you are grinding. Consider the way the tool rest will be attached. A carriage bolt can be put directly through the surface that the grinder is mounted on or it can be mounted through a separate board first, which is then screwed or clamped in front of the grinder. If you're doing the latter, factor in the thickness of the mounting board.

The table of the tool rest shown in 3–3 and 3–4 is 3 x 5 inches. The base is exactly the same length. A 7-inch carriage bolt passes through the block supporting the table. When the knob is tightened down, the table is captured securely.

The block is formed from a pair of

³/₄-inch-thick pieces, each dadoed half the diameter of the bolt, and then glued together to make the passage for the bolt. To keep the

3–3. Side view of a shop-made tool rest.

3–4. Back view of the tool rest.

halves aligned during glue-up, drive a couple of very small brads into one glue surface; nip them off so that ¹/₁₆ inch of the nail protrudes. When the halves are put together, the brad stubs will prevent the parts from slipping. The base is mortised across its width in the center to allow for adjustment toward and away from the grinder. Sandpaper glued to the bottom prevents the base from slipping.

ing that the direction of rotation is always down, onto the tool rest.

The same tool rubbed lightly on the revolving wheel will remove glazing. This is especially important with gray Carborundum wheels, which glaze over quickly. Glazed wheels result in slower grinding and faster heat buildup. Despite the friable bond, the recommended aluminum-oxide wheels also glaze slightly (seen as black streaking). Notice the way it feels to grind with a freshly dressed wheel; it seems to bite into the steel. The sparks emitted wrap all the way around the wheel as you grind. As the wheel glazes, the biting slowly changes into a skating feel and the stream of sparks gets shorter and shorter.

If you feel the tool bumping or pounding on the surface when grinding or dressing the wheel, then the wheel requires truing. Further evidence is patches of glazing or discoloration on the wheel, indicating the high spots contacting the tool while grinding. When the wheel is out of true, grinding is difficult to control and significantly slower because only a small portion of the wheel is being used. It is important to correct the situation. A dressing stick or star-wheel dresser is not effective for truing; it simply rides on the existing contours of the wheel. A diamond dressing stick (available from woodworking catalogues or industrial supply companies) mounted in a simple jig works well (see page 47).

Honing Stones

In my lexicon, "honing" is sharpening a blade by hand, progressing with graded abrasives that range from coarse to fine until the blade is razor-sharp. My preference for honing is synthetic Japanese water stones. They hone an edge to a very high degree of sharpness, very quickly, while being reasonably priced. Among the various brands I have tried, King is my favorite, combining quick cutting with good wear resistance and an extremely fine-grit stone that yields a superb level of sharpness.

Other brands I have used cut more slowly, wear more quickly, and don't produce the same degree of sharpness. Get two grits: 800 and 8,000 (in King nomenclature, the 8,000-grit water stone is designated G-1 or G-3, depending on the thickness). The surface of an 8,000-grit stone blackens from carbon deposits, which can slow down the sharpening. A "nagura," a small block of abrasive, is used to clean the surface and develop a slurry that speeds sharpening.

The 800-grit stone quickly removes grinding scratches left by even a 36-grit wheel. The 8,000-grit stone removes scratches left by the 800-grit stone, producing a mirrored surface in moments. I find no need for intermediate stones. Amazingly, if the grinding is accurate enough, you may even skip directly from the grinding wheel to the 8,000-grit stone, achieving the keenest edge in under a minute.

Like the recommended grinding wheels, water stones are friable—which is why they cut so quickly—but, by definition, they wear rapidly too. When they are handled properly, wear is not a problem, and can even be used to an advantage, as described below. You should get years of use from the stones. After 12 years of intense everyday use, mine still have life in them.

What of some alternatives? Oilstones are slower; and good-sized stones, as well as those with the finest grits, can be expensive. Ceramic stones are slower and are unavailable in grits as fine as those for water stones. Also, if a ceramic stone is not perfectly flat (something that is often desirable), there is nothing that can be done about it. Check its flatness before buying one. Diamond stones cut fast, but they too are unavailable in fine enough grit to yield the same sharpness that water stones produce. Check these too for flatness, before buying. Coarse diamond stones are very good for flattening the backs of plane irons. They have the advantage of remaining flat through an intense session of use—that is, if they start out flat. There are also natural, quarried water stones, but they do not seem to be a good value compared to synthetic water stones.

The truing jig (3–5) holds the diamond dresser securely and allows for a controlled cut, creating a wheel both true in circumference and straight across the face. A wooden block is drilled to accept the dressing stick. The block is mounted to a platform with three screws from below: two hold the block to the platform, and one pulls the saw kerf tight to clamp the dressing stick (an option is to drill all the way through the block and squeeze the kerf with a stove bolt [a bolt with a domed head] and knob, as shown in 3–5). The platform has a lip on the bottom at the back, formed by sawing off a portion of the platform or by gluing on a strip of wood. The lip registers off the back of the grinder tool rest to produce the straight cut across the wheel.

Mount the jig on the tool rest. Adjust the angle of the tool rest so that the dressing stick is aligned with the radius of the wheel (3–6). Rotate the base of the tool rest so that its back edge is perpendicular to the plane formed by the side of the wheel (3–7); the face of the wheel will thus be trued square to its side.

Shim the jig away from the wheel with three strips of masking tape applied to the back of the tool rest where the jig will register (refer to 3–5). Bring the jig into position, capturing the tape shims. Loosen the clamp holding the dresser, bring the dresser into light contact with the wheel, and retighten the clamp. Remove the tape shims to effect a cut into the wheel equal to that same thickness.

Next, start the grinder and bring the dresser into light contact with the wheel, working it back and forth over the face of the wheel. When the tool has cut into the wheel a distance equal to the thickness of the three strips of tape, the lip of the jig contacts the back edge of the tool rest, which guides a straight cut and limits any further cutting. Stop the wheel and examine the face when the dresser ceases cutting. The entire circumference should appear freshly cut. If there are still low spots as yet untouched, shim the tool rest with tape and reposition the dresser into light contact with the wheel, as before. Remove the shims and dress the wheel again. Continue in like fashion until the wheel is completely trued. Once done, the wheel is unlikely to ever need truing again unless it is removed from the grinder and then remounted.

3–5. A diamond dresser mounted in a truing jig. Note the masking tape shim between the lip on the bottom of the jig and the back of the tool rest.

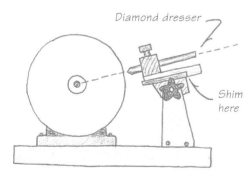

3–6. The dressing stick in the truing jig is aligned with the radius of the grinding wheel.

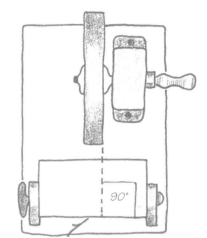

Plan View

90°

Back edge of tool rest

3–7. The back edge of the tool rest is positioned perpendicular to the side of the grinding wheel.

3–8. A honing workstation. It consists of a wall-mounted countertop, inset water bucket, plywood cover, water stone cradle, mist bottle, flattening stick, wooden straightedge, granite lapping plate (for flattening stones), and a rag.

Honing Workstation

A dedicated place for honing (3–8) increases your comfort while working and contains the slurry that water stones develop in use. A section of counter-top mounted to the wall makes a good surface. To determine a comfortable working height, stand by the wall where you are mounting the table, feet shoulder-width apart, arms relaxed at the sides, fingers outstretched. Mark the wall at your finger-tips. Use that measurement for the height of the tabletop. The work surface should accommodate a lidded tub for soaking the coarse water stone.

There also must be a means of firmly anchoring the stones while they are being used, that is, a cradle for the stones. Their aggressive cutting

action teamed with a suction effect between the blade, stone, and water film creates significant resistance. Without an anchor, the stone will skate across the table while you attempt to hone. Suspend the tub by its rim, fitting the tub tightly into the countertop so that it will not jiggle. The bottom of the cradle registers on the rim of the tub. I've used the cradle shown in 3–9 for years. Four dowels are placed two at each end to capture the 800-grit stone; the same four dowels fit holes in the bottom of the 8,000-grit stone base. Finally, put up a hook to hang a dish towel for wiping the iron and fingers clean.

Care and Use of Water Stones

If you work regularly, leave the 800-grit stone immersed in water. It will not be harmed and will be ready for immediate use. Most 800-grit stones are quite porous and must be fully saturated or there will be no water on the surface available for lubrication. If the shop is unheated, do not let a saturated stone freeze; the result is a pile of loose abrasives. If sharpening is an occasional thing, let the stone dry out between uses—it is a little more convenient to check and flatten a completely dry stone.

Stones that are 8,000-grit are relatively imperme-able, so they need not be soaked prior to use. A squirt of water and they are ready.

Checking and Flattening Stones

Check the stones for flatness across their length and width with a 12-inch straightedge (refer to Straightedge on page 37 if there is any doubt con-cerning proper technique). Blot them dry first if they are wet. Observe their middles and edges. Dips are easiest to rectify; humps require an extra step. Stones can be flat-tened by dry- or wet-sanding in con-junction with a true reference surface.

3–9. A stone cradle that accommo-dates two different-sized stones.

Making a Stone Cradle

Ilus. 3–10 shows another version of a stone cradle. If the 8,000-grit stone came mounted on a wooden base, remove the "feet" of the base and cut it down in width and length as close to the size of the 800-grit stone as possible (but do not saw into the stone). Select a water-resistant wood such as cedar, redwood, teak, or mahogany for the cradle that is 1 to 1¹/₂ inch thick. Cut the stock about five inches longer than the longer stone and ¹/₄ inch narrower than the wider stone. The stones are captured by a wedge.

Build up a ledge at each end by gluing on two pieces of wood about ³/₈ inch high. One piece has a square end to register against the stone; the other has a slightly tapered end to register against the wedge. There must be enough room between the ledges for the largest stone and a wedge. Use waterproof glue. Using nipped-off brads as described in Making a Tool Rest on page 45 will prevent the ledges from slipping as they are glued. If the stones are much different in length, a different-width wedge may be needed for each.

Cut dadoes across the bottom of the cradle corresponding to the rim at the ends of the soaking tub. Make them deep enough so that the ends of the cradle sit on the countertop without bottoming on the rim. Depending upon the shape of the rim, you may opt for a close fit to secure the cradle to the tub, or allow some room and use a wedge to take up the slack.

3–10. Another version of the stone cradle. The stone is captured by a wedge.

The reference surface for dry-sanding can be a jointer or table-saw table. For wet-sanding, use a 12-inch square of ¹/₄-inch or thicker plate glass with the edges seamed (knocked off). The reference surface determines the flatness of the stone, so make sure that it is flat side to side and across the diagonals. A food tray under the glass catches any drips.

Dry-sanding is fastest, but the stones must be quite dry or they will immediately clog the sandpaper. Clamp a 24-inch strip of 6-inch-wide 100-grit paper to a jointer or table-saw table.

If the stone only has dips, proceed as follows: Lay the face to be trued down on the sandpaper and grip the stone in the middle with the thumb and curled forefinger of each hand (3–11). Push right through the center of the stone and stroke the stone the length of the sandpaper, stopping when the leading edge reaches the end of the paper. Pick the stone up and start over again at the start of the paper.

Each stroke should be very deliberate and uni-directional (no scrubbing back and forth). Every few strokes, sweep away the accumulated grit from the sandpaper with a stiff brush—wear a dust mask—and then carefully scrutinize the surface of the stone being sanded. You will notice zones of varying color: the lighter areas have been abraded; the darker spots have not been touched yet. Continue just until the moment the entire surface of the stone becomes

3–11. A balanced grip for flattening water stones when dry-sanding.

a uniform color. Check again with a straightedge to be sure the stone is flat.

If you grab the stone and flail away thoughtlessly, things ultimately go slower, not faster, and sufficient accuracy will not be achieved. Chances are good, in fact, that a hump and/or a wind will be sanded into the stone, creating more work for yourself.

Humps are troublesome to correct because of the tendency to continually rock on the hump while sanding, never making any progress (other than thinning the stone). If a hump is detected on the stone, do this: Create a very slight dip by sanding on a piece of sandpaper that is narrower than the stone. If the stone is humped widthwise, cut a piece of sandpaper $1/2$ inch narrower than the width of the stone and sand the stone lengthwise, without hitting the long edges, using unidirectional, deliberate strokes (3–12). If the stone is humped lengthwise, the paper should be one inch shorter than the length of the stone and the strokes should go crosswise without touching the ends of the stone. Simply put, you are sanding where the reading from the straightedge indicates high spots and avoiding areas that are already low. Do not overdo it; sand only until the slightest amount of dip is observed with the straightedge. Return to the full-sized sandpaper and, with a few strokes, sand just until the dip is obliterated.

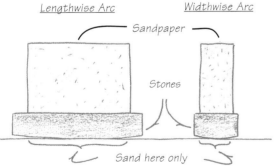

3–12. *Where to concentrate sanding to flatten water stones with lengthwise and widthwise humps. The sandpaper is appropriately sized to facilitate this.*

Wet-sanding is used when the stones are wet. This applies primarily to the 800-grit stone, as the 8,000-grit stone is likely to be dry before you start honing and should be checked and flattened then. The stone should be clean and the surface blotted dry with a paper towel before proceeding. Next, check it for flatness. Set up the 12-inch square of glass on a food tray and flood the glass with water. Lay a piece of 100-grit wet-or-dry sandpaper, abrasive side up, on the glass. The water gently adheres the sandpaper to the glass. Flood the paper with water.

Now stroke the stone on the sandpaper in small circles, utilizing the entire sheet of paper and applying as much force as can be comfortably and completely controlled. Blot the stone dry every so often and scrutinize the stone. As with dry-sanding, you should see the same two zones of color as mentioned before; proceed until the stone becomes a uniform color. Final-check the stone with the straightedge. Treat humps in the same manner as described for dry-sanding, using wet-or-dry sandpaper.

Further smooth the flattened stones by briefly rubbing the faces of the 800- and 8,000-grit stones against each other. This removes the scratches left on the stone by the rather coarse sandpaper and markedly increases the sharpening efficiency of both stones. Take care to carefully rinse the 8,000-grit stone afterwards, to remove particles of 800 grit from its surface.

Finally, chamfer every corner to save your fingers from painful nicks. Tip the stone at 45 degrees and sand in the chamfers (3–13). This also protects the corners from flaking from the pressure exerted while you hone. The stones are now ready for use.

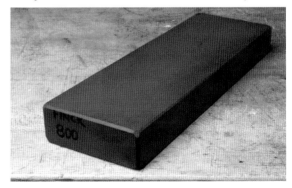

3–13. *This water stone has chamfered edges.*

SHARPENING PLANE IRONS

The following discussion is geared to plane irons, but holds equally true for spokeshaves and chisels. Knives are generally treated differently unless one face of the blade is meant to be perfectly flat, as with some marking and Japanese-style knives.

The Back Side

Do not underestimate the importance of preparing the back of the iron. It plays a significant part in determining the ultimate sharpness of the blade and how consistently it sharpens. Mistakes here can be costly in terms of time spent making corrections. Pay close attention and work carefully.

The first task is twofold: to flatten the back and polish it to a mirror shine (3–14 and 3–15). Generally, when grinding the beveled side of the iron, or honing it with an 800-grit stone, a small burr develops on the back side. This burr is easily removed by honing the back side with the 8,000-grit stone if both the stone and the back of the iron are flat. If the iron or stone is not flat, the task becomes chancy and leads to problems. The worst temptation is tipping the back edge of the blade up in order to concentrate pressure at the spot where the burr is. So doing drastically widens the wedge angle (3–16), and the performance of the plane plummets.

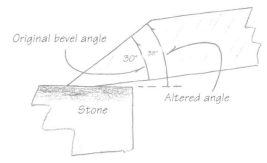

3–16. Tipping the blade up while flattening the back increases the wedge angle. You must avoid this.

Coarse grind marks on the back of a plane iron form nicks in the cutting edge that leave corresponding raised lines in the wood being planed (3–17). The flattening process eliminates the coarse grind marks. Polishing with successively finer stones leads to a mirror finish. When the back is polished to the same high degree as the beveled side, the edge will be its sharpest, leaving a slick, smooth surface on whatever is planed.

With a small straightedge, check the back of the blade for flatness across its width, as near to the cutting edge as possible. Do not be concerned if the blade shows a hollow beginning $1/16$ inch or more back from the cutting edge. In fact, its presence is

3–14. The polished back of a plane iron.

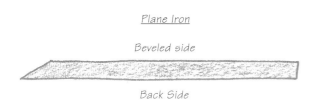

Plane Iron

Beveled side

Back Side

3–15. The two sides of a plane iron.

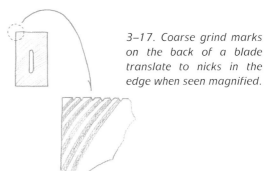

3–17. Coarse grind marks on the back of a blade translate to nicks in the edge when seen magnified.

beneficial, speeding the flattening and polishing process, because there is less metal to remove. Japanese blades are purposely made that way for this very reason.

Also check for flatness along the length of the blade. Concentrate on the last inch of blade nearest the cutting edge (3–18). This is the amount that will overlap the stone when the back side is honed. Pay closest attention right at the cutting edge. If you notice the back rolling away from the straightedge right there, the wedge angle will be too wide and you will not be able to remove a burr without tipping the blade when honing the back; this means some extra flattening work has to be done (refer to 3–16).

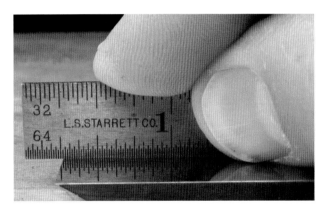

3–18. Checking the back of the iron for flatness lengthwise with a small straightedge.

Sharpening Technique

Select the iron to sharpen. I suggest you begin with the one from your block plane because it will need to be in top shape for plane-making. Make sure the stones are flat and well secured to the work surface. A stone with any dips or bumps will transfer inaccuracies to the back of the iron.

Now, prepare a "flattening stick" from a piece of wood that is $3/4$ x $1^1/4$ x 6 inches (3–19). The $1^1/4$-inch-wide surfaces should be flat. Nicely round all the sharp edges. The flattening stick allows energy to be focused on the middle of the iron, eliminating the natural tendency to inadvertently hone more material from the outer edges of the iron (creating

3–19. Iron and flattening stick in position on stone.

an arc rather than the desired flat). The stick allows more pressure to be exerted on the iron, speeding the progress, and helps you keep the iron flat on the stone.

Dip the stick in water and grip the plane iron and stick together as shown in 3–20. When you have the proficiency, plane the $1^1/4$-inch-wide surfaces. The flatness and smoothness of the planed stick grips the plane iron even better. Overlap half the width of the stone with the plane iron to equalize wear on the stone and give the iron enough support while honing, to avoid tipping it back to front. The goal is to create a flat surface on the back of the plane iron, from side to side and extending back at least $1/16$ inch from the cutting edge (3–21).

3–20. Gripping the iron and flattening stick.

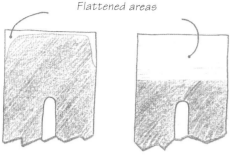

Flattened areas

3–21. Acceptably flattened plane-iron backs as revealed by polished areas.

Next, center yourself in front of the 800-grit stone. Make sure the stone is sopping wet and keep water on the surface with an occasional squirt from the water bottle. Begin honing with a back-and-forth motion covering the first third of the stone—try about six times back and forth. Then glide over the center and concentrate your efforts on the back third of the stone for six cycles. The harder you press, the faster the back will be flattened, but stay in complete control. Dip the iron in the stone's water tank and wipe it clean.

Sharpening requires a constant dialogue between you and the tools. You ask the questions and the tools give the answer. However, you must know what questions to ask and how to interpret the response. And beware of false assumptions.

Look at the back of the iron under bright light and you will see a zone of lighter gray developing where the iron has been contacting the stone. Finer-grit stones leave a brighter surface. The distribution of the zone corresponds to the high points

observed with the straightedge. If the center was humped, then it should show signs of wear without the corners' being touched. If the center was dipped (3–22B), the opposite holds true. An arc in the iron should show honing marks at the cutting edge and about an inch back, with the center untouched. If the cutting edge rolls away from the flatness of the back, then the back will be honed except right at the cutting edge (3–22C).

Check the honed areas against the straightedge. If they do not correspond, then there is a problem. Recheck the stone for flatness. For instance, if the iron is humped widthwise, but the stone has an even greater arc lengthwise, then the corners of the iron will be honed first and more of an arc will be produced across the iron. If the technique is faulty and you are rocking the plane iron widthwise or lengthwise while honing, you cannot rely on what is indicated by looking at the plane iron. The flattening stick is very useful to minimize these problems. As you gain confidence in your ability to read the plane iron, the straightedge will be relied on less and less, and will eventually be reserved perhaps for a final check.

As you progress, flip the stone end for end and hone on the other half of the same face. Then use the other face of the stone in the same fashion. Continue honing until the back is flattened as described and all of the coarser grinding marks in the flattened region have been replaced by the finer scratches of the 800-grit stone.

Needs work

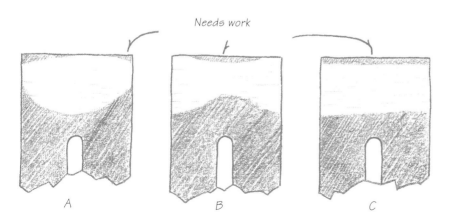

A   B   C

3–22. Plane-iron backs that need more flattening. The lack of polish at their cutting edges indicates problems. A: Plane iron with low corners. B: Plane iron with a hollowed center. C: Plane iron with a cutting edge that is rolled away.

If preferred, this initial flattening may be done using a coarse diamond stone lubricated with water. The diamond stone has the advantage of not wearing as you hone. Be sure the stone is flat before proceeding. Remove the scratches left by the diamond stone with the 800-grit stone.

Move to the 8,000-grit stone. This is contrary to the doctrine that one must progress slowly through intermediate grits before arriving at the finishing stone, but experience has taught me that the 8,000-grit stone cuts quickly enough to bypass this. (If it takes considerable time to polish off the scratches from the 800-grit stone, by all means use an intermediate stone to speed the progress— a 1,200-grit stone is a good choice.) Prepare the stone with a squirt of water and circular swipes of the nagura stone, covering the entire surface. Scratch several grooves on the bottom of the nagura with the sharp corner of a file tang to help it glide over the stone easier. Use the same honing technique as with the 800-grit stone. Rewet the stone and clean it with the nagura as the stone dries and blackens with use. The flattened area of the blade should take on a uniform mirror polish within moments—how soon is determined by how much pressure is applied while honing. Sometimes the bright polish will reveal scratches that are coarser than those of the 800-grit stone or slight defects in flatness that have not been noticed. Return to the 800-grit stone to rectify these problems; then advance again to the 8,000-grit stone to finish the work.

Now that the flattening and polishing have concluded, never hone the back of the iron again with anything but the 8,000-grit stone. That would only scratch the finely polished surface and lengthen the sharpening process.

The Beveled Side

The intersection of two planar surfaces creates the cutting edge for many conventional woodworking tools. The angle between the surfaces directly influences the working characteristics of

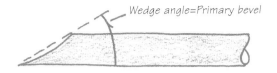

Blade with one bevel

Wedge angle=Primary bevel

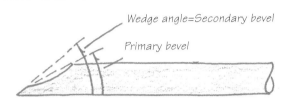

Blade with two bevels

Wedge angle=Secondary bevel

Primary bevel

3–23. Blade bevel and angle terminology. The two blades shown are the same thickness. Typically, thick blades are prepared with one bevel and thin blades are prepared with two.

the edge. The "wedge angle" (3–23) is the angle continuous with the cutting edge of the blade. The cutting edge is simply a wedge of steel, but the angle of that wedge, precisely where the cutting occurs, is of crucial importance. If the wedge angle is made too narrow, the cutting edge is weak, nicking and dulling easily, but as long as it remains sharp it will slice wood effortlessly. If the wedge angle is too wide, then the cutting edge cannot easily enter the wood to slice off a shaving—instead it tends to skitter and scrape across the surface. But the cutting edge is more durable—that is, it better resists dulling and chipping (this is called better "edge retention").

The wedge angle that best resolves the conflict between ease of slicing shavings and edge retention is 30 degrees. This is a serviceable angle for all woods. But woods do come in a great variety of hardness and with varying abrasive qualities. For example, a softwood like white pine planes beautifully with a wedge angle a couple of degrees narrower than 30 degrees without noticeably affecting the durability of the edge. A little experimentation may pay off with good results.

The terms "macro-bevel" and "micro-bevel" are often used interchangeably with "primary" and "secondary bevel."

Sharpening the Beveled Side of Thick and Thin Blades

Consider two different approaches for sharpening the beveled side of plane irons based on the thickness of the blade. Anything $1/8$ inch thick or less I categorize as a thin iron. Such a blade is prepared with two bevels: the *primary* or *macro-bevel,* formed with the grinder; and the *secondary* or *micro-bevel,* honed right at the tip. If the blade is thicker than $1/8$ inch, it is a thick iron and it receives only a primary bevel. For a thick iron, the wedge angle is the same as the primary bevel. The wedge angle on a thin iron is the same as the secondary bevel. The key to this approach is to combine the speed of water stones with the flexibility of freehand honing (as opposed to using honing jigs or guides).

The thicker the blade, the wider the bevel at a given angle. Thick irons have a bevel wide enough to balance upon easily, making freehand honing simple to master with consistent results. The bevel on a thin iron is too narrow for that (3–24). Thin irons require a modified approach that is a little trickier to master, though still quite effective.

Wooden planes will accommodate specialized irons that are even thicker than "thick" replacement blades designed for metal planes. A major plus of making your own planes is capturing the sharpening advantage that the thickest irons offer.

GRINDING AND HONING GUIDELINES

Knowing when to grind and when to hone requires some considered judgment. Choosing properly increases sharpening efficiency and will get you planing again more quickly. In general, think of the grinder for quick metal removal and precise setting of bevel angles. Hone when little metal needs to be removed to achieve razor sharpness, to obliterate small nicks, and to fine-tune the shape of the edge, whether it is straight or slightly arced. Grinding and honing techniques are given below.

Grinding Techniques

First and foremost, grinding establishes and maintains the primary angle in a reliable manner. Whenever the wedge angle has wandered a few degrees away from 30 degrees, grinding is the first step to reestablishing the mark. Grinding quickly obliterates nicks and reestablishes the edge of an overly dulled blade. Honing can also be used to do this. The choice between grinding and honing in these situations depends on your skills at both jobs. Whichever achieves the goal more quickly should be the method of choice.

Grinding with the circumference of a wheel creates a corresponding arc in the bevel on the blade called a "hollow grind" (3–25). The hollow

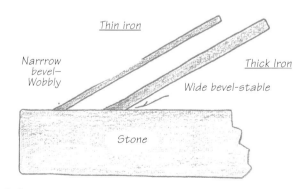

3–24. Freehand honing is difficult while attempting to rest on a thin bevel. A wide bevel offers more support and eases the task.

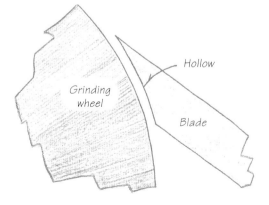

3–25. The arc of a grinding wheel imparts the same arc on the bevel of a blade, resulting in a hollow grind.

grind provides two points of contact at the toe and heel of the bevel, providing a stable platform when honing the wide bevel found on thick irons (3–26). Repeated honings flatten out the hollow grind. Regrind the entire bevel once the honed flats that develop occupy one-half to two-thirds of the bevel (3–27).

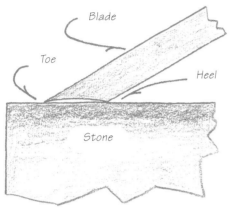

3–26. Honing a hollow-ground blade on a stone with the bevel resting on its toe and heel.

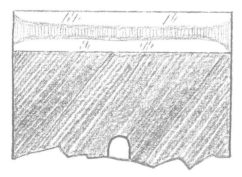

3–27. Polished flats, the result of honing a hollow-ground blade, occupy more than two-thirds of the bevel. It is time to regrind.

Grinding should help create the final shape, or very close to the final shape, of the cutting edge. It should be straight across for jointing and truing, and slightly arced for polishing surfaces. Grind to restore a wavy or hollowed cutting edge to its proper shape. Finally, if the angle formed by the cutting edge and a side of the blade is way off of 90 degrees, there may not be sufficient lateral adjust-ment in the plane body to bring the cutting edge into parallel alignment with the bottom of the plane. Grinding is the best way to restore that angle to 90 degrees.

Determining Whether the Bevel Angles Are Correct

The primary angle of a thin iron should be 25 degrees, and the secondary angle should be 30 degrees (3–28). A thick iron should have only a primary angle of 30 degrees. The reasons for both are given below. Gauge the primary bevel with the type of protractor shown in 3–29. The secondary bevel is a little trickier because generally it is quite small. Try rolling the beam of the protractor up to the secondary bevel while sighting at a bright light source. Concentrate your gaze right at the tip of the cutting edge, where a small dot of light should be seen. When that dot of light finally disappears, with the tip of the blade tucked right into the vertex of the beam and base of the protractor, you should be

3–28. Thin iron with ground primary bevel and honed (pol-ished) secondary bevel.

3–29. Gauging the primary bevel with a protractor.

exactly on the cutting edge of the secondary bevel, where the reading is meaningful.

If the iron has been honed freehand, chances are the bevel directly influencing the wedge angle has been domed in the process. This makes it difficult to get a precise protractor reading. More importantly, a blade in this condition usually has an excessive wedge angle. The primary angle probably started out in the 25- to 30-degree range. Each time the iron is rehoned, there is a natural tendency to tilt the blade higher and higher, producing a domed or rounded bevel. The wedge angle may end up at 35 degrees or higher (3–30), resulting in poor performance regardless of edge sharpness.

Here's a trick to assess the flatness of the bevel forming the wedge angle: Position yourself with a light source above and behind you. If the bevel is flat, the reflection is uniform and will reflect light to your eye when the iron is held at *one specific angle*. If the bevel is domed, the reflection scatters and light reflects to your eye as the iron is rotated over *a range of angles* (3–31). The wider the degree

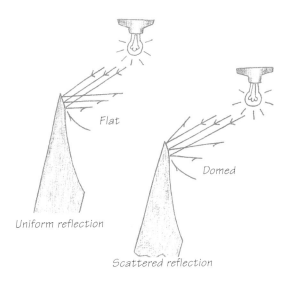

3–31. *A flat bevel reflects light uniformly. You will see a reflection with the blade at a specific angle. A domed bevel scatters the reflection. It can be seen over a range of angles.*

of rotation, the more of a dome there is, and the steeper the wedge angle.

Setting the Tool Rest

With the grinder at rest, place the blade, bevel side down, on the tool-rest platform and bring the bevel up to the wheel until the two contact. Sight from the side and observe where the wheel contacts the bevel: at the toe, middle, or heel (3–32). A bright light, white wall, or a piece of white mat board on the far side of the wheel greatly facilitates visibility and, thus, accuracy. The existing primary-bevel angle

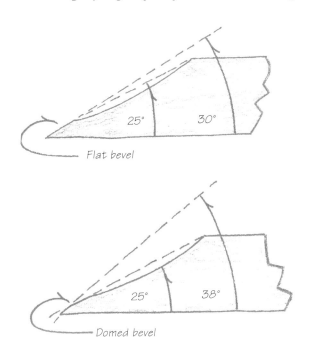

3–30. *A domed secondary bevel unacceptably increases the wedge angle.*

3–32. *Checking the angle of the tool rest. Observe how the arc of the wheel relates to the bevel of the blade.*

will be maintained if the arc of the wheel contacts the bevel in the middle, or along its entirety. The primary bevel will be widened if the wheel contacts closer to the toe, and it will be narrowed if the wheel contacts closer to the heel of the bevel (3–33).

It is easy to effect accurate adjustments of the tool rest described in this text. First, adjust the tensioning bolt that holds the tool-rest platform so that the platform is held snugly but can still be rotated by hand without straining. Roughly set the proper angle of the platform. Then position the tool rest so that the front edge of the platform is $1/8$ to $1/4$ inch from the outer face of the wheel and tighten the

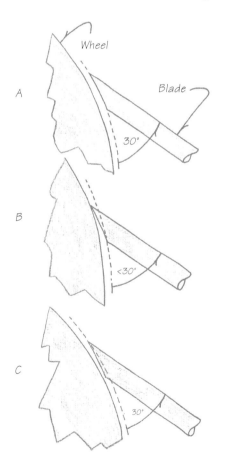

3–33. Sighting the grinding wheel and blade from the side indicates the effects of grinding on the existing primary-bevel angle.
A: A maintained bevel angle. B: A widened angle.
C: A narrowed angle.

base firmly in place. Sight again on the contact point of wheel and bevel. If the adjustment looks good, you are set for a trial grind. If the adjustment is off, proceed as follows.

It is more difficult to get an accurate setting while angling the platform up, so always start with the platform tilted too high in the front. Use the blade itself as a depth stop to make minute movements of the platform. Bring the bevel into contact with the wheel, and then back it away $1/32$ to $1/16$ inch. Pinch the blade snugly to the platform with your fingers and rotate the platform and blade together into the wheel until the blade bottoms on the wheel. Continue moving incrementally like so until the platform is angled precisely as you want it. If you overshoot, back up and try again.

Make a trial cut with the grinder by simply touching the bevel lightly to the moving wheel. Look at the bevel and see if the fresh grind mark is in the right place. Continue adjusting the platform and making test grinds until you are satisfied. If planning to alter the existing angle, you won't have a good idea of the exact angle you are grinding at until the new bevel is ground out sufficiently wide so that a reading can be taken with the protractor. Alter the current angle by a degree or so each time, until you close in on the 25- or 30-degree mark.

It should be noted that if an angle slightly greater or smaller than the targeted angle cuts well and holds its edge, by all means stick with it. With some experimentation, the performance of different blades can be optimized this way.

Gripping the Blade

As a right-hander, I lightly grasp the blade in my left hand as shown in 3–34. The thumb on the right side of the blade and the middle finger on the left control side-to-side movement. The index finger is the heat sensor. Keep it in the middle of the blade and quite close to the tip, within $1/4$ inch or so. Take care not to grind your fingertip; this is a potential danger, but is unlikely to happen if you concentrate on the task at hand. Should the blade warm to the

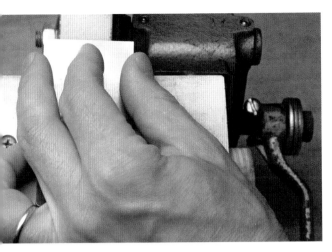

3–34. Blade-grinding grip.

point where the finger can no longer be comfortably positioned there, it is time to cool the blade. If the blade is short enough, about 3½ inches long or so, the pinkie can capture the end of the blade; this is insurance against the blade's slipping backwards while grinding, and falling to the floor.

For a smooth motion and clean grinding results, the hand and fingers must be relaxed, with the fingers slouched over and the rear palm of the hand resting lightly on the blade or the tool rest (3–35). The thumb and middle finger should glide over the tool rest as the iron is slid from side to side while grinding. Remember, the rotation of the wheel down onto the tool rest will naturally keep the blade down. Only the lightest downward pressure is needed. If the fingers are elevated and tense, move-

3–35. The fingers should be slouched over and relaxed.

ments will be herky-jerky, resulting in a poor grinding job. Excessive downward pressure will also alter the adjustment of the tool-rest angle. Practice the grip and side-to-side movement with the grinder off.

Determining Straightness and Arc in the Cutting Edge

An acceptable *straight* contour for the cutting edge is fairly easy to verify, and is described in the following section. When sighted with a straightedge, the range may vary from no discernible light-filled gaps along the edge to very slight gaps, at the corners only, that extend perhaps for ⅛ to 3/16 inch. The proper degree of arc, however, is more nebulous, and the amount of arc needed is related to the type of surface desired. If a surface that feels flat and smooth is desired, the arc will be minimal. If a scalloped feel is desired, that calls for considerably more arc. In neither case are the corners of the edge simply clipped off. That always results in a harsh "stairstep" feel to the surface. Likewise, a hollowed contour yields the same effect.

When determining the arc on the blade, place a straightedge on the cutting edge. It should roll smoothly on the arc. Experimentation and practice will move you toward your goal.

When polish-planing and taking those last few strokes that will be the finished surface, the shaving thickness should be around .001 to .002 inch. For a flat surface, free of discernible scalloping, those shavings must be nearly the full width of the blade. Clearly, the arc must be very small to achieve this, but it must be present or the corners of the blade iron will dig into the wood.

Assessing the Contour of the Cutting Edge

Make a small hardwood straightedge to check the condition of the edge. Fine-grained wood like maple, beech, and pear or boxwood works well. Mine is 3/16 inch thick, 3 inches long, and ½ inch tall. A steel straightedge may be used, but wood seems more at home against a steel cutting edge. Hold the straightedge against the cutting edge and sight against a bright light (3–36). The union of the two should be seamless if the cutting edge is straight. Alternatively, if the blade is properly arced it will rock ever so slightly on a hump in the center of the blade. The light should reveal a point of contact in the center with gradually wider light-filled gaps toward the corners. If the blade is hollowed, there will be contact points at the corners and a light-filled gap in the center.

3–36. Assessing the contour of the iron's cutting edge with a hardwood straightedge.

Grinding the Blade

The critical skill in grinding is maintaining the bevel of the iron flat on the wheel while sliding the iron from side to side. If the blade pivots while you are grinding, only a corner of the wheel contacts the bevel, making it difficult to achieve the desired result, but very easy to grind a wavy or hollowed edge.

It is extremely helpful if you can see clearly the relationship between the cutting edge and the wheel while grinding. Position your body in line with the axis of the wheel, off to the side of the grinder. From there, it is possible to sight down over the wheel and see the point of contact between the iron and wheel. If the blade pivots away from the wheel slightly as you are grinding, a small, but readily visible, angled shadow line occurs, providing instant feedback to make an adjustment (3–37). A light touch gripping the iron, combined with some practice, eventually allows you to *feel* when the iron is flat on the wheel as you

are grinding, but until then a direct visual cue is a great boon.

3–37. The correct sight line reveals an angled shadow line between the wheel and the cutting edge (evident below the index finger) if the bevel is not flat on the wheel.

Before you begin grinding, you should know when to stop. This is when the bevel is at the correct angle, the edge contoured properly, and a very slight burr has been raised at the cutting edge from corner to corner on the back of the iron. Furthermore, the grinding should obliterate any previous traces of honing from heel to toe of the bevel. The presence of the burr is very important; it indicates that the bevel and back meet at a crisp line and are ready for honing. Until the burr arises, a rounded or dulled condition still exists at the cutting edge (3–38).

Assess your goal and current conditions before you start grinding. Is the objective a straight or arced cutting edge? Is the edge already properly contoured or does it need reshaping? Is the wedge angle correct? Does the angle of the cutting edge relative to the side of the blade need adjustment? Has the blade been honed previously or is it new? Typically a new blade will require grinding only if the primary bevel angle is off or the cutting edge is blunt. In the case of a thick iron, is there a hollow grind present? The answers to these questions guide your intent as you grind.

Turn on the grinder and gently bring the bevel to bear against the wheel. Even with light pressure, and a clean (unglazed), coarse wheel, there may be

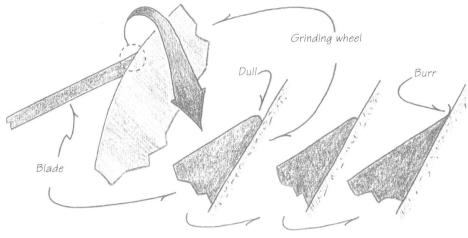

3–38. Development of burr during grinding: it appears when the beveled side and the back meet at a knife edge.

Grinding wheel

Dull

Burr

Blade

Grinding progress

some overheating. Cool the blade in a can of cold water if your heat-sensing finger gets too hot. Pushing hard against the wheel heats the tool rapidly and may also cause the bevel to ride up on the wheel and off the tool rest, altering the angle of the bevel. Begin sliding the iron from side to side while maintaining full contact between the bevel and wheel. The object is to grind the full bevel from corner to corner. Every 10 seconds or so turn the iron over and examine your progress.

If the edge contour is correct to begin with (straight or arced) and the blade has been previously honed, the shiny honed area at the cutting edge offers a road map to guide your grinding progress. The grinding should shape the honed area into an even band parallel to the cutting edge. It is likely, though, that the band will taper, or be wider in some spots than others. With the bevel still kept flat on the wheel, and while you are still moving the iron from side to side, linger on the areas that need more grinding and avoid or quickly pass over the areas that are overground. When the honed band at the cutting edge has been evened out, resume corner-to-corner grinding again.

There may be a tendency to overgrind the center of the bevel. To counter this, linger at each corner before passing through the center. Continue checking on the progress of the grinding until the honed area

at the tip is almost completely gone, having been replaced by newly ground metal. If the honed area is already gone at the heel, then the primary angle has been narrowed. If there is more honed area remaining at the heel than at the tip, the primary angle has been widened. You may wish to slightly adjust the tool-rest angle to correct this.

As you come to the finish, the honed area at the tip should completely disappear at once, and the burr simultaneously develop all across the back side of the edge. Carefully diagnose the extent of the burr with a fingernail pulled upward from the rear of the blade over the edge (3–39). A fingernail

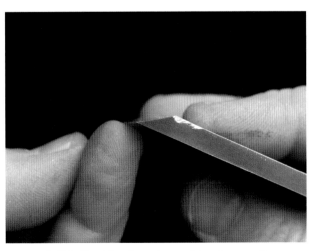

3–39. Checking for a burr with a fingernail.

will catch on the slightest burr, but if the pad of the finger is being used the burr may not be detected until it has grown relatively large. Check all along the edge for the burr. If it is not present the entire way across, continue grinding, but avoid the spots where the burr has developed already. If you continue grinding those areas, the edge will become hollowed there.

If the contour of the edge is inadequate to begin with, make use of the straightedge to assess the situation. If the edge is hollowed in the center, linger at the outer edges while grinding. If the edge is overly arced, then linger in the center. If the edge is wavy, concentrate on keeping the bevel in full contact with the wheel. If the edge is skewed left or right and you wish to restore it to square, again simply spend more time grinding whichever side is high (in contact with the square when taking a reading). Do not entirely neglect the low side. Feather the strokes there occasionally. Feathering consists of grinding on the "high" side and then moving slightly toward the "low" side. This is repeated, moving farther toward the "low" side with each succession.

In summary, do the following: Keep moving from side to side over the iron, keep the iron in full contact with the wheel; and devote extra grinding time to those spots that register as high with the straightedge. Of course, the contour of the cutting edge does not change until the new grind marks have reached the edge and a burr has developed. Once you have effected a change, roughly gauge the progress with the straightedge, which will give only a rough reading because of interference from the burr. When the cutting edge is close to a final contour, hone the burr away with the 8,000-grit stone (read on about honing technique), and then obtain an accurate reading with the straightedge. As you will discover below, the shape of the honed flat that develops on the bevel also cues you to the condition of the contour. You may need to hop from wheel to stone a few times until satisfied with the result. Be very picky! If the task cannot be completed with

the wheel, do as much as possible with it and finish the job honing with stones. Before long, properly grinding an iron will take just a moment.

Honing Technique

When honing, the objectives are speed, accuracy, and, most of all, utmost sharpness. Hone in the following situations: after grinding the edge; any time the edge has lost razor sharpness and can be reconditioned quickly with the stones; and to obliterate minor nicks. Honing also tailors the shape of the edge, be it perfectly straight or slightly arced.

You may feel that the more time spent honing, the sharper the edge will get. This is simply not true. With a clear grasp of the fundamentals and a knowledge of what to look for, honing typically requires 30 to 90 seconds. Longer sessions are usually counterproductive. Excessive honing erodes the hollow grind of a thick iron and alters the wedge angle of a thin iron. Literally, then, it's back to the grinding wheel.

When honing, grasp the iron as shown in 3–40, with the three fingers (or two for narrow irons) as low down to the stone as possible, but without allowing them to drag on the surface. The low grip allows energy to be transferred efficiently to the cutting edge and, in the case of thick irons, is key to creating stability while honing. Slight upward pressure from the thumb and pinkie tucks the iron into the palm or against the heel of the hand. With the wrist held firm, the iron, hand, and forearm become a single unit that guards against wobble and gives close control over the selected honing angle. *Caution*: If your fingers consistently contact the stone while honing, the skin will be worn off; bloody streaks on the stone are the first indication (ouch!).

Stand with knees relaxed and slightly bent. Place one foot about six inches in front of the other, and feet a little more than shoulder-width apart. Hone in a tightly looping circular pattern, letting the corners of the iron overlap the long sides of the

3–40. Honing grip for plane irons.

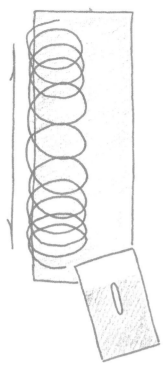

3–41. Circular honing pattern. Use the whole stone and pass over the center quickly.

stone by $1/4$ inch or so (3–41). The circular motion originates almost entirely from the shoulder; hold your wrist and elbow firm, but without tension. Traverse the length of the stone while circling; because the center is contacted twice for each time an end is hit, linger at the front and back thirds and pass quickly through the center to spread wear evenly. The front-to-back movement is effected by moving the *entire* upper body with the *knees*, not the arm, making it much easier to maintain the angle of the forearm and, hence, the wedge angle.

Use as much pressure and circle as rapidly as you can while maintaining complete control. More pressure and speed lead to a quicker honing job. Be gentle while learning the motions. It is all too easy to inadvertently slide off the stone, chipping off a chunk of it in the process. Another consideration about pressure concerns the size of the iron. If the pressure from your hand is constant, then the narrower the blade, the higher the developed pressure (pounds per square inch) on the cutting edge, so

smaller tools sharpen more quickly. You may on occasion need to back off, to avoid excessively sharpening the blade or gouging the stones. With expe-rience, speed and pressure can be tailored to the specific tool.

I do not use other honing patterns for plane irons, finding that they are slower, more difficult to control, and promote uneven wear of the stones.

Honing Thick and Thin Irons

Thick irons are honed with the primary bevel laid flat on the stone. As described above, proper grip and motion, along with the wide bevel, should allow you to hone with no trace of wobble. As you hone, *two* polished flats develop: one at the cutting edge and one at the heel of the bevel. They should grow at equal rates as you hone, and show no evidence of doming. Doming indicates wobble; concentrate on focusing the force of the fingertips right through the middle of the bevel if troubles persist.

Honing thin irons is somewhat more demanding. Recall that the primary bevel of a thin iron is too narrow to balance on while honing with any measure of stability. It is used simply as a reference. At rest, place the bevel on the stone and gently rock the iron until you sense that the bevel is flat on the stone. The blade is now at 25 degrees if the bevel was ground correctly. Pick up the heel of the blade very slightly, increasing the angle of the blade to approximately 30 degrees. Think of the iron as the minute hand of a clock pivoting at the cutting edge, and note that merely one minute of travel on a clock face corresponds to six degrees of rotation.

Now hone the secondary (micro-) bevel using the same technique described earlier. Only one polished flat should develop, right at the tip. The heel of the bevel should remain untouched. Check the amount of doming on the micro-bevel (refer to 3–31) each time you go to resharpen. If it exceeds more than a few degrees, it is time to reestablish the primary angle with the grinder. With practice, you will have little problem maintaining the wedge angle for several sharpenings before returning to the grinder.

Honing Irons with a Ground Edge

For irons that have been freshly ground to a knife-like edge and have a burr present (this includes most new irons), begin honing at what is usually considered the final honing stage, that is, with the 8,000-grit (finish) stone. Don't be skeptical. The 8,000-grit stone will quickly polish the bevel and simultaneously remove any burr on the back side, regardless of the coarseness of the grinding wheel used on the bevel. This works not only because water stones cut quickly, but also because tremendous pressure is developed at the edge when a freshly ground blade is being sharpened. The surface area being honed is very small, so consequently the PSI is very high. Following this advice minimizes time spent honing and time spent grinding irons and flattening stones. Also,

the accuracy of freehand honing is greatly enhanced by minimizing contact time with the stones.

The burr obscures both the contour of the cutting edge and the presence of nicks. Polish the bevel briefly to obtain a reading of the shape of the edge: about five seconds of honing to develop a flat $1/64$ inch wide should be sufficient. If the 8,000-grit stone is kept meticulously flat, it can reveal if the shape is straight, wavy, arced, or hollowed, and to what degree. The location and extent of the polished bevel amplify the condition of the cutting edge (3–42). It is important to keep pressure in the middle of the iron while honing, to avoid false readings. You will also get false readings if the stone is out of flat.

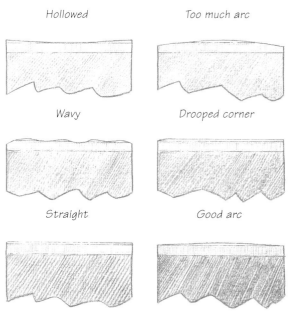

3–42. Assessing the grind of a plane iron. A brief honing polishes the bevel, giving a diagnostic of the shape of the cutting edge.

If the contour is off, always apply this rule: Grind away the shiny area(s) of the bevel just honed, while avoiding the spots that have not been honed. Honing on a *flat* stone always reveals the high spots of the cutting edge. If the center is hollowed, the ends will polish first and must be ground down. Likewise, the center will polish first if it is overly arced and will need grinding down. A good straight contour is revealed by a perfectly even line of polished bevel the full width of the iron. A good arced bevel is polished in the center and gradually peters out toward the edges (refer to 3–42). Alternate grinding and taking a reading with the finish stone until you achieve the proper contour, straight or arced; then finish honing on the 8,000-grit stone. If controlling the grinder proves to be too difficult at this stage, substitute the coarse stone to achieve the same effect.

Balanced pressure while honing with the coarse stone yields a straight edge. To arc the edge, simply alternate pressure at the corners of the bevel. If your index, middle, and ring fingers are supplying downward pressure, press harder with the index finger while circling up the stone; then press harder with the ring finger while circling back down. The blade will be arced in no time. To tell if you are on the right track, check the burr; it should be more prominent toward the corners than in the center. Honing similarly on the 8,000-grit stone yields an evenly polished bevel, though arced, from corner to corner.

Another, more elegant method of arcing the edge is easier still, but may not work for everyone. Despite the care I take to distribute wear over the stone's surfaces, they still eventually hollow slightly in length and width, but they do not progressively worsen. They reach a certain point and hold. I noted this once to a friend and he responded that the woodworker Toshio Odate reserved just such an arced stone for shaping his irons. By simply honing the bevel with balanced pressure, the arc of the stone is transferred to the iron. Now I keep an additional coarse stone, which I never flatten, and it always produces a nice arc on my irons. Use the alternating-pressure method on the 8,000-grit stone to polish the entire arc.

Obtaining the optimum arc requires finesse at the stones and experience with the planes. The planes must be in perfect working order and there must be precise control over the depth and lateral adjustments in order to evaluate the iron. Sometimes I think I've arced the blade properly, but the results are not what they should be. In this case, I return to the coarse stone, remove or add a little arc as required, finish-hone, and try the blade again. Sometimes this might take two or three attempts, but these efforts are always rewarded when the plane starts slicing lacy shavings without a trace of the corners of the blade marring the planed surface.

Once the edge is properly shaped, finish-hone the bevel with two or three trips up and down the 8,000-grit stone, polishing it to a high sheen. Then hone the back side. Use the same technique as when flattening the back, except there is no need to use a flattening stick; just use your fingers. Since honing the bevel probably already removed the burr, the purpose here is simply to keep the back side nicely polished and free of corrosion. A few short strokes at either end of the stone, avoiding the center, suffice and prevent the stone from hollowing.

Checking for Sharpness and Nicks

After honing, objectively assess whether the edge is free from nicks and sufficiently sharp for planing. You must determine if the blade needs more honing, a return to the grinder, or is ready for use. While it is very satisfying to shave off hairs to test a freshly sharpened blade, this method delivers no information about the presence of small nicks. Nicks in the blade leave raised lines in the wood as you plane. Also, the hair-shaving test presents a threshold: the blade either is, or isn't, sharp enough to do it. Some woods demand the very sharpest blade, and the thumbnail-drag test reveals sharpness along the continuum. A touch will indicate just how sharp the blade is.

Hold your thumbnail on the edge of the blade as shown in 3–43. Drag the tip of your nail along the length of the blade. Be careful to angle your thumb sufficiently so that its tip does not contact the edge, or you will get a nasty slice! If your nail gliding along the edge feels frictionless, like a knife edge dragged across ice, the blade is very sharp, free of defects, and ready for use. If your thumbnail seemed to catch here and there, you have located nicks in the edge. The bigger the catch, the bigger the nick. You may need to rehone with the coarse stone or even go back to the grinder to remove the nicks; both can do the job, so it's a matter of experience deciding which will use your time more efficiently. If you feel uniform friction while dragging your nail across the blade, the blade is not sharp enough and may indicate the continued presence of a burr left from grinding or coarse honing; return to the fine stone to remove the burr and further sharpen the edge. Continue the process until a sharp, nick-free edge is achieved. An iron with softer steel usually requires only one cycle. The entire process of coarse and fine honing should take about 30 to 90 seconds.

3–43. Thumbnail-drag test.

Rehoning the Cutting Edge

Several cues indicate the blade needs resharpening. The presence of raised lines on the planed surface correspond to nicks in the blade edge. You may notice after planing for some time that the plane starts producing dust and the blade needs to be advanced to continue taking a fine shaving. Perhaps the surface now exhibits tear-out whereas before the blade cut cleanly. Observing the bevel with the blade still installed in the plane may show a white line at the cutting edge when viewed with bright light. The worn edge of the blade has rounded and scatters light to give this appearance. All of the above indicate it is time to resharpen.

Again, the decision to rehone rather than regrind takes some experience, the final arbiter being which technique will get you back to planing more quickly. Generally, a blade that is simply dull can be quickly restored by honing, as can one with small nicks. A thick blade still possessing adequate hollow-grind should also be rehoned, as should a thin blade that is not overly domed at the microbevel.

Begin with the 800-grit stone. The primary purpose of this step is to form a crisp knife-like edge where the bevel and the back side of the blade meet. Just as with grinding, this occurs the moment a burr is discernible on the back edge of the blade. Until a burr arises, the cutting edge still exhibits rounding that occurred from the abrasion of planing. The edge contour should still be satisfactory, so hone to maintain a straight or arced edge as needed.

Use the 800-grit stone sparingly. When I use the 800-grit stone on plane blades of particularly hard steel, circling up and down the stone two times will usually create a burr. This takes about 30 seconds. Of course, this varies with blade hardness and how dull and, consequently, how rounded the cutting edge was to start with. A blade of softer steel, typical of most thin irons, often needs only one trip down the length of the stone. For some irons, even one straight stroke—with no circling at all—can develop the burr. This takes just a few seconds. Remember, any time spent beyond the absolute minimum required to achieve the barest possible burr is unnecessary and wasteful. Also, note that only the beveled side of the iron has been worked on the 800-grit stone. Remember, once the back side has been flattened and polished with the 8,000-

grit stone, it should never contact the 800-grit stone again. Proceed to the 8,000-grit stone and finish honing as directed above.

Producing an Extremely Sharp Blade

Though the 8,000-grit stone produces sharpness sufficient for most occasions, I sometimes seek an even higher level of sharpness for extremely demanding situations. Stropping with 14,000-mesh-equivalent diamond compound (available through lapidary supply sources) does the job. To prepare a strop, glue a $2^1/_2$ x 12-inch piece of unsplit cowhide, smooth side out, to a backing board. Charge the surface with dots of compound (3–44). Press the bevel firmly on the strop as if preparing to hone. Drag the iron *away* from the cutting edge while holding the angle steady. Beware of rounding the cutting edge. Always stroke away from the cutting edge or the strop will be quickly sliced up. Repeat this four or five times, and then drag the back side a time or two. The thumbnail-drag test will reveal an even slicker, thus sharper, edge. The compound lasts for many stroppings; recharge as necessary.

SHARPENING STRAIGHT CHISELS

The principles for honing and grinding, and deciding which approach is needed, are precisely the same for chisels as for plane irons. The technique is a variation on the theme established with plane irons.

Grinding Narrow and Wide Chisels

For chisels to work well, it is important to maintain a crisp, straight cutting edge that is at a 90-degree angle to the side. This can be a challenge. Typically, chisels that are somewhat narrower than the width of the grinding wheel, perhaps $^3/_4$ inch wide and under, are clumsy to grind with the side-to-side motion introduced for plane irons. Their width, insufficient to register on the face of the wheel, and the extended length of their handles combine to create a wobbly situation. These narrower chisels demand a different grinding technique. With the tool rest supporting the chisel at the proper angle (see below), gently prod the grinding wheel with the chisel tip, not so much moving the chisel in and out, but pulsing the *pressure* on and off the wheel while maintaining contact. Keep the chisel properly oriented to the face of the wheel to yield a cutting edge 90 degrees to the side. It may help to clamp a guide block to the tool rest to guide the side of the chisel.

Remember, for a given amount of force applied, the narrower the chisel, the higher the PSI developed while grinding. Thus, chisels grind and heat up rapidly. Feel for overheating and be sure to back off the pressure when grinding narrower chisels.

Chisels that are wider than the wheel call for the side-to-side motion used to grind plane irons. With the full width of the wheel registering against the edge, controlling the chisel is not much more difficult than grinding a plane iron.

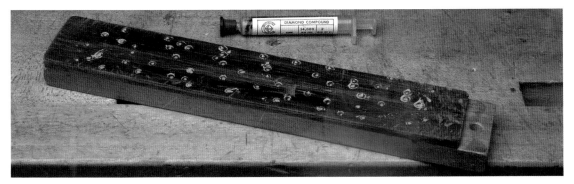

3–44. A strop charged with compound.

3–45. The proper chisel grip for honing.

Despite the thickness of most chisels, treat the bevel angles the same as those on thin irons: the primary bevel should be ground to 25 degrees, and the secondary bevel honed at 30 degrees. Chisels cannot be adequately gripped for honing in the same way as thick irons: when the fingertips concentrate pressure over the bevel, the handle cantilevers out too far, creating an unbalanced arrangement. Additionally, narrow chisels do not have a wide enough bevel to provide a stable platform.

Preparing Chisels for Sharpening

Chisel backs are flattened and polished the same way as plane-iron backs, but since chisels have handles there is no need for a flattening stick to aid in the process.

Honing the Bevel

Depending on the width of the chisel, place your index finger or your index and middle fingers on the back of the chisel about $1/2$ inch from the edge. Press the chisel handle against your wrist and the heel of your palm by squeezing up against the chisel with the pinkie and ring finger (3–45). The chisel should feel like an extension of your forearm. Keep your forearm at a constant angle while honing and the chisel will follow, producing a precisely honed secondary bevel.

Because of the high pressure developed when honing narrow chisels, those under one inch are quickly done with a few straight strokes. Start at the far end of the stone, and rest the chisel securely on the primary bevel. Tilt the chisel up slightly, just as with thin plane irons, to arrive, approximately, at a 30-degree secondary bevel. Apply balanced pressure to the cutting edge with your finger(s) resting on the back, and drag straight toward yourself along the length of the stone. Use your legs to make the movement, rather than your arms or shoulders, and there will be no trouble maintaining the angle. A burr should develop in one to three strokes on the 800-grit stone.

Thicker chisels may require the circular motion if the burr does not develop right away with straight strokes. Observe the microbevel: if you notice that it tapers in width from one side of the chisel to the other, the pressure exerted on it is unbalanced and the edge will eventually lose its

90-degree relationship to the side of the chisel (3–46). Make an adjustment with the next stroke to even out the microbevel. If one finger is supplying pressure, reposition it slightly toward the side where the microbevel is narrower. If using two fingers, simply press down a little harder with the finger on the side that needs more pressure.

Tapered microbevel

Shift to the 8,000-grit stone. Hone the microbevel two or three straight strokes for narrow chisels, or up and down the stone with a circular motion for wider chisels. Hone the back side briefly, and then check for sharpness. Repeat if necessary. Stropping with diamond compound is reserved for special situations when that extra level of sharpness is required.

3–46. Too much pressure on the left side of the chisel creates a tapered flat on the bevel. This will lead to a skewed cutting edge.

SHARPENING SPOKESHAVE IRONS

Irons for the No. 151-pattern spokeshave are usually less than $1/8$ inch thick, and are treated in precisely the same manner as thin plane irons. Locking the short iron into your hand at a precise angle while honing poses a modest difficulty.

SHARPENING KNIVES

Knives are tricky to sharpen because it is difficult to set the bevel angles reliably. Knives work best when they start slicing at a very low angle. If the blade must be angled up significantly in order to start cutting, it will not perform well regardless of how sharp; it will tend to skitter across the surface or dive in deeply. Shoot for a combined wedge angle of 20 to 25 degrees.

Hone the knife on a narrow side of the stone to prevent hollowing the face. Start on the 800-grit stone. For a double-beveled knife, lay the blade flat on the stone. Then elevate it to about 10 to 12 degrees; use a protractor to help you estimate this at first. Hold that angle and, with a looping spiral motion, work your way along a section of the stone (3–47).

Hone the other bevel following the same procedure. Look closely at the edge with help from a bright light, and even a magnifying glass. Make sure that you have honed out to the cutting edge. It may take a bit of honing to overcome an excessive wedge angle if the knife has been improperly sharpened in the past. Continue honing until a burr can be discerned (use the thumbnail-drag test); the burr indicates that you are ready to proceed to the 8,000-grit stone. Use the same technique as for the 800-grit stone, although the backing board and narrower thickness of the 8,000-grit stone force you to hone on the face. Drag your thumbnail across the edge again to test for sharpness, making sure that the burr has been removed. A final stropping with diamond compound brings the knife to razor sharpness. Once again try to maintain a consistent bevel angle; do not roll the blade while stropping. Stropping is essential because it is difficult to hone knives consistently at the correct angle.

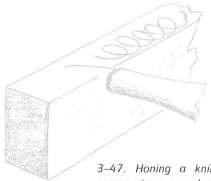

3–47. Honing a knife using a coarse stone on edge. Hone the knife with a circular pattern.

Making a Carving/Marking Knife

The blades on most marking and carving knives feel too thick and bulky for my taste. The types of knives shown in 3–48 are easily made and perform beautifully for marking and also for carving delicate details. Discarded saber-saw blades make good knife blanks, combining springiness and good edge retention. Shape the blade slowly and carefully with a grinding wheel, taking care not to draw the temper of the steel.

Alternatively, this project provides a good opportunity to become acquainted with the basics of heat-treating metal—annealing, hardening, and tempering—which can be easily done on this small scale. The advantage is that the blank may be easily shaped with the steel in a softened state, and then rehardened and tempered.

Heat-treating employs high-temperature heat sources and potentially flammable materials. Caution must be taken. Use gloves and safety glasses, and it is wise to have a fire extinguisher on hand. First anneal, or soften, the steel. Hold the knife blank with vise grips and heat the end that will become the cutting edge with a propane torch until it is cherry red. It is easiest to observe the colors of annealing and hardening in a darkened shop. Allow the blade to cool slowly by thrusting the heated blade into a can of wood ashes. When it is at room temperature, the metal can be worked with a file, grinder, or belt sander, with no concern for overheating the steel.

When the blade has been shaped, harden it by heating it to cherry-red and then quenching the blade in a can filled with motor oil or water, swirling it around until the metal has cooled. The blank should now be brittle-hard. To harden it properly, you must know the type of steel and the appropriate medium for quenching (which could be water, oil, or various inert gases), although water usually works well enough. Buff one face of the knife end of the blank to a shine with 150-grit wet-or-dry sandpaper in order to see the run of colors during the tempering process. Apply the torch, fitted with a heat spreader, to the edge of the knife blank opposite the cutting edge, and heat the edge very gently (from a distance).

Be aware that the thinnest part of the blade will heat fastest, so keep

3–48. Shop-made knives.

Making a Carving/Marking Knife *(continued)*

the heat away from this area. The metal will turn a straw color and then indigo. This progression of colors moves rapidly across the blade from the hotter edge to the cooler edge. When the cutting edge has acquired a straw tinge, *quickly* quench it in the motor oil or water to arrest the tempering process. Indigo-colored metal is too soft to hold an edge; straw-colored is just right. If you undershot, heat the blade a bit more and quench it again. If you overshot the mark, reharden the blade and try tempering it again. (See Alexander Weygers's book *The Making of Tools* for more information on heat-treating.)

Next, saw an oversized handle blank in half and rout out a cavity that will accept the shank of the blade (3–49). Epoxy the blade into the cavity and glue the two halves together with yellow glue in one operation (3–50). (Alternatively, you may use polyurethane glue for the entire operation.) When the adhesives have dried, wrap the blade several times with electrician's tape or sink it into a cork to guard against cuts. Shape the handle with the band saw, rasps, files, and sandpaper. Remove the tape and hone the edge (3–51).

3–49. Making a knife: The handle has been resawn and routed, and the blade has been shaped.

3–50. A glued-up knife (the handle has been preshaped before gluing where it meets the blade).

3–51. The finished knife.

CHAPTER FOUR

Making a Plane

C hapter 1 contains information on resawing the plane blank into the two cheeks and the midsection. It also shows how to determine which would become the front, back, top, and bottom of the blank, and how to mark these parts out with a cabinetmaker's triangle.

Following are the remaining techniques for making hand planes (4–1). Also included is a list of the tools needed for these procedures.

TOOLS AND SUPPLIES NEEDED

- Six-inch combination square
- Protractor
- Pencil
- Block plane
- Practice stock: straight-grained hardwood, about 18 inches long, $3/4$ inch thick, and 3 inches wide
- Dowels ($5/16$ x 2 inches)
- Brad-point drill bit ($5/16$ inch)
- Drill press or power hand drill
- Dovetail saw or razor saw
- Chisel ($1/2$ inch)
- Clamping cauls: two pieces of $3/4$-inch particleboard or plywood about 12 inches long and 3 inches wide
- Router with a $1/2$-inch guide bushing and $3/8$-inch bit

4–1. Wall rack of shop-made planes.

Optional Tools and Materials

- Double sticky tape—thin type for carpet
- Plug cutter ($5/16$ inch)
- Sanding drum (3-inch diameter)

PREPARING THE GLUE SURFACES

The plane blank has been resawn into the two cheeks and the midsection, and the front, back, top, and bottom have been marked. The next step is to smooth and flatten the adjacent surfaces of the cheeks and the midsection that eventually will be glued back together. With experience, hand tools quickly do the job: a plane can be used to smooth the surfaces or a scraper can be used to remove defects like raised lines left by a chips in the planer knives. Avoid hand-sanding because the outer margins tend to get rounded, which only accentuates the glue lines. Another option is to leave the surfaces as they are off the machine; the glue lines may be apparent once the plane is assembled, but it should hold together securely.

LAYING OUT AND SAWING THE FRONT AND BACK BLOCKS

Determine the position of the throat opening on the midsection and lay out the angles that when sawn will create the front and back blocks. A strong word of caution: The layout and cuts occur on the *midsection*; be sure to separate it from the cheeks before proceeding. The plane blank is ruined if the cheeks are sawn mistakenly.

The throat opening will be slightly more than halfway along the bottom of the mid-section, closer to the front end than the back. (If you feel stranded without precise measurements, a throat opening located five-ninths of the total length will do. To determine this, multiply the length of the blank times five, divide this number by nine, and measure that result from the *back* end of the blank.) The exact location is not critical, but why should the throat plate be in this area? One of the most demanding planing tasks is preparing boards for edge-joining. It requires precise control of the plane. The planing stroke begins at a standstill and ends with the plane in motion. With the throat opening forward of center, less of the sole of the plane is resting on the board when the blade begins its cut, but the plane is easy to control because it is motionless. Because of the throat opening placement, when the blade finishes its cut more of the sole will be in contact with the board, which helps you balance the plane while it is in motion.

From the point of the throat opening, lay out a 45-degree line angled back toward the rear of the plane. This defines the back block and the ramp that the plane iron will eventually rest upon. From the point of the throat opening, move forward about $1/16$ inch and draw a line angling to the front of the plane at 62 degrees. The center block is now divided into three sections: the back block, the triangular center section, which becomes scrap, and the front block, forming both the front of the throat opening and the front portion of the plane (4–2).

The front block is angled at 62 degrees for several reasons. It's about the steepest slope that gives sufficient clearance for shavings to exit between the

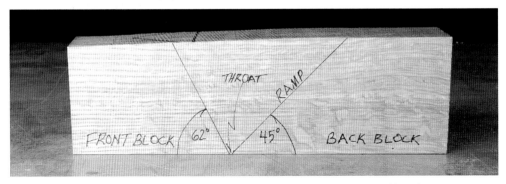

4–2. A plane blank with front-and-back-block layout on the midsection.

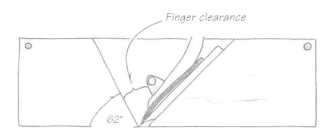

Finger clearance

Curve increases clearance

4–3. Finger clearance between the cross-pin and front block must be wide enough to conveniently extract jammed shavings.

4–5. The curved front block increases finger clearance between it and the cross-pin.

front block and the cross-pin while allowing enough space for most people's fingers to remove an occasional jammed shaving (4–3). If it were much steeper, the space between the cross-pin and front block would be so tight that if shavings collected and jammed there, removal would be an irritating task requiring a pencil point or needle-nose pliers.

The angle can be made lower, but that may interfere with the shaping of shorter planes. Also, as the bottom of the plane wears, the throat opening widens; the lower the angle of the front block, the faster the widening occurs. One of our goals and one of the advantages of making your own plane is that the plane can have a very narrow throat opening (4–4); it pays to maintain this narrow opening as long as possible. Alternatively, the front block can be cut with a curve, keeping the angle steep at the throat opening and sweeping away in the vicinity of the cross-pin (4–5). This is a good solution.

Still, I prefer a straight cut for the first plane because you can practice truing that cut before advancing to the critical job of truing the ramp of the back block, using the same techniques.

Prepare the band saw for making the cuts along the angled lines by precisely squaring the blade to the table. The band saw may not seem the natural choice for this task over the table saw, but in actuality *neither* machine will make the cuts accurately enough. Making these angled cuts on short, thick stock feels dangerous with a table saw, and requires some setup time. I prefer to use the more benign band saw, carefully make the cuts freehand, and cleaning up the sawn surface to perfection with a block plane. Saw to the waste side of the lines— within the triangular area. Make the 45-degree cut first and don't be concerned if the saw kerf nicks a bit of the 62-degree line (4–6). Save the triangular scrap.

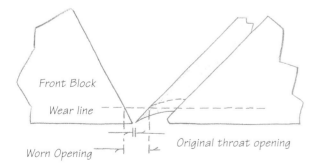

Front Block

Wear line

Worn Opening

Original throat opening

4–4. An enlarged view of the throat opening. It widens as the bottom wears. The steeper the angle at the tip of the front block, the slower the process.

4–6. The sawn-out front and back blocks.

Now clean up the cuts to produce smooth, square, and straight surfaces on both the front and back blocks. Use the block plane to do this. In experienced hands the task is completed in one or two minutes for each block. A complete novice may require half an hour for the first block and five or ten minutes for the second. This is time very well spent, for in the process you will have touched on almost all the skills needed for just about every other type of planing task. It is a challenging way to start off—trial by fire, if you will—but persevere and there will be great rewards.

CLEANING UP THE CUTS

Adjusting the Block Plane

The block plane must be tuned up and effectively sharpened for the work to proceed smoothly (see Chapters 2 and 3). Set the blade for a very fine cut with the blade protruding evenly across its width. Back off the blade until it *does not* protrude through the bottom. View the cutting edge from the back of the plane with the plane turned upside down. As you slowly bring the blade forward, see if the cutting edge is skewed in relation to the bottom of the plane; it should appear parallel (4–7). To make adjustments, pivot the blade, bringing one corner up and the other down, using the plane's lateral

adjuster. For some inexpensive block planes that lack adjusting mechanisms, the blade is brought forward and adjusted laterally by gently tapping the back of it with a two- to three-ounce hammer, and it is backed up by tapping the back edge of the plane itself (see Making an Adjusting Hammer on pages 102 and 103). The plane must be properly tensioned for this to work well (see Chapter 2). You will probably find it more precise to adjust the plane with a hammer even if it has a mechanical lateral adjuster.

When the blade is nearly protruding, let your sense of touch guide the adjustments. Gently caress both sides of the throat opening with the pad of the thumb while bringing the blade forward (4–8). Both corners of the blade should simultaneously become barely discernible. If not, make lateral adjustments until the same amount of slight drag is felt on the thumb at both corners. If the throat opening is very fine, you will be very close to the final setting. If the throat is wide, the blade will most likely need to come out a bit further yet. That is because the pad of the thumb dips into the larger opening and can feel the blade before it actually extends beyond the bottom of the plane.

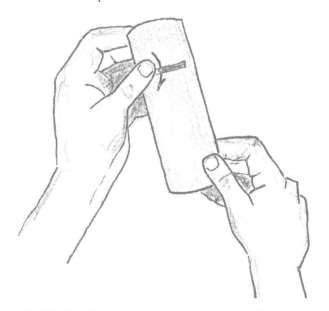

4–8. The thumb is used to feel for the protruding cutting edge.

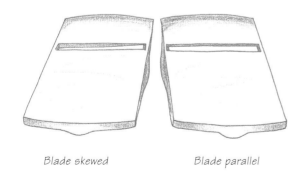

Blade skewed   Blade parallel

4–7. Bottom view of a block plane. Set the cutting edge precisely parallel to the bottom of the plane.

Final Adjustments

Begin a stroke on the practice stock. If the blade thunks against the wood and you feel yourself tensing to shove it through, stop: the blade is out too far. Though it is difficult to suppress the urge, there is no need to continue; the only likely result is damage to the planed surface, be it a serious dig or planing it out of true. Back the blade up and try again.

Ideally, the first stroke should either produce no shavings or take the smallest bit, requiring little if any effort to slide the plane across the wood. The shaving should be so thin that it falls apart and is almost dusty. This is because the jointed surface of the wood is not smooth, but slightly scalloped by the action of the jointer cutters; the blade hits the high points of each scallop and misses the low. Always adjust the depth of cut in this fashion, progressing from no shaving to a very thin shaving to the final setting. In this way, you will eliminate accidental digs and the frustrations of dealing with them.

To produce a shaving of equal thickness across its width requires setting the lateral adjustment of the blade exactly. The blade edge must be perfectly parallel to the bottom of the plane. This is crucial; if not done properly, it is very difficult to adequately true or polish a surface. When the blade takes a deeper bite from one side of a surface, either each subsequent pass dips it lower and lower or that corner of the blade may leave a prominent dig.

To check the lateral blade setting, take two shavings, first utilizing only the left side of the blade, and then only the right. The plane is held flat on the practice stock but offset to the left, and then the right, rather than planing right down the middle of the stock (4–9 and 4–10). Compare the thickness of the two shavings and be sensitive to the amount of resistance you feel; it takes more effort to produce a thicker shaving. You may find that one side takes a small bite and the other side produces nothing. Adjust the blade in the direction of the lesser cut and try again, until the resistance feels identical

4–9. Planing with the left edge of the blade.

4–10. Planing with the right edge of the blade.

when planing with either corner of the blade. It may also be necessary to readjust the depth of cut.

The shavings are of the proper thickness when they lose their "woodiness" or stiffness; instead they feel fluffy and soft when bunched together, like a cotton ball (4–11). Practice your stroke (see

4–11. "Cottony" shavings on the left; "woody" shavings on the right.

below) until continuous shavings can be consistently made from one end of the practice stock to the other. If the board gets out of true from the initial efforts, true it with the jointer; otherwise, it's difficult to produce a continuous, thin shaving.

With only a little experience, peeking at the throat opening and stroking your thumb across it will reveal almost all that is needed to know to set the blade properly. Practice stock becomes unnecessary. It takes just a few minor adjustments as you begin planing to set the blade; this is done without a second thought and with no time lost.

Gripping the Plane

Make sure the test scrap is straight. The blade will be protruding only one to two thousandths of an inch for this fine cut. If the wood is out of true more than that, you won't get intelligible results from the trial cuts. A careful pass on the jointer is called for. Carefully examine the grip shown in 4–12. The left thumb is placed gently in the center of the front of the plane with the fingers curled underneath and registered against the side of the wood. The thumb gives balance, and the fingers guide the position of the plane on the wood like a fence on a table saw.

4–12. Gripping the block plane for a practice cut.

The right hand cradles the back of the plane, fingers and thumb gripping the sides of the plane.

Try to avoid pressing hard on the cap iron or back of the blade with the palm of your hand as this may knock the blade out of adjustment and result in a major blister. Some block planes just have lousy ergonomics in this latter respect. Note that in 4–9 the hands are held low to the plane and slant to the back; this aligns the bones in the hand with the direction of motion as much as possible. This will increase the control of the stroke and minimize chatter. For the same reasons, the right forearm is held low, directly in the line of travel, the elbow an inch or two above the planed surface. These instructions should be reversed for left-handers.

The Stroke

Handling a plane well consists of much more than just shoving it across a board. You must choreograph the pressure of your hands, use your legs and hips, and be conscious of the position of your forearm, elbow, and shoulder. It *is* a bit of a dance, but easily mastered. Take the time to do this right and soon it will take no more thought than breathing.

The basic pushing stroke is covered here, for that works best for truing the ramps of the plane. Other strokes are covered in Chapter 5. Position yourself behind and to the left of the end of the practice stock. Feet should be spaced apart shoulder-width distance plus half again as wide, the left foot should be forward, knees slightly bent, and legs should feel springy.

Set the front of the plane flat on the wood, the blade slightly shy of contact. With the elbows held close to the sides, initiate the cut, *not* with the arms and shoulders, but by rocking forward slowly with knees and hips. Come forward slowly until you just feel the blade engage, let the plane hesitate slightly while your knees continue forward, and then allow the plane to continue. Once the plane is fully supported by the wood, free up your arms and shoulders to finish the cut. The hesitation prepares your body for the

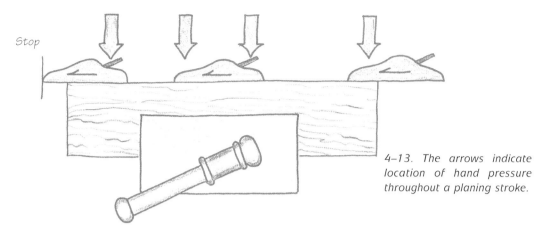

Stop

4–13. The arrows indicate location of hand pressure throughout a planing stroke.

beginning of the cut, getting you off to a smooth start, and ensures that the plane is sitting flat on the stock. Of course, this is all done in one fluid motion.

Try to be critically aware of your body while practicing planing. Take a stroke, concentrating on just one of the above points, and see if it can be adopted. Concentrate on the additional points as you are able until the whole stroke is second nature. The goal is a balanced posture that applies smooth, controlled power to the plane without tiring you out.

One last, very important, point: As alluded to above, it is important that the plane bottom be registered flat on the stock at the start of the cut. Do not let the end of the plane droop. Use downward pressure with the front (left) hand only. Once the plane is fully supported by the stock, gentle downward pressure is distributed to both hands. As the cut ends, pressure shifts entirely to the back (right) hand so that when the blade exits the wood the back part of the plane is squarely registered on the stock. Stop the motion of the plane while it is still in firm contact with the stock (4–13). Do not allow the plane to shoot off the board or you will find that the stock dips at the end and probably twists to the left or right too. Once the plane stops, pick it up and start a new stroke.

Planing the Ramps

Gauge the initial condition of the front block with a square, plane it true, and then repeat this proce-dure for the back block. For consistency, always register the square off the same side of the block. Measure near the tip of the ramp and near the other end. Also check for straightness along the length of the ramp (4–14 and 4–15). Plane away the areas that read high—the points in contact with the blade of the square—and avoid planing what is already low.

4–14. Gauging the ramp for straightness.

4–15. Gauging the ramp for square.

Keep this in mind: Due to the angled cut, you are planing a hybrid grain direction that is more like end grain than side grain (4–16). End grain offers more resistance to planing than side grain. It will be easier to start the cuts, owing to less initial resistance, if the plane is skewed about 30 degrees to the side of the block (4–17). The direction of the stroke is still parallel to the sides and must favor the grain direction—toward the tip of the ramp. There is also some danger of chipping out the tip of the block with a poorly executed stroke. To avoid a mishap, stop the plane with it still firmly registered on the ramp.

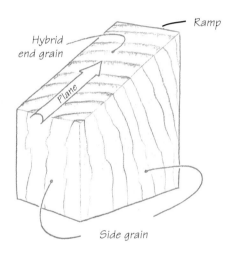

4–16. The ramp, because of its angled cut, has hybrid end grain. It must be planed in the direction indicated.

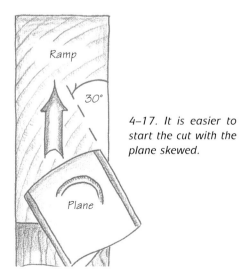

4–17. It is easier to start the cut with the plane skewed.

Concentrate on squaring the ramp first. Realize that until the saw marks are planed off, you will not get complete shavings like those on the practice stock. For better efficiency, set the plane for a slightly heavier cut to remove the saw marks; then readjust the plane to the finest setting again. Start with the front block to get the hang of the task at hand, before attempting the more critical back block. To minimize chatter, clamp the block firmly in a vise, with the ramp parallel to the vise's top and as close to the vise jaws as possible. Leave sufficient room to keep the fingers from harm's way as you plane.

Out-of-true surfaces—surfaces that are slanted, humped, or have wind—are all corrected with the same approach. High spots (identified as points of contact with the blade of the square) are planed first, and then feathered (gradually worked) toward the low area(s) with methodically placed strokes. *The plane is always kept flat on the planed surface.*

If the ramp reads high on the left side, plane a shaving on the left side with half of the blade hanging over the edge. Make a couple of strokes the length of the ramp, and then move the plane to the right—about $1/2$ inch. Take another couple of strokes. Move the plane back to the first position and take a stroke; then move it to the second position and take a stroke. Next, move the plane so that the right side of the blade is even with the right side of the ramp and take a stroke (4–18). In this manner, an angular adjustment is made while the flatness of the ramp is maintained from side to side. Increasing or decreasing the amount of overlap between adjacent strokes speeds or slows the rate of change. Pop the block out of the vise and take a new reading for squareness. Continue in the same fashion until the ramp is precisely square all along its length.

If the ramp is humped along its length, running from end to end, take short strokes from the middle only, beginning and ending the strokes about an inch from the ends. Make a stroke from the left side, one from the middle, and one from the right. Repeat until the plane no longer takes a shaving, a

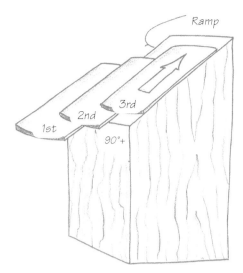

4–18. The planing pattern used to square a ramp that is high on the left.

sign that the ramp has been flattened. Finish with long strokes covering the full length of the ramp, again planing left, center, and right. A widthwise hump down the center running the length of the ramp is treated similarly. Make full-length strokes right down the center until no more shavings will come. Finish with full-length strokes left, center, and right (4–19).

The seemingly trickiest situation is when the

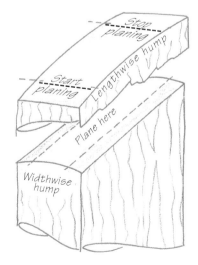

4–19. Flattening ramps with lengthwise and widthwise humps.

ramp has wind, because the ramp angles out of square in different directions at opposite ends. Once more, plane away the high spots by planing the diagonal of the ramp. Take two strokes from corner to corner, and then a stroke slightly to the left and one to the right, still on the diagonal. Again plane from corner to corner, to the left and right, and then a bit farther to the left and right. If the ramp is square at one end, but out of square at the other (still considered a wind), maintain square-ness by planing that end evenly, but direct each stroke to the side that is high on the out-of-square end. Always finish off with straight strokes the length of the ramp. The finished surface should be silky smooth and entirely free of digs or bumps (4–20).

4–20. The front ramp has been smoothed with a minimum of work—just the shavings seen here. For stability it has been clamped low to the bench top.

The surface of the hard wood you are truing consists primarily of end grain and can offer a fair amount of resistance to even a finely set, well-sharpened blade. If you are having trouble obtaining a smooth, chatter-free cut, try a slight variation on holding the plane that helps to generate more controlled power. Keep everything as before, but plant the right elbow firmly into the right side, just above the hip bone. Keep your elbow there throughout the stroke, letting the *leg* muscles do all the work (4–21).

4–21. *To brace the plane for a firm stroke, plant your elbow in your hip.*

If this is your first go at accurate work with a hand plane, don't get discouraged. This is not an easy task. It frequently takes a great deal of work to true the ramp. First you are off one way, and then the other. Eventually you get tired and the plane starts to dig or won't take a nice shaving anymore. The fact is, the more accuracy demanded of the blade, the duller it has become.

Remember, most block planes have blades of very soft steel; they will not hold a keen edge long—perhaps only a few minutes. Try planing the ramp as accurately as possible and then stop for a resharpening break. Set the plane up again for a very fine cut and finish planing the ramp. You will be rested, the plane will be at optimum performance, and, no doubt, the ramp will be completed perfectly in no time as all.

As a final test of the ramp's flatness, place it down on a flat surface (like a machine table). Try to rock the block by applying a rotational pressure. If it sits there steady, and the perimeter of the ramp meets the table seamlessly all the way around, the task is complete. If it does rock a bit, that indicates a wind (4–22). Note the corners that the ramp is rocking on and plane those down a touch using the same technique as before. Perfect trueness is not mandatory for the front block, but this is practice for the back block, where it is a major concern. Now move on to the back block, where the work will go much quicker. Be very critical of the results. The plane iron will be resting on the 45-degree ramp; if it is not perfectly trued, the blade may pivot or chatter while planing.

When the back block has been perfected, plane a $1/8$-inch chamfer into the tip (4–23). The chamfer protects the fragile fibers at the tip of the ramp from

4–22. *Testing for wind on a flat surface—note the tight fit of the ramp against the table-saw table.*

4–23. *A chamfered ramp.*

chipping; they are prone to damage if the corner end of a board jams into the throat opening when a poorly executed planing stroke dives down at the finish. The plane does *not travel* straight across the width of the block to form the chamfer; that would cause the fibers at the end of the stroke to tear out. Instead it travels slightly upward, in the direction of the grain. It also helps to skew the plane in that direction.

THE THROAT OPENING

The bottom of the front block presses down on the wood as the blade lifts a shaving from the surface. The nearer the downward pressure can be brought to the cutting edge, to oppose the lifting action, the less likelihood there is of tear-out occurring when difficult woods are planed (4–24). That is the very important advantage of a small throat opening.

Setting the Throat Opening

Indexing the front and back blocks to the cheeks with $5/16$-inch dowels determines the initial throat opening. The opening is purposely set too tight for the blade to pass through. After glue-up, the bottom of the plane is trued and the opening is widened by smoothing the bottom of the plane and filing the tip of the front block until the blade just pokes through the opening. The goal is to produce a plane that, when the blade is set for a very fine cut (shavings .001 to .003 inch thick), the opening has a corresponding size across its full width. Any wider and the shavings will have less support as they are planed off the board; any narrower and the shavings will quickly jam the opening. It should be pointed out right now, though, that should your efforts produce a plane with a wider opening, it will still function perfectly well with all but the most demanding woods. Also keep in mind that a plane is frequently needed to take heavier shavings, so you must also have a plane with a wider opening.

A heavy shaving might fall in the .010- to .015-inch range, which is four to six times *narrower* than $1/16$ inch. Even a "wide" throat opening on these shop-made planes is pretty narrow compared to what is found on most factory-made planes.

Before establishing the throat opening, take special note: The blade in the wooden plane is oriented with the *beveled side down* when laid in the plane. That's the reverse of the block plane. Make sure the blade is oriented correctly in the following steps or the throat opening will mistakenly be set much too narrow and pinch off the space between the cross-pin and front block. Despite the significantly lower inclination of the blade in a block plane, the "cutting angle" is similar to that of a wooden plane (4–25).

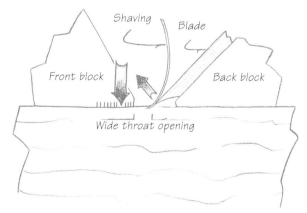

4–24. *A wide throat opening does little to oppose the lifting action of the blade as it takes a shaving. The front block is too far from the cutting edge to influence the quality of the cut. With a narrow throat opening, the front block supports the surface fibers of the stock against the lifting action of the cutting edge, thus minimizing tear-out.*

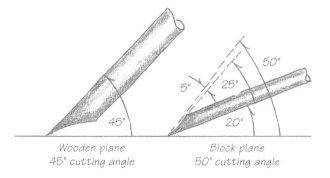

4–25. *The orientation of the blade bevel in the plane influences the cutting angle.*

Reassemble the plane blank in its original form, minus the triangular scrap. Lay it on its side with the rear of the plane to the left. Remove the cheek that is now on top and set it aside for the moment. Line up the rear of the back block with the rear of the cheek it is resting on (let's call it the "layout cheek") and align the bottoms of the two parts flush.

Next, sharpen a pencil point on fine sandpaper or a file to produce a chisel-shaped tip (4–26). Mark the position of the 45-degree ramp on the layout cheek (4–27). The flat face of the pencil point goes up against the ramp as you mark, producing a line with no offset, a great boon to accuracy. Mark the tip of the ramp of the front block ⅛ inch up from the bottom of the block. One way is to set the blade of a six-inch combination square to protrude ⅛ inch from the square face of the handle. Reference off the bottom; then mark the front and side at the corner (4–28).

4–27. Marking the position of the 45-degree ramp of the back block on the "layout" cheek.

4–28. Marking the tip of the front block ⅛ inch up from the bottom.

4–26. Chisel-tipped pencils.

Place the front block back on the layout cheek in its approximate position. Use the cheek that was removed to align the front and back blocks flush with the bottom of the layout cheek (4–29). Make sure the 45-degree ramp of the back block is on its line, put the plane iron on the ramp, *beveled side down*, and bring the cutting edge up close to the bottom of the plane. Hold the back block steady. Jockey the front block and the blade until the cutting edge aligns with the ⅛-inch mark on the front

4–29. Aligning the bottoms of the blocks and the layout cheek using the other cheek.

block. Be sure the plane iron is resting flat on the *45-degree ramp* and that the bottoms of both blocks are flush with the bottom of the layout cheek. Without jostling the front block, carefully mark the location of the 62-degree ramp on the layout cheek (4–30 and 4–31).

Reassemble the plane blank with each piece properly oriented. Set the whole unit, bottom down, on a clean, flat surface so that the bottoms of

the cheeks and blocks will all sit flush. Clamp up the blank with very light pressure. Use a hammer to tap the front and back ramps onto their respective layout lines on the layout cheek; then line up the other cheek evenly with the layout cheek. Check again to see that the front and back blocks are properly aligned, and gently tighten the clamps; there should be enough pressure to hold the parts together firmly, but not so much that the surfaces are marred. As one final check, place the blade in the plane (bevel side down!) and see that the cutting edge contacts the front block at the 1/8-inch mark. If it is high or low, lay the plane assembly on a flat surface again, loosen the clamp holding the front block, and tap the block forward or back as needed. Tighten the clamp again and you are set to drill the indexing holes that lock the blocks in place with the cheeks (4–32).

4–30. Marking the layout cheek for the position of the front ramp. This determines the initial throat opening.

4–31. The layout cheek marked for both ramps; the pencil lines are enhanced with ink for better visibility.

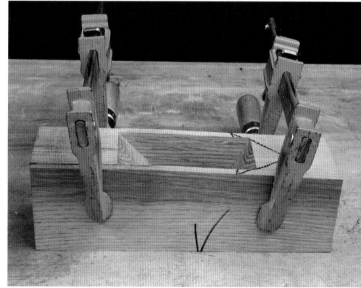

4–32. Clamped-up plane ready to have index pins drilled into it.

A drill press, hand drill, or horizontal boring machine can be used to drill the index holes. Place the clamps so that the handles are on the same side of the plane blank, and then drill the opposite side. The holes should be twice the depth of the cheek thickness—about ⅝ inch deep—and located in the upper corners of the blank (4–33). Tape wrapped around the drill bit or the depth stop on the drill press gauges the depth.

4–33. *Index pin holes drilled in the plane. Note that holes have been drilled on the opposite side as well.*

4–34. *Spacer blocks elevate the plane above the clamp jaws for drill-press drilling of index pins.*

Usually, the clamp handles are in the way and must be reversed so that index holes can be drilled on the other side. To avoid shifting the blocks, use a third "helper" clamp. Snug it on next to one of the clamps in use with its handle pointing in the opposite direction. Remove the adjacent clamp and reposition it in like manner next to the unaltered clamp, which is then removed. The position of the clamps may make for awkward drilling on the drill press. A pair of equal-thickness spacer blocks give the clamps clearance over the table (4–34).

The dowel indexing pins should fit the holes precisely to do their job well. If they are too tight, it's a bother disassembling the plane prior to glue-up. If they are too loose, the blocks will slide around during glue-up, adversely affecting the throat opening. Make a practice hole in the triangular scrap and test-fit the dowel. If the fit is too tight, sand the dowels lightly or tap them through a dowel sizer. If the dowels are too loose, try some others or a different drill bit. Letter-designated

bits are available in intermediate sizes: the "N" bit is slightly smaller than ⁵⁄₁₆ inch in diameter.

You may have surmised from the position of the index pins that the blocks are free to pivot. An alignment stick is clamped across the bottom of the blocks during glue-up to lock everything in place. Do not omit the alignment stick and add extra index pins in an effort to capture the blocks. That makes disassembly prior to glue-up more difficult, and chances are the blocks will still shift during clamping anyhow. The pins will be cut away when the plane is shaped.

Once the holes are drilled, tap the dowels home and remove the clamps. Trim off the excess dowel with the dovetail or razor saw, getting close but being careful not to gouge the cheeks. Clamp up the plane blank as shown and pare each dowel end flush to the cheeks. During glue-up, the blank will be faced with particleboard or plywood ("clamping cauls") to both spread the clamping pressure and protect the cheeks from damage. If the dowel ends protrude at all, the caul is held away from the cheek and no clamping pressure is transferred there.

Pare the dowels flush with a very sharp $1/2$-inch chisel. Lay the chisel flat on the cheek and, using the thumb of your left hand to supply force, push the *corner* of the chisel through about $1/16$ inch of the dowel per slice (4–35). If the elbows and shoulders are used to do the work, a slip can be disastrous because the range of motion might be nearly two feet or so. Any body part in the path will be seriously stabbed. The thumb supplies forceful, controlled pressure with a range of motion closer to $1/2$ inch or so, and accuracy and safety are considerably enhanced. Work your way across the dowel in this manner, slicing off only about $1/16$ inch of wood with each pass. This is one of the keys to clean, accurate chisel work. Take rapid *light* cuts. When too big a bite is attempted with a chisel, its wedge shape forces it deeply into the wood, making it difficult to control the cut. Trim the ends of each dowel flush.

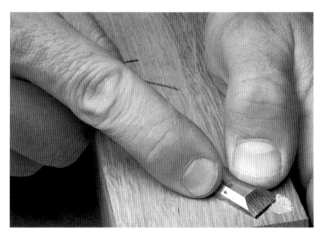

4–35. The thumb guides the chisel to pare dowel ends with power and precision.

LOCATING THE CROSS-PIN

Crosscut a length of cross-pin stock (refer to Chapter 1) $1/16$ inch shorter than the width of the fully assembled plane blank. Remove one of the cheeks from the plane-blank assembly. If the index pins are

tight, try placing the blank on end and fitting the point of a chisel between the cheek and block in line with the pin. Tap down, gently forcing the cheek and block apart about $1/8$ inch (4–36). Reverse the blank and do the same at the other end to the same cheek. Gently pry the pieces apart by rotating the chisel in the gap. Avoid waggling the parts or the holes will quickly become enlarged.

4–36. Separate the cheeks from the blocks by wedging them apart with the tip of a chisel.

Marking Cross-Pin Location

Lightly pencil the margin of the two ramps on the cheek that is still in place, making sure that the bottoms of the blocks are flush with the bottom of the cheek. Pivot the blocks out of the way and lightly mark a line on the cheek, within the triangle just drawn, that is $1^1/4$ inches up from the bottom of the cheek (4–37). That is the height of the center of the cross-pin off the bottom; placed lower, the wedge may not clamp the blade properly, perhaps shifting in use. The cross-pin might also choke off the space between itself and the front block, causing shavings to jam. Put the cross-pin much higher and you find yourself limited to rather tall shapes for the plane, whereas most people favor low-slung shapes for this style of plane.

4–38. *Locating the face of the cross-pin on the height line 3/16 inch from the chip breaker.*

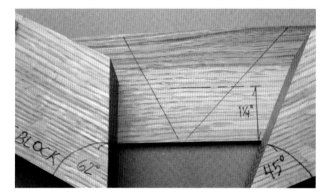

4–37. *Lines showing margin of front and back ramps (the outer extent of the sloped portion of the front and back blocks) and cross-pin height.*

There must be space between the *face* of the cross-pin that contacts the wedge (avoid the mistake of measuring off the centerline of the cross-pin) and the 45-degree ramp, to accommodate the blade, the cap iron, and the wedge. Pivot the back block into position and place the iron and the chip breaker on the ramp (remove the cap screw, which will be in the way). Measure away from the chip breaker 3/16 inch—representing the eventual thickness of the wedge—along the line giving the height of the cross-pin and make a mark (4–38).

Place the cross-pin stock that has been trimmed to length end up, so that the diagonal of the cross-section of the cross-pin is on the height line and a corner is touching the mark made on the line. Take a sharp pencil and lightly trace all around the cross-pin hole (4–39). A line across the other diagonal of the traced square gives the center point of the cross-pin on the height line and the placement of the cross-pin hole.

Drilling for the Cross-Pin Hole

Before drilling the cross-pin hole, you may wish to skip ahead to Making the Cross-Pin on pages 92 to 97. One convenient method of forming the round

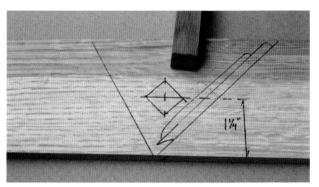

4–39. *Tracing around the cross-pin stock and locating its center.*

tenons at the ends of the cross-pin is with a 5/16-inch plug cutter. If using this method, first be sure to select a drill bit for the cross-pin hole that mates tightly with a sample plug or is slightly undersized. An alternate method sizes the tenon to fit the existing cross-pin hole.

Mount the 5/16-inch brad-point drill bit in the drill press and check to see that the bit is perpendicular to the table; if you drill and the bit is askew, the cross-pin will not be parallel to the 45-degree ramp, necessitating a double-tapered wedge to compensate. Place a backing board beneath the cheek to prevent tear-out when the bit exits the cut. Drill the hole for the cross-pin (4–40).

Next, assemble the plane blank and lay the blank on its side with the drilled cross-pin hole facing up. Using the existing hole as a guide for placement, carefully bring the spinning bit down through it (do not enlarge the hole), and drill the other cheek

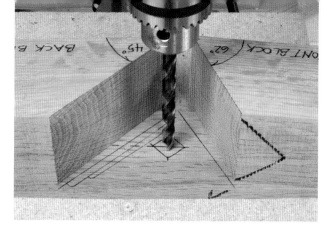

4–40. Drilling the first hole for the cross-pin in the marked cheek.

(4–41). Lightly countersink the cross-pin hole on the inner and outer surfaces of both cheeks. On the inside, the chamfer helps guide the cross-pin into place during glue-up and gives clearance around the base of the cross-pin tenon where there may be a little difficulty in cleaning up the waste. On the outside, it looks attractive.

4–41. Drilling the other cheek for the cross-pin through the first hole.

CAP SCREW CLEARANCE SLOT

The plane iron and chip breaker are assembled with the cap screw. The cap screw faces down on the ramp when in use, requiring a clearance slot. The slot must be slightly deeper than the thickness of the cap screw. Should the cap screw bottom-out on the slot, however slightly, the blade will pivot at that point, skewing out of adjustment with the first passes of the plane. The slot must extend far enough so that it does not prematurely limit the forward adjustment of the blade. It is quite frustrating finding out after the plane has been glued up that the blade cannot be brought forward far enough to take a shaving!

The slot width is made $3/16$ inch wider than the diameter of the cap screw, to avoid the risk of binding up the blade assembly and limiting its lateral motion. The length of the slot is determined by the position of the threaded hole in the chip breaker that accepts the cap screw. When the chip breaker is screwed to the blade, its tip is set back from the cutting edge about $1/32$ inch. When the assembly is set in the plane to make a cut, the cap screw will always be in the same position on the ramp, even as the blade wears over the years. With this in mind, use the blade assembly to mark the extent of the slot (4–42). Lay the blade assembly so that it overlaps the 45-degree ramp, as shown, with the cap screw resting on the side of the ramp. Slide the blade down the ramp until the cutting edge contacts a straightedge or block of wood held flush with the bottom. Observe the location of the cap screw relative to the edge of the ramp and mark the ramp $1/8$ inch beyond the leading edge of the perimeter of the cap screw (toward the tip of the ramp). The extra $1/8$ inch provides assurance that the cap screw will not bottom out on the end of the slot. The bottom of the plane will be dressed later on, further extending the reach of the blade.

Carry this mark over to the face of the ramp and lay out the slot width too. The slot may be chiseled by hand, but it is best done with a handheld router and a simple template.

4–42. Using the blade assembly to mark the extent of the cap-screw clearance slot that will be routed on the face of the 45-degree ramp.

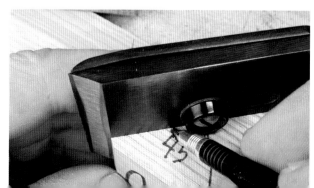

A template collar guide mounted to the router base is the key to this simple fixture (refer to Chapter 1) that is used to rout the ramp slot as described on page 91. The template guide is a concentric ring that encircles the router bit. The cut is guided when the collar contacts the template. A slot-shaped template will create a similar, but smaller, slot in the ramp. Since the outside diameter (O.D.) of the bit must be smaller than the inside diameter (I.D.) of the guide, the slot will be narrower and shorter than the template slot, resulting in an offset. Select a guide of smaller O.D. than the actual slot width, and a straight router bit with a diameter at least $1/8$ inch smaller than the guide I.D—for example, a $5/8$-inch guide with a $1/2$-inch straight bit.

CALCULATING OFFSET

The offset between the bit and template slots equals the radius of the router bit subtracted from the outside radius of the guide collar.

TEMPLATE LAYOUT

Start with a 7 x 7-inch squared-up piece of $1/2$-inch-thick multi-laminate plywood. (Baltic birch is a good choice; another option is to glue up the thickness from two pieces of more readily available $1/4$-inch lauan plywood.) Carefully mark a center-line at one edge (4–43). An accurate way to do this is to measure the entire width and divide by two (there's more to it than that): here the result is $3 1/2$ inches. Set this length with your combination square and make two marks mea-

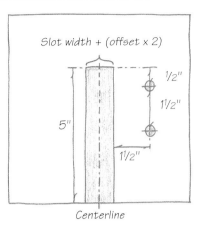

4–43. A plan for laying out a template that aids in routing the ramp slot.

suring in at the edge that amount by registering the handle of the square off both sides. The two resultant marks will either overlap perfectly, indicating the dead center of the board, or they will be slightly offset, in which case the center of the small space between the two marks is simply eyeballed. The width of the template slot is the desired width of the cut plus *twice* the offset. Center this amount on the centerline.

The length of the template slot is made oversized so that the router is well supported by the template at the start of the cut. Mark a line denoting five inches on *both* sides of the plywood; the line should be cen-

tered and slightly longer than the width of the template slot. Setting up with the aid of the marked template, use the band saw and the fence to cut one of the sides of the slot. Cut down to the five-inch line and carefully back out of the cut. Maintain gentle pressure against the fence while doing this to avoid skewing the template, which could catch the blade and pull it off the wheel. Alternatively, shut off the saw and allow the blade to stop before pulling out of the cut.

Next, flip the template over so that the opposite edge registers off the fence and saw the other side of the slot, stopping at the five-inch line marked on the back side. Saw away most of the waste in the center with the band saw, stopping just shy of the five-inch line. Clean up the end of the slot with a chisel. Drill and countersink the attachment holes.

Mark a vertical line on the side of the template slot that spaces away from the end of the slot by the amount of the offset; when the template is mounted on the ramp for routing, this mark is aligned with the actual slot length marked on the ramp (4–44).

4–44. A template with its slot cut out, holes drilled and countersunk, and "end-of-slot" mark transferred to the inside edge of the slot.

ROUTING THE RAMP SLOT

True a piece of 2 x 2 x 12-inch softwood scrap on which to mount the template. Orient the 45-degree ramp of the back block horizontally and clamp it flush with the scrap in a vise. The ramp and one-inch-wide surface must make a uniform flat surface or the routing will be adversely affected (4–45). Point the open end of the template slot *away* from the tip of the ramp and set the template down on the ramp. Center the template slot on the ramp lay-out lines and align the "end-of-cut" mark of the template with the end of the slot laid out on the ramp. Clamp it temporarily or tack it with thin carpet tape; then screw the template to the scrap with two $1^1/4$-inch drywall screws (4–46).

Install the template guide and bit in the router. Set the depth of cut by placing the router in the template and bottoming the bit against the ramp. Adjust the depth stop to give a cut equal to the thickness of the cap-screw head plus $^1/16$ inch, or note the required setting on the depth-of-cut scale. To avoid overloading the bearings and the subsequent squall of the router, make the slot depth in two passes—half the full depth for the first pass and full depth on the second. Position the template guide within the template slot without contacting the edge of the ramp.

Start the router. The direction of bit rotation causes the router to move to the left as the cut is started. For smooth operation, begin the cut with the guide contacting the left side of the template and go all the way around the template, keeping the guide against the side until the bit exits the cut. Stop the router and carefully remove it from the template; if the template slot is inadvertently nicked with the spinning bit, subsequent use may transfer the divot to the ramp. Reset the depth of cut and repeat the procedure (4–47).

Before removing the template, place the cap screw upside down in the ramp slot to be sure it is routed deeply enough. Then remove the template

4–45. The scrap board and ramp clamped flush in a vise.

4–46. The template clamped and then screwed to a scrap board.

4–47. The routed slot.

and double-check the length of the slot. Place the blade assembly on the ramp with the cap screw in the slot. Will the cutting edge extend beyond the bottom of the back block? Rout it longer if it does not.

This template with its screwed-on fence can be shimmed to rout narrower-width planes. If you will be making many planes, you may wish to modify the template by adding an adjustable fence that allows the template to be centered on a ramp of any width quickly and easily (4–48). The fence registers off the side of the ramp and is set so that the centerlines of the ramp and template coincide. The "end-of-slot" line on the template is lined up with the slot layout on the ramp and then the template and ramp are clamped together, firmly butted, in a vise.

4–49. Marking the length of the cross-pin.

4–48. A ramp-slotting template with an adjustable fence, which also provides a means of clamping the template to the ramp.

MAKING THE CROSS-PIN

Assemble the plane blank and clamp it lightly, ensuring that the cheeks are fully contacting the front and back blocks. Lay the cross-pin stock across the plane, one end flush to the outside of a cheek. Space in about $1/16$ inch from the outside of the plane and make a notch on the cross-pin with a knife (4–49). Extend the mark using a knife and square.

Consider the portion of the cross-pin that is captured between the two cheeks. The grain of the installed cross-pin is 90 degrees to the grain of the plane body. The cross-pin will not perceptibly change in length with changes in ambient humidity, but the width of the plane body will. You must be sure the cross-pin will not be trapped against the cheeks if the plane body shrinks in width (4–50). The plane adjusts very poorly if this occurs; there's even a risk of the plane delaminating.

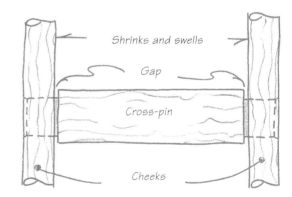

4–50. The cross-pin requires clearance between the cheeks as the plane shrinks and swells following seasonal changes in humidity.

Think about the atmospheric conditions of the shop and the moisture content of the wood. If it's winter and the plane blank is fully dried and acclimated to the dryness of the warm seasons, expect little, if any, shrinkage. Therefore, the shoulders of the cross-pin can be nearly flush with the inner surface of the cheeks. The humidity of summer causes the blank to swell. Unless the shop is dehumidified, it is wise to leave more space between the shoulders and cheeks during this time of year: $1/16$ inch overall will do.

To mark the shoulders, place the cross-pin stock across the top of the plane blank, centering its measured length. The ends of the cross-pin (one actual, one only marked, as yet) should each be just shy of the outer surface of the cheeks. Place the knife flush to the inner surface of the cheek and bring the cutting edge up against the cross-pin. To create the clearance referred to above, rotate the knife, pivoting the cutting edge away from the inner surface of the cheek, and make a notch on the cross-pin that is the appropriate distance from the inner face of the cheek (4–51). Do the same for the other shoulder.

4–51. Marking out the shoulders.

Cutting and Fitting the Tenons

There are probably as many ways of producing the round tenons on the ends of the cross-pins as there are woodworkers. No matter the method, the tenons must fit the holes well and they must be coaxial—that is, the central axes of the tenons should be directly in line (4–52). The method described below employs a plug cutter to create

the tenon and a table saw to establish crisp shoulder lines.

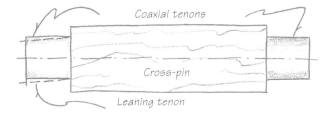

4–52. Cross-pin tenons must be coaxial.

Clamp, screw, or use carpet tape to attach a scrap of straight plywood to the rear of a table-saw sled or miter gauge. Next, make a fresh saw kerf in it with the blade set higher than the thickness of the cross-pin stock. If a miter gauge is being used, the plywood should be $3/4$ inch thick. Now, the marks on the cross-pin can be aligned with the saw kerf, which indicates precisely where the blade will cut (4–53). Set the blade height to $1/16$ inch and make a test cut in some scrap to be sure that it is no higher. The shoulders of the tenon will be established with the next cuts without intruding on the tenon itself.

4–53. A crosscut sled with a clamped-on plywood backer. The sled shows a fresh saw kerf that is higher than the cross-pin thickness.

Align a knifed mark designating a shoulder with the saw kerf in the plywood. Make sure that the waste portion of the kerf falls on the tenon side of the mark. Register the end of the cross-pin with a stop clamped to the plywood (4–54). Make four saw kerfs completely around the cross-pin to delineate the first tenon shoulder. Stop the saw and reset the stop, registering off the same end of the cross-pin, so that the kerf in the plywood is aligned with the mark for the second shoulder (4–55). Again, be certain that the waste portion of the kerf falls on the tenon side of the cut.

4–54. A close-up that shows the plywood saw kerf aligned with the mark for the tenon shoulder, the stop in place, and the cuts made.

4–55. The setup for the opposite tenon shoulder, with the cuts made.

Next, make the cuts. Raise the blade, align the length mark on the cross-pin with the kerf in the plywood, and cut the cross-pin to length (4–56). Do not accidentally cut off a tenon-to-be. Take similar caution with your own fingers. Stay alert at all times when working with small stock. Use a clamp or a stick to hold the work if you feel uncomfortably close to the blade.

4–56. The crosscut cross-pin.

Use a dadoed scrap of wood to position and hold the cross-pin vertically on the drill press while forming the tenon with a $5/16$-inch plug cutter. The scrap should be milled true at least 1 inch thick, 12 inches long, and so its width is about $1/2$ inch less than the length of the cross-pin. The dado goes square across the width of a face, oriented, as shown in 4–57, in the center of the scrap.

Mark the dado directly off the cross-pin; the cross-pin should be a snug fit. Set the table-saw blade to cut slightly above the thickness of the scrap and cut the plywood backing the miter gauge or sled so that the kerf will be visible with the scrap in position. Lower the blade height to cut the full thickness of the cross-pin or about half the thickness of the scrap. Cut out the dado with multiple crosscuts, lining up the kerf in the plywood and the marks on the scrap (refer to 4–57). Check the fit. Enlarge the dado if it's too tight or shim the cross-pin with a piece of tape if it's loose.

Ascertain that the drill-press table is set up perpendicular to the chuck. Draw diagonal lines from corner to corner on the end of the cross-pin to find its center. Temporarily chuck a $1/16$-inch bit into the drill press to aid centering the dado. Place the cross-

4–57. Cutting a dado in the cross-pin holder.

pin fully in the dado, position the fixture so that the bit centers on the intersection of the diagonals, and clamp it in place on the table (4–58). Replace the bit with a $5/16$-inch plug cutter and form the tenon with the plug cutter. Be careful to avoid damaging the shoulders of the tenon (4–59). Reverse the cross-pin end for end—keep the same face pointing out to ensure that the tenons will be colinear—and form the other tenon.

Pare across the shoulders of the tenon with a very sharp $1/2$-inch chisel, as shown in 4–60, to clean up any waste. The thumb of the left hand works in

4–58. A small drill bit is used to center the tenoning jig.

concert with the thumb, index finger, and middle finger of the right hand. Using only the range of motion of these digits, the chisel can be manipulated with control and power while minimizing the risk of injury from a stabbing slip.

4–59. Drilling a tenon with a plug cutter.

4–60. Paring the shoulders of a cross-pin tenon.

Try the tenon in a hole drilled in a piece of scrap. It should rotate freely, but with no trace of wobble. Use a smooth or mill bastard file if the tenon needs a little shrinking. Keep the safe edge of the file against the tenon shoulder to prevent dings.

Select the straightest, smoothest face of the cross-pin to register off the wedge. Nicely round the corners of the opposite face to create more clearance between the cross-pin and front block (4–61). A file or block faced with sandpaper will do the job. A parabolic shape, in cross-section, gives even greater clearance. Drill a $5/16$-inch hole in a piece of scrap (such as the triangular waste piece), to act as a stand. Place a cross-pin tenon in the hole. Take light downward cuts with the chisel to establish the direction of grain run-out (4–62). If the cuts want to dive into the wood, flip the cross-pin and approach from the other end. Do most of the shaping with the chisel, and then switch to the block plane.

A handy way of planing small stock is to set the plane for a fine cut and then clamp *the plane,* upside down, in the vise. Drag the cross-pin across the stationary plane to make the cuts (4–63). Leave the facets from the planing, if you find them pleasing, or sand the cross-pin smooth. Break the

remaining sharp corners of the face that will contact the wedge with a couple of plane strokes. Finally, lightly dome the ends of the tenons, first with slightly arcing strokes of a smooth or mill file, from the perimeter to the center, and then with 220-grit sandpaper (4–64). This helps the cross-pin pop right into place during glue-up and to look nice installed in the cheek.

Alternate Approach to Making Cross-Pin Tenons

Square tenons can be cut on the table saw, and then rounded by hand with a file. Establish the shoulders as described before, and then make multiple passes

4–61. Shape the cross-pin into a parabolic cross-section or simply round the corners that are opposite from where it registers against the wedge.

4–62. Rough-shaping the cross-pin with a chisel while it is secured on a stand.

4–63. Shaping the cross-pin by dragging it over a stationary plane.

4–64. The finished cross-pin.

to form the tenons. Set the blade height with the scrap end of the cross-pin stock so that the thickness of the tenons ends up barely larger than the diameter of the cross-pin hole. Knock the corners of the tenon off with the file to form an octagon. If the file has a "safe" (smooth) edge, keep it against the shoulder of the tenon to avoid abrading it. Use arcing strokes to further shape the octagon into a cylinder. Check the end to see if it is circular and sight the length of the tenon to be sure that it is not leaning.

As you approach the final size, fit the tenon employing a series of three holes drilled in the triangular scrap from the plane blank. When you can just get the tenon into the first hole, give it a few twists to burnish the surface; this gives a clear indication of precisely where to file. Alternate burnishing and filing until the tenon fits all the way in. The first hole has been enlarged in the process, so try the tenon in the second hole. The cross-pin should rotate freely, but not wobble from side to side. Make any adjustments and then check the final fit with the third hole. Repeat with tenon number two.

GLUING UP THE PLANE BLANK

In preparation for gluing up the blank, take a file and lightly chamfer the ends of the index pins that protrude from the front and back blocks. The chamfer guides the pins into the cheeks and prevents stray fibers from breaking off the pins; these fibers will inevitably get trapped between the cheeks and block, adversely affecting the glue joint. The pins need not be glued in place, but assembly is simplest if they are all placed in the blocks.

Dry-assemble the plane blank, *including* the cross-pin, clamping lightly in the vicinity of the index pins, and check that the pin ends are flush with the cheeks. Any protrusion must be trimmed back now. Shift the clamps to a point about halfway down the front and back ramps, but not over the open area between the front and back blocks.

Now, test the rotation of the cross-pin. You should be able to move it with your fingers without straining. If it flops about loosely, try for a tighter fit next time or make a new cross-pin. If it is too tight, rotate it several times (use pliers with the jaws padded, if they are needed) to burnish the tenons. Make sure that the tenon ends are also flush with the outer surface of the cheeks or recessed. Disassemble the plane and touch up the tenons if need be.

Preparing the Clamping Cauls and Alignment Stick

Cut two cauls the length and height of the plane blank from 3/4-inch-thick particleboard, plywood, or trued lumber. The cauls distribute clamping pressure and protect the cheeks from the clamps. The alignment stick should be a sturdy piece of wood as long as the plane blank, about 3/4 inch wide and 1 1/2 inches thick. The 3/4-inch-wide edge must be straight along its length (4–65). The alignment stick is clamped to the blocks during glue-up to properly register the blocks with the cheeks.

Dry-Clamping

Clamp up the plane blank, positioning the cauls, alignment stick, and clamps as they will be for the actual glue-up, *but with no glue*. This is a chance to

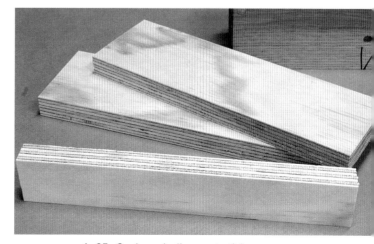

4–65. Cauls and alignment stick.

calmly practice the moves; make sure that you have everything needed, and final check all the fits. Assemble the plane. Clamp on the alignment stick. Positioning the clamps near to the throat opening gives the best registration, since the ends are held in place by the index pins (4–66).

4–66. The alignment stick clamped to the plane bottom.

Now, position the cauls evenly and apply a clamp to one end, a little below center. Clamp the opposite end a little below center too. Add the intermediate clamps, staggering them high and low. Do not clamp the open area between the blocks; that might distort the plane. Instead, locate a pair of clamps near the tips of the front and back blocks (4–67). It is this portion of the plane that is under constant stress exerted by the wedge, so it pays to clamp it securely.

With all the clamps on, try rotating the cross-pin. (Did you remember to install it? It is easy to forget. When disassembling the plane prior to the glue-up, leave the cross-pin installed in one of the cheeks at all times so that you won't forget it.) If the cross-pin still seems tight, it may indeed need one more little trim, but also check to see that the shoulders are not binding between the cheeks. Now check all the seams between the cheeks and the blocks: those down in the throat opening; at the ends; and on the bottom and the top. If there are any gaps now, they won't glue up very well. Take the time to investigate and make corrections.

4–67. Complete dry-clamping of the plane.

Glue-Up

Remove all the clamps except those holding the alignment sticks, which may be left in position. If glue will be applied to both surfaces, before removing the cheeks from the blocks lightly pencil the margin of the 45- and 62-degree ramps on the cheek that is unmarked so that you will know where *not* to put glue there. Also remove any unwanted marks in the exposed triangular area of the cheeks. Choose the front and back blocks if applying glue to only one surface.

Make a little glue spreader from a piece of wood about 2 inches wide, 4 inches long, and $1/8$ inch thick by notching the end about $3/32$ inch deep every $3/32$ inch with the band saw. Do not stroke, as with a paintbrush, when using the spreader. Zigzag glue across the wood with a squeeze bottle, hold the spreader perpendicular to the surface, and firmly scrape through the glue, right off the edge. The glue dammed up on the spreader will adhere for a moment, long enough to reposition the spreader for the next pass. Practice on a piece of scrap to get the hang of it (4–68).

Before spreading the glue, take a moment to consider how much is enough. Ideally, after the separate pieces are clamped up, small, evenly spaced beads of glue will appear along the joint. If no squeeze-out appears, chances are there is insufficient glue. A gush of squeeze-out leads to a messy cleanup job. Open-pored woods like oak and ash will accept more glue than close-pored

4–68. Practice gluing with a notched spreader.

species such as maple or beech. Glue can be applied to both surfaces of an oak plane, but to only one surface of a maple plane. Try to avoid squeeze-out down at the throat opening where it is difficult to clean out. Hold back the glue about ¹/₈ inch along the ramps.

Use carpenter's yellow glue (aliphatic resin) such as Titebond. The bond is very strong and clamping time is short: one hour is sufficient. If you are dealing with a waxy or resinous tropical hardwood, like coco bolo for instance, scrub the glue surfaces with acetone or denatured alcohol (observe proper safety precautions) just prior to gluing to achieve a good glue bond. Use fresh glue; it should be free-flowing and not appear thick, stringy, or lumpy. Polyurethane glues also work well on these types of wood.

Have on hand a dampened towel and a sharp ¹/₂-inch chisel to aid in cleanup. Cover up the bench top to catch glue drips. Install the cross-pin in one of the cheeks! Apply glue to one side of the plane (4–69). Put that cheek in place, flip the plane, glue the other side, and apply the cauls and clamps. Now that the clamps are on and tightened up, remove the alignment stick so that it is not accidentally glued to the bottom of the plane by squeeze-out. Do not be alarmed if the blocks are not perfectly aligned with the cheeks; they are usually slightly recessed, which is fine. Illus. 4–70 shows the glue-up with a reasonable amount of glue squeeze-out.

Remove all squeeze-out from the bottom of the plane and the ramps. Firmly scrape off the glue with your chisel, wiping it clean with the damp

4–69. Gluing one side. Note the cheek with the cross-pin installed.

4–70. The glued-up blank with a reasonable amount of glue squeeze-out.

cloth after each swipe. Do not bother with the top and ends; that squeeze-out will be sawn away in the shaping. Leave the plane clamped for an hour and let it dry for three or four more hours, if not overnight, before continuing. In the meantime, tune up the plane iron and chip breaker or skip ahead a bit and make a temporary wedge and adjusting hammer (if you need a hammer).

OPENING THE THROAT

Sight down the 45-degree ramp at a bright light to reveal any remaining traces of glue. Chisel them away if there are any, for the plane iron must bed securely on the ramp. Lay the plane iron on the ramp, beveled side down, and check to see that the cutting edge butts against the front block. It should not pass through the opening! By the time the bottom is trued and the opening carefully filed, the tip should just squeak through, revealing a minute band of light at the opening when the blade is set to take a whisper-thin shaving. That is your ultimate goal.

Tensioning the Plane with a Temporary Wedge

Just as with the block plane, the wooden plane must be under its normal operating tension whenever the bottom is trued. Because it is exceedingly dangerous to pass the plane over the jointer knives with the plane iron and chip breaker installed, it is necessary to make a temporary wedge that is thick enough to take up all the space between the cross-pin and 45-degree ramp to tension the plane.

Use a piece of the wedge stock that's prepared as discussed in Chapter 1. It should be the same width as the plane iron. Cut a six-inch length. Measure the space between the cross-pin and 45-degree ramp with the flat of the cross-pin set parallel to the ramp (4–71). Lay out a low-angle wedge on the side of the wedge stock (4–72). Set up the band saw with the table set square to the blade. Saw out the wedge freehand, just taking the line (4–73). Try it for a finger-tight fit. If the wedge slips too far under, mark it $1/4$ inch beyond the cross-pin and trim to that line. If it does not go under far enough, it must be thinned slightly. Clamp the wedge in the vise with its sawn surface up and use the block plane to thin it. Use the same methodical technique as when truing the ramps.

One final, most important point: When pressed home finger-tight, the wedge should fit snugly

4–71. Measuring the space between the ramp and cross-pin.

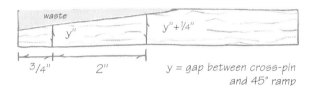

4–72. Temporary wedge layout. The tip of the wedge must go fully under the cross-pin and extend beyond it about $1/4$ inch. The wedge slope rises $1/4$ inch vertically for every 2 inches of horizontal travel. The gap measured between the cross-pin and the 45-degree ramp ("y") falls on the wedge $3/4$ inch from its tip, accounting for the $1/2$-inch thickness of the cross-pin and the $1/4$-inch extension. Draw the vertical line "y" at that point, measure up from the bottom of the wedge the distance between the cross-pin and 45-degree ramp, and mark it. The $1/4$ x 2-inch "rise over run" must pass through that point. Make another vertical line two inches from the first. Set the combination square so that the blade extends from the handle the length "y," plus $1/4$ inch. Measure up from the bottom on the second vertical line that amount and make a mark. Connect the two points on the two lines, and the layout is complete.

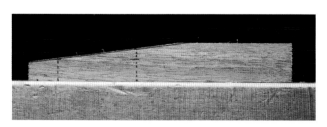

4–73. The sawn temporary wedge.

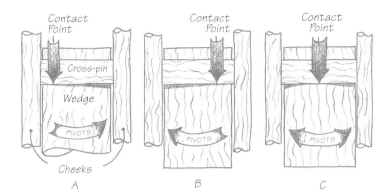

4–74. Diagnosing a pivoting wedge. In A and B, the thickest side of the wedge tightens first, and then the end of the wedge pivots toward the thin side. In C, the wedge pivots easily once it is pressed into place, because of a hump at the point of contact between wedge and cross-pin or on the bottom of the wedge (possibly a protruding cap screw, when the final wedge is diagnosed).

and evenly across its width and lock into place without the least tendency to pivot. If it pivots as it is pressed into place, there is a mismatch between the wedge and cross-pin. This is not critical for the temporary wedge, but the final wedge must fit perfectly for the plane to adjust well and hold its adjustments. You may wish to practice fitting the temporary wedge before working on the final wedge.

Fitting the Wedge

Illus. 4–74 illustrates three conditions that lead to a pivoting wedge. To differentiate conditions B and C, check across the width of the wedge with a straightedge, at the point of contact with the cross-pin. Make adjustments to the wedge with the block plane. Plane away humps in the center of the wedge until the plane cannot take a shaving. A slight depression in the center is fine (for the final wedge) because pressure is then directed toward the edges of the plane-iron assembly, minimizing the chance that the blade will skew while planing.

To alter the thickness of the wedge from side to side, use the same strategy used for squaring the ramps. Plane the sawn surface. This time the objective is not squareness, but a tight fit between the wedge and cross-pin. Take a couple of full-length strokes from the high side and progress toward the low side, keeping the wedge flat across the width while doing so (4–75). Try the wedge in the plane. Keep fitting until the wedge slips under the cross-pin the right amount, tightens up with-

out pivoting, and feels locked into place with just finger pressure when you try to wiggle the wedge from side to side. Of course, it will come loose if wiggled with sufficient force, but when the wedge is fit just right, you will feel it break free suddenly, without having to pull it out (4–76).

4–75. Planing the temporary wedge.

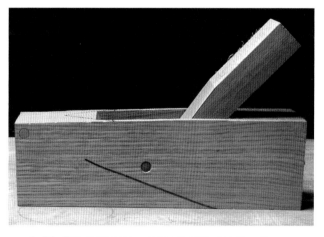

4–76. The temporary wedge installed in the plane.

Making an Adjusting Hammer

Use a length of 5/8-inch-diameter brass rod for the head. If ordering through an industrial supply catalog, remember that the minimum length will provide for many hammer heads. Smaller lengths may be found at a hardware store or machine shop. Saw off a segment 2 1/2 inches long, face the ends with a sander, and then round the sharp edges.

Now the trick is to drill a perfectly centered hole crosswise through the rod. To do this, make a simple fixture from a squared and trued length of hardwood that's approximately 12 inches long x 1 3/4 wide x 1 inch thick. In the center of the stick draw two connected lines half the length of an edge and face and mark the exact centers (4–77). Drill a 5/8-inch hole through the mark on the face. Then insert the brass rod so that the ends protrude from the fixture the same amount. The rod must be a snug fit. If it is too loose, shim it with a wrap of tape.

Chuck a 3/8-inch brad-point drill bit in the drill press. Lay the fixture on the drill-press table, edge up, and use the point to perfectly center the bit at the centerpoint on the line. Clamp the fixture securely. Drill down to the rod, but not into it. Replace the bit with a 3/8-inch metal-cutting bit and drill through the rod (4–78).

Make a handle from a 12-inch-long x 1-inch-wide x 1-inch-thick stick of tough, springy hardwood such as hickory, ash, or oak. Shape one end to a 3/8-inch-diameter to fit the hammer head. The stick is longer than the handle will be, so the waste end may be clamped in a vise while the handle is worked with a spokeshave. Lay out the shape of the handle on one face; the shape should taper to 3/8 inch at the hammer-head end. Saw out the shape on the band saw, remaining outside the lines. Lay out a second set of lines on the sawn face, again tapering to 3/8 inch at the head end, and saw those as well (4–79). If dealing with gentle curves, place the concave surface down, to prevent the stock from rocking, while the second set of lines is being sawn.

Use a spokeshave to shape the handle (4–80). Form the 3/8-inch-square end of the handle into an octagon and then, with very fine cuts, shape it into a circle. Try the hammer head until it just gets started on the handle. Twist the head back and forth to burnish the handle and you will see exactly where to remove wood to improve the fit. Fit the handle snugly through the head and let it extend about 1/8 inch beyond. Simply trim off any excess if it goes through further. Cut the handle to length and trim up the end.

Next, saw a narrow kerf in the thin end of the handle, for wedging the hammer head in place. Saw it in line with, and 1/8 inch shy of, the full

4–77. Fixture layout for drilling a centered hole in a hammer head (holes already drilled on centers).

4–78. Drilling a handle hole into the hammer head.

4–79. *Sawing the handle. The first set of lines are already cut, and the second set are being sawn.*

another piece of wood that will act as a temporary table (4–81).

Now prepare a low-angled wedge from some ³/₈-inch-wide stock. The wedge should take up most of the length of the kerf, without bottoming, before it jams. Install the hammer head, squeeze a little glue into the saw kerf, and tap the wedge into place. When the glue has dried, carefully pare the end of the handle and wedge, leaving them both a bit proud of the hammer head (4–82).

4–80. *Shaping the handle with a spokeshave.*

4–81. *Kerfing the handle for a wedge. The scrap below the handle stock serves to close off the wide band-saw throat plate; otherwise, the narrow handle end might drop in and jam.*

diameter of the hammer head. The kerf is visible only at the end when the hammer head is installed. It is difficult to clamp the tapered shape of the handle and make the cut with a handsaw, so use the band saw, running the handle against a straight piece of stock. Close off the throat plate of the band saw by sawing into

4–82. *A view of the finished hammer showing the pared, wedged end.*

Truing the Bottom

Flattening the bottom with the jointer cleans up any misregistration between the cheeks and blocks while simultaneously widening the throat opening. The goal is to have the bottom true and square to a side while leaving a $1/32$- to $1/16$-inch margin between the bottom and the point where the cutting edge of the blade contacts the front block. That margin allows room to carefully widen the throat with a file, making critical adjustments, until the iron just pokes through. Slip the plane iron into the plane and make a mark, from below, where the cutting edge contacts the front block (4–83). The mark should be about $1/8$ inch up from the bottom.

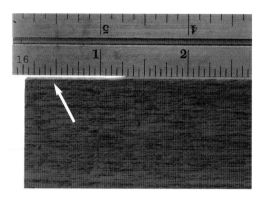

4–84. This test shows the jointer depth of cut. Note the light-filled gap between the wood and the ruler.

4–83. Marking the front block where the blade contacts it.

Set the jointer for a fine cut, about $1/32$ to $1/64$ inch, and make sure that the fence is square to the table. Make several test passes on a piece of scrap, checking for square. Watch your technique: keep the side firmly against the fence as the stock is fed over the cutters. To accurately gauge the depth of cut, joint the first inch of the board and then pull back. Lay a straightedge on the partially jointed edge and you can see the depth of cut directly (4–84).

Recall that any time the bottom is trued, the plane must be under normal operating tension. *Remove the blade* and install the temporary wedge. Tap the wedge in *gently* with the adjusting hammer. "Gently" means lightly grasping a two- to three-ounce hammer, choking up so that your thumb is about three inches from the head, and swinging only from the wrist. What is the right amount of wedging force to generate? Use your ears. The first light tap sounds hollow, and even makes a rattling sound. As the wedge tightens, the sound transforms to a pleasing percussive note, like tapping a solid block of wood. That sound indicates the right amount of wedge tension; do not go beyond it.

Check that the side of the plane that registers off the jointer fence is free from any protrusions. Take a pass and examine the bottom. Is the bottom entirely smoothed? How much margin is there between the bottom and the mark on the front block? Examine the bottom after every pass and answer those two questions. When the bottom is flat and the margin has been reduced to $1/16$ to $1/32$ inch, you are finished truing with the jointer. If you should notice that one side of the throat opening is becoming wider than the other, stop immediately. That indicates the bottom is going out of square. Reexamine the fence setting and check your technique with practice stock. If no improvements can be made, go on to the next step. Just a little more filing is needed to correct the situation.

Carefully sand the bottom smooth with a 24-inch length of 100- to 150-grit sandpaper clamped to a flat machine table. Devise a grip to balance and center the pressure of your hands on the plane (4–85). Focusing hand pressure to the center will help prevent rounding the ends or sanding a wind

4–85. *A balanced grip produces an accurately sanded plane bottom.*

into the bottom. Just as with truing the block plane, make a single stroke forward, lift the plane off the sandpaper, and start over again. Brush the sawdust off the sandpaper every couple of strokes. Do not scrub back and forth. A disciplined approach will quickly smooth away the scallops left by the jointer, leaving the bottom nicely trued. Sight the bottom at a low angle toward a light to see if it has been uniformly sanded. Check for flatness lengthwise and widthwise. Once again, remember to have the plane under wedge tension during the truing operation.

Filing the Throat Opening

Correct execution of this critical stage distinguishes a decent plane from a truly fine one, so be certain you understand the procedures before proceeding.

Generally, the cutting edge is set *parallel* to the bottom of the plane to perform correctly. The throat opening—the gap defined by the cutting edge and the front block—should be even across the width of the plane and just wide enough for a thin shaving to pass through when the above condition is met. To achieve this, *the front edge of the throat opening—the part formed by the front block—must be oriented parallel to the cutting edge when the cutting edge has been positioned parallel to the bottom of the plane.*

Recognize that the above discussion makes no mention of registering the blade off the inside of the cheek or butting the cutting edge fully against the front block when determining where to file the opening. Neither action necessarily orients the cutting edge parallel to the bottom of the plane.

The shape of the edge will influence the reading, so the edge must be properly arced, or straight, before the front block can be filed. If the plane may have either type of blade in it, use a straight cutting edge to make the readings.

Determine where to begin filing. Place the blade in the plane with the cutting edge contacting the front block. Turn the plane upside down, holding it as shown in 4–86. Viewing the plane from the back, pivot the blade on the front block until the cutting

4–86. *Holding the plane for aligning the cutting edge parallel to the plane bottom. The middle fingers hold the blade in position.*

edge is parallel to the bottom, as shown in 4–87. Pinch the blade firmly to the ramp and, without allowing it to shift, sight through the throat toward a bright light to assess the point of contact between the cutting edge and front block (4–88).

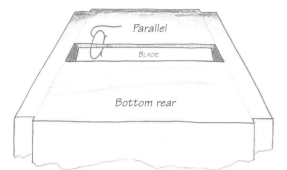

4–87. The cutting edge is seen parallel to the bottom of the plane and contacts the front block at some point.

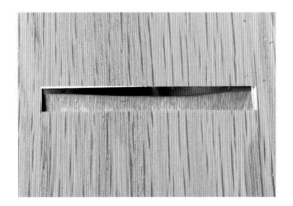

4–88. The cutting edge is still held parallel to the bottom of the plane. The assembly is then sighted toward a bright light. Here, the cutting edge contacts the tip of the front block at the right corner, showing where the front block must be filed to increase the opening and obtain a parallel gap.

If the two meet seamlessly across the full width of the blade, then file evenly across the width of the tip of the front block. At the start, it is more likely that the blade will contact the front block at a corner, leaving a gap across the rest of the opening. Begin filing at the point of contact (4–89). Mark an "X" there to avoid an error.

Clamp the plane vertically in the vise, front down and the bottom facing you. Angle the tip of the file

4–89. Sighting the throat opening. The cutting edge was set parallel to the bottom of the plane. The cutting edge is clearly not parallel to the tip of the front block. The right corner of the blade is contacting the front block at the "X."

slightly toward the front of the plane so that the flat filed on the front block leaves the angle of the tip of the front block at less than ninety degrees (4–90). If this isn't done, the shavings will have insufficient clearance over the chip breaker and clog the opening. Allow the file to lie flat on the top of the front

4–90. Filing the tip of the front block to widen the throat opening. The file tip is canted or angled slightly toward the front of the plane.

block and proceed in a manner similar to the approach used on the ramps of the plane to true and alter the angle: two strokes at the point of contact with the blade, and then one just beside it; then back to the first position, and to the second position; then a little further over, and so on. In this way, you influence the angle while maintaining a straight line, which should successively narrow any gap observed between the cutting edge and front block each time the throat opening is checked. Should inaccurate filing produce a hump or dip in the front block, file at the point(s) of contact indicated by the next reading until the cutting edge mates evenly with the front block again.

As you begin, remember that the work will go very quickly because a small portion of wood—the tip of the front block—is being filed. Hold back. File in one direction, from the bottom toward the top of the plane. Be very methodical and do not press hard on the file. When the file is up against the inside of a cheek, turn the "safe" edge there to avoid marring the surface.

Every few strokes, remove the plane from the vise and check your progress by sighting as described above. Keep filing the points of contact. Every stroke allows the tip of the blade to creep forward. Soon the blade comes right up to the surface of the bottom. Stop before it pokes through. Now is the time to shape the final wedge so it can be used to securely hold and position the blade for the most accurate final result.

MAKING THE FINAL WEDGE

The method for making the final wedge is much the same as used for the temporary wedge. There is one major difference: the space the wedge fits into is made smaller by the presence of the chip breaker and iron. Make the final wedge out of the temporary one. Measure the distance between the cross-pin and the top of the chip breaker/blade assembly. Transfer this measurement to the first vertical line,

nearest the tip of the temporary wedge, and make a mark (it should be about $3/16$ inch from the bottom [4–91]). Draw a line with the same slope as the temporary wedge through the point on the vertical line. This is the basic contour of the final wedge.

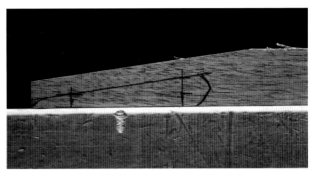

4–91. Lay out the final wedge on the side of the temporary wedge.

Before proceeding, consider a few more points. The wedge needs to be sized and shaped to promote convenient adjustment of the iron with a hammer. The end of the wedge must also be durable enough to withstand repeated taps of the hammer without chipping. At this point, decide whether the wedge will be curved or flat. The flat style is fitted in exactly the same manner as the temporary wedge; this is quickest and easiest. The disadvantage of this type is that the end of the wedge remains close to the surface of the blade so you may, on occasion, accidentally rap the blade when intending to tap the wedge. Curving the wedge away from the blade affords more clearance between the two. The wedge can also be made longer, without obscuring the end of the blade, so you may easily grasp the wedge and jiggle it from side to side to remove it and the iron when it's time to sharpen the iron. The blunt end of the blade must be accessible for adjusting forward and laterally with the hammer.

Making a Curved Wedge

Continue the layout. Measure up the slope of the final wedge $1/2$ and 2 inches from the intersection with the first vertical line and make marks. The sweep begins at the ¹/₂-inch mark and ends at the 2-inch mark (4–92). Draw the curve freehand, or use an aid like a French curve or a lid about the diameter of a gallon paint can. If there is not enough wood to make the curve needed, transfer the layout to the other end of the stock to provide more room to work with.

4–93. A sanding drum set up for fairing a wedge curve. Note how the fingers are used to influence sanding.

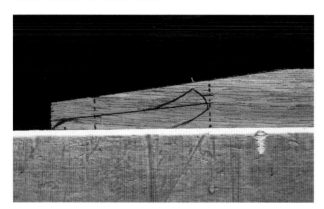

4–92. The layout of a curved wedge on the side of the temporary wedge.

Saw out the curve on the band saw. The curve may be left rough from the saw, or touched up with a scraper (see Chapter 7), file, and sandpaper. Another approach is to refine the curve using a 3-inch-diameter drum sander fitted with 150-grit sandpaper and chucked in the drill press. A backing board of ³/₄-inch plywood with a 3¹/₂-inch hole cut in it allows the drum to be dropped level with the backing board. Run the drum at about 900 rpm. Check that the drum is 90 degrees to the backing board and shim the board if necessary.

Downward pressure through the wedge, on the backing board, keeps the wedge parallel to the drum. The trickiest part of the process is keeping the wedge flat across its width, especially at the eventual point of contact with the cross-pin. The following technique helps: Place a single finger in the center of the wedge directly behind the point of contact with the drum. Gently stroke the curve against the direction of rotation to smooth out the saw marks and fair the curve; apply pressure to the drum with that single finger alone (4–93).

Also stay alert to the possibility of incorrectly tapering the wedge across its width as you proceed. View the wedge end-on at its tip to monitor this. If a taper develops, move your index finger lower or higher, to favor pressure over the thicker part of the wedge. Try the wedge for a fit with the plane-iron assembly in place.

Once the saw marks are cleaned up, the curve looks good, and the wedge has been started under the cross-pin and is flat across its width, the rest of the fitting and thinning may be done with greater control on the bottom side of the wedge using the block plane and that now-familiar technique. If the drum-sanding left a hump in the center, skip to Chapter 7 and the discussion of scrapers. A scraper will rapidly remove the hump. It is okay to leave a scant hollow in the center of the wedge as long as its outer edges contact the cross-pin correctly.

Be extremely critical of any pivoting of the wedge as it tightens. Check that all the points where the wedge contacts the cross-pin and chip breaker are flat. As the wedge is pushed in and out, it starts to develop burnished areas that indicate the contact points. These are best seen by looking at the wedge with a bright light projected at a low angle. The top of the wedge should show a shine all across its width at the cross-pin location (4–94). If the shine tapers off to one side, the shiny side is too thick and

4–94. Examining the wedge for burnished areas. Note the shiny band across the full width of the wedge indicating a good fit.

4–95. Dimpling the wedge for cap-screw clearance.

needs thinning. A shine only in the center indicates a hump. The back of the wedge should burnish at its sides as well as under the location of the cross-pin. Also, make sure that the wedge is flat length-wise on its back side. Continue shaping the wedge until it fits precisely. Review the discussion on fitting the temporary wedge (page 101) for reminders.

A frequent trouble spot occurs when the cap screw protrudes through the chip breaker, however slightly, creating a pivot point for the wedge. Check the bottom of the wedge for a burnished spot in the vicinity of the cap screw. If there is one, either grind the screw down a bit or dimple the back of the wedge at that point with a drill bit, to provide clearance. Chuck a $1/2$-inch bit in the drill press, level the wedge with a prop, and drill a small depression. Rather than center on top of the bur-nished spot, offset the bit slightly backward, toward the thicker portion of the wedge, because the wedge will now seat a little deeper (4–95).

Finally, the tip of the wedge should extend $1/4$ to $5/16$ inch beyond the cross-pin. Trim it back to that extent if it is longer. Arc the tip of the wedge to a knife edge, so it will not be a dam for shavings. Do this with a finely set block plane, skewing it and angling the stroke as when forming the chamfer at the tip of the 45-degree ramp. Do not let the arc intrude upon the area of contact with the cross-pin (4–96).

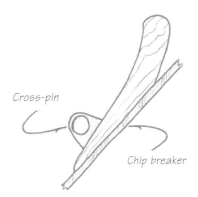

Cross-pin

Chip breaker

4–96. Side view of the wedge and cross-pin.

Finishing the Wedge and the Throat Opening

At this point, if the end of the blade rises less than $1/4$ inch above the cheeks when installed in the plane, you must saw out a sweep to provide access for making blade adjustments with the hammer. Lightly pencil the position of the 45-degree ramp on the outside of one cheek. Lay the blade on that line as though it were in the plane ready to take a cut. Pencil in a shallow sweep that will expose about $3/8$ inch of the end of the blade (4–97).

Saw the sweep on the band saw. Install the blade assembly with the cutting edge up against the front block. Install the wedge with a firm push of a finger. Turn the plane upside down and sight the cutting edge against the tip of the front block as was done

4-97. Lay out an access sweep for the blade in the plane cheeks.

previously when the throat opening was filed. Adjust the blade laterally until the cutting edge is parallel with the tip of the front block. Be extra careful not to chip out the bottom of the plane while doing this.

Now that the blade has been carefully adjusted and is held firm, sight through the opening as before to determine where to file the final strokes. Remove the blade assembly, file, and check again. Repeat this process until the edge pops through. Be aware that the presence of the chip breaker will keep the blade from slipping all the way through the opening; once the very edge of the blade pops through, you are finished (4-98).

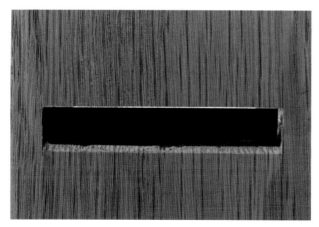

4-98. The completed throat opening is all but undetectable. Sighting it against a bright light reveals a hair-thin opening sufficient to allow a thin shaving to pass.

Final Shaping of the Wedge

Before the plane can be tested, the wedge must be trimmed to size so that it does not obscure the end of the blade. Set the blade assembly in the plane, with the chip breaker bottomed against the front

block, and insert the wedge. Keep in mind that the blade should be about 3^1/$_2$ inches long. Any longer and it may rub the hand annoyingly in use. If it's too long, cut it to length, and then use a grinder or belt sander to smooth the edges and corners. The chip breaker should be about ^{1}/$_2$ inch shorter than the blade. This allows a clear shot at the blade with the hammer when the blade is being adjusted.

For a wedge with a straight top surface, mark the wedge at a point slightly higher than midway between the top of the chip breaker and the end of the blade. Crosscut the wedge there and "break" (soften with a file or sandpaper) the sharp corners with a file so that they won't be susceptible to chipping when struck by the adjusting hammer. Lightly break all the other sharp edges too, except the tip of the wedge, so the wedge feels comfortable when handled.

An upswept wedge may be left a little longer, providing more wood to grasp when the wedge is being removed. Mark it about even with, or a little longer than, the end of the blade. Curve the bottom end of the wedge off the chip breaker too, to get more clearance between the blade and wedge (4-96 and 4-99). Shape the end of the wedge into a durable profile that will withstand the repeated taps of the hammer (4-100 and 4-101). Cut the wedge out on the band saw and use a file and sandpaper to finish the sawn surfaces.

4-99. Final marking of the curved wedge.

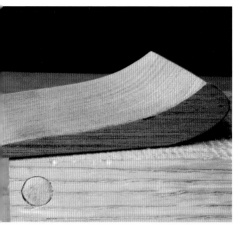

4–100. The finished wedge.

4–101. A gallery of wedge shapes.

SETTING UP THE PLANE

Even though it looks like a crude block of wood, your first plane should be ready to work! Make the first attempt worthy of all your efforts so far; let the first shaving be a beautiful, lacy-thin one—not a fat, hogged shaving, which is likely to jam up the opening anyway. Here's how to set up the plane properly:

1. Sharpen the iron to your utmost and install the chip breaker so that its tip is parallel to the cutting edge and set back about $1/32$ inch. Don't mash the cap screw down; just tighten it until you cannot shift the chip breaker on the iron with your fingers' supplying moderate force.

2. Slip the plane-iron assembly into the plane, letting the chip breaker bottom against the front block, and center it between the cheeks. Drop in the wedge. Cup the bottom of the plane, in the center, with your left hand. Grasp the iron with the thumb and middle finger of your right hand, bracing your palm against the top of the plane. Retract the blade assembly about $1/16$ inch—just enough so that the edge no longer protrudes. Then tighten the wedge by pressing lightly with your index finger to lock the blade (4–102).

3. Flip the plane over so that its bottom is now up, while still holding it in the middle with the left

4–102. Holding the plane, blade, and wedge while initially setting the blade. The right index finger sets the wedge.

hand. Sight the cutting edge against the tip of the front block—you are eyeballing the plane from the back end to the front as was done so many times while the throat was being filed—and bring the blade up even and parallel to the bottom with light taps of the hammer.

4. Hold the plane with the right hand too, freeing the left thumb to slide around the plane and feel all across the opening for the blade protruding above the bottom. The initial adjustment is set when the edge of the blade just barely scrapes the pad of the thumb and it feels as though it protrudes evenly across the width of the plane. Of course, if the edge

is arced, it should be felt more in the center of the plane than at the edges.

5. Tighten the wedge with a few light taps of the hammer. Do not overtighten it. Listen to the sound of the hammer tapping the wedge. Remember, it goes from a hollow, rattle-like tone to a solid, musical note that sounds like a solid chunk of wood being rapped. That is when to stop tapping the wedge. The blade should not have budged a bit. If it did, there is a problem. Skip ahead to Troubleshooting Techniques on pages 113 and 114.

To retract the blade if you overshoot, simply give the back end of the *plane body* a fairly sharp rap with the hammer. The inertia of the blade assembly causes it to lag a bit as the plane is struck and sent forward. In effect, the blade retracts. This action may also loosen the wedge, so always check afterwards for that solid sound with a light hammer tap.

TESTING AND ADJUSTING THE PLANE

Try the plane, at first, on the edge of a straight-grained board that's about $3/4$ inch thick, 6 inches wide, and 2 feet long. A width of $3/4$ inch is enough to balance the plane on relatively easily, making it easier to determine how well the plane is performing. The edge should be carefully straightened on the jointer. The objective is to evaluate the plane, not dress a rough board. To take a very thin shaving, the surface being planed must be true.

Don't rush while planing. Handle the plane carefully. Apply your experience with the block plane. Register the front of the plane on the edge of the board and bring the blade up to the corner, hesitate, and then start the push. If the plane was adjusted properly, the first stroke should effortlessly produce dust and fragments as the blade skips across the tops of the scallops left by the jointer knives, or there should be nothing at all. Tap out the iron a bit farther if nothing was produced.

If the blade clunks into the corner of the board, and it seems to take some force to start the cut, the edge is already out too far. Back the plane off and retract the blade. Try the edge with your thumb to feel if the blade moved; then reset the wedge, adjust the blade, and try again.

Depending on the size of the throat opening, planes feel different to the testing thumb. The wider the throat opening, the more the pad of the thumb can dip into that space. The blade will be felt sooner, even before it is actually protruding at all, on a plane with a wider throat. You will get to know your plane in this way.

The second or third stroke should start to produce continuous shavings. Try to produce a shaving that stretches from one end of the board to the other and is thin enough to reveal the porous nature of the wood when held up to the light (4–103). A bunched-up shaving should hold together and have a cottony feel. It is too thick if it feels brittle and woody.

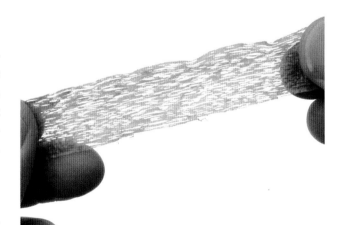

4–103. A thin shaving produced with a new plane.

Now check that the blade is set parallel to the bottom of the plane. Use the same method as with the block plane: make a shaving using the left side of the blade and then the right side. Compare the thickness of the shavings and the required force. Adjust the blade laterally until both sides of the blade perform the same.

TROUBLESHOOTING TECHNIQUES

Sometimes there is one glaring, easily detected problem holding back the proper performance of the plane. At other times, it is a combination of subtle flaws taken in total that create the mischief. Each of the critical areas must be carefully examined and the problem identified; then the outlined requirements for that area must be fulfilled with all precision. With perseverance, you will get the plane to work beautifully if you are encountering difficulty.

Below is a discussion of some of the problems, the reasons for these problems, and the solutions:

1. The plane does not produce a thin shaving.

A. *The plane bottom is not true.* Check the bottom of the plane for flatness with a straightedge as long or longer than the plane. A new plane often moves somewhat to begin with. There may be a slight concave arc the length of the plane, or a small hump directly behind the throat opening. These imperfections lift the blade off the surface being planed at some point in the cut. True the bottom on sandpaper as before. Remember: Retract the blade and have the plane under normal wedge tension.

B. *The blade is not sharp enough.* If the blade is not truly sharp, it cannot take very thin shavings. Review Chapter 3 and evaluate the edge.

C. *The wedge is too tight.* If the wedge has been overtightened, adjusting the blade is difficult. Review the information on setting the wedge.

D. *The wedge slope is too gradual.* If the upper and lower surfaces appear almost parallel, the wedge will not tighten properly and tends to grip the blade too tightly. Review Making the Final Wedge on pages 107 to 111 for information on wedge layout. Be especially critical when analyzing the point of contact between the wedge and cross-pin; the slope at that point is what really matters.

2. Shavings jam the opening.

A. *The shavings are too thick.* Try to get the thinnest shavings possible; most of the planing will be done with very fine shavings. You may simply be trying to force a shaving that is too thick through the fine opening.

B. *The throat opening is insufficient.* If even the thinnest shavings jam the opening, clean out the plane, reset the blade for a thin shaving, and then sight the opening against a bright light. An even, hair-thin gap should appear across the width of the plane. If it pinches down to nothing here or there, mark those spots on the bottom, remove the wedge and blade, and file the opening judiciously.

C. *The throat opening is filed at an incorrect angle.* The flat created on the front block by filing the throat may lean toward the chip breaker, rather than away from it, providing inadequate clearance and directing the shavings down against the chip breaker. Completely darken the filed surface of the opening with a pencil. Clamp the plane in the vise (see Filing the Throat Opening on pages 105 to 107 for information on filing the opening). Make sure that the tip of the file is canted toward the front block. File very carefully, being sure not to widen the throat opening. The pencil mark will show your progress. File until a band of pencil mark that's about $1/32$ inch wide is left at the tip of the front block.

D. *There's a gap between the chip breaker and blade.* Release the wedge and carefully extract the blade after a jam-up. Are any shavings caught *under* the chip breaker? If so, there is a gap between the blade and chip breaker that must be eliminated. (Review Making a Chip Breaker on page 30 for information on jointing the chip breaker.)

E. *The wedge is too long or incorrectly profiled.* If the wedge extends more that $1/4$ inch beyond the lower edge of the cross-pin, it may interfere with the shavings. The tip of the wedge should also be rounded to a knife-like edge to allow shavings to flow up and over the wedge. (Review Making the Final Wedge on pages 107 to 111.)

3. The blade skews in use.

A. *There is a pivot point.* Possibilities include: the cap screw protrudes beyond the chip breaker and contacts the wedge; the wedge does not fit against the cross-pin properly; the bottom of the wedge is humped. Look for burnished areas in the wrong places on the wedge and correct the causes. Review Fitting the Wedge (page 101) and Making the Final Wedge (pages 107 to 111) for solutions.

If the clearance slot in the ramp is not deep enough, the cap screw will bottom out and become a pivot point. The slot must be deepened, or a thinner-headed screw must be used.

4. The blade pops back during use.

A. *The wedge angle is too steep.* Review Making the Final Wedge on pages 107 to 111 for information on wedge layout. Be especially critical when analyzing the point of contact between the wedge and cross-pin.

5. The blade corners dig.

A. *The cutting edge is shaped incorrectly.* The edge must have a slight arc in it. Check it against a small straightedge. If the edge is hollowed or straight across, the corners will protrude and dig. Review Chapter 2 for information on sharpening.

B. *The blade is adjusted incorrectly.* You may be taking too heavy a shaving or the blade may not be set parallel to the bottom of the plane. Review Testing and Adjusting the Plane on page 112.

C. *The plane bottom is humped across its width.* A hump down the center of the plane, going from side to side, especially right in front of the throat opening, shields the center of the blade, allowing only the corners to cut. Review Block Plane on pages 37 to 40 for information on flattening.

SHAPING THE PLANE

Getting the Feel of the Plane

Get to know the feel of this plane in use before shaping the body. There is a temptation to customize the body to a certain grip that is favored, to carve ripples, handles, and notches that fit the fingers like a glove. Hold off. A problem may arise. In the middle of a planing session, you may wish to shift the grip, spreading the work to some other muscles, but can't, because the plane only feels right held that one particular way. It may even be discovered that for some tasks the shape of the plane is entirely uncomfortable. This is true of metal planes and their handles, which dictate a certain grip.

Use the plane for a while. Try some of the different grips and techniques described in Chapter 5: push and pull strokes, one-handed techniques, and side and edge-joining strokes. You will begin to arrive at some ideas for shapes that work for your hands for a variety of grips. As you make more planes, no doubt some will be shaped for a "glove-fit." For now, just soften the harsh edges of the plane slightly to avoid blisters and splinters as you get acquainted with the plane.

Shaping Guidelines

After working with the plane a while, it is time to shape the body. You may wish to make a quick mock-up from softwood to test the hand fit and check the visual appeal, or to start shaping the plane immediately. There are several basic guidelines that must be followed:

1. Leave at least $5/16$ inch of the cheeks above the cross-pin. If you encroach farther, the cheeks may split from the force exerted through the cross-pin by the wedge.

2. Heeding the first point, remove enough wood from the cheeks and back block to afford clear access to the blade. You must be able to tap the blade forward and from side to side.

3. Do no more than lightly break the leading edge of the plane bottom. Stray shavings often litter the surface being planed. If a shaving is run over, it gets jammed in the throat opening if the front edge is overly rounded or chamfered. Usually the blade must be removed to clear the blockage.

This is a needless waste of time. Keep the front edge as described above and stray shavings will be swept off the board by the plane.

Shaping Techniques

Follow these procedures when shaping the plane body:

1. Clean up the side of the plane. Planing it is preferable, but just sand carefully if you don't have the skills or the plane to do it yet. Keep the side square to the bottom. Now sketch the shape of the plane on the side of the blank (4–104). Do this free-hand or with the aid of French curves.

2. Saw the profile on the band saw (4–105). *Caution:*

Sawing takes considerably less force when the space between the front and back block is reached and the blade is exposed between the cheeks.

Angling the plane on edge while using the band saw to cut away excess material is an unorthodox and *potentially unsafe* technique (4–106). I maintain a tight grip on the plane and never bury the blade in more than about $1/2$ inch of wood. If too heavy a cut is taken, there may be enough force to pivot the plane downward, dragging your hand into the blade or breaking the blade. If using this technique, be aware of the risks involved. The safer alternative is to simply take a little more time in the next step when shaping the plane with hand tools.

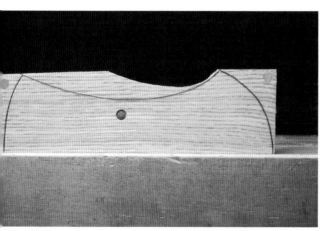

4–104. The shape of the plane is sketched on the side of the blank.

4–106. This unorthodox band-saw technique is potentially dangerous, so be very careful.

4–105. The shape is sawn out with the band saw.

4–107. The band-sawn plane.

3. The body can also be shaped with spokeshaves, files, and scrapers, as shown in 4–108 to 4–110. (See Chapter 7 for guidance with scrapers.)

4. The long bottom edges can be chamfered (4–111), to reduce friction between the plane and board. Leave a 1/16-inch flat between the edge of the chamfer and the throat opening.

5. File off all sharp corners very lightly only at the leading edge of the bottom (as directed above), for comfort and aesthetics elsewhere.

6. As discussed previously, the tip of the 45-degree ramp was chamfered prior to glue-up. If that has been obliterated in the process of truing the bottom, reestablish it now. First be absolutely positive that the back block and not the front block is being worked on; if not, that sweet opening you worked for will be swiftly destroyed. Use a knife to mark a line 3/32 inch back from the tip of the back block that is the same width as the opening. Place the tip of a wide chisel in the scribe line and, with a tap of a mallet, reestablish the chamfer.

A completed plane is shown in 4–112.

4–108. Shaping the front end with a spokeshave.

4–110. Scraping the back block.

4–109. Shaping the center curve with a spokeshave.

4–111. Chamfers on the bottom.

4–112. The completed plane.

SOLES AND INSERTS

Any time a plane is made from wood that does not wear particularly well, it should be fitted with a sole or an insert of durable wood to extend the life of the precisely fitted opening and protect the bottom from marring. A sole is a complete covering for the bottom of the plane, while an insert is an inlay for the area of the bottom just in front of the throat opening where most of the wear occurs. Larger planes made with lighter, faster-wearing woods are especially good candidates for this approach. The size of the plane gives it enough weight, and the sole provides the durability.

In the sections below, I describe how to make soles and inserts.

Soles

Select a very hard and dense wood for the sole. There are many choices: Lignum vitae is a classic.

South American ironbark, secupira, and cocobolo are all very hard-wearing. Among domestics, Osage orange (sometimes called hedgeapple or bodark) and mulberry are very durable; they are more likely to be found in a firewood pile than the lumberyard, though. Resaw several oversized pieces and dry them in the shop for a few months if you have raided the woodpile.

Soles are best applied to the trued-up plane blank just prior to resawing the cheeks and center block. Mill a sole to a finished thickness of $3/16$ inch. Size it $1/4$ inch wider and longer than the plane blank. Align the grain of the plane body and the sole so that when the cheeks and midsection are milled, the grain run-out of the two is compatible. Glue the sole to the blank, backing it with a $3/4$-inch-thick caul. Make sure that the sole overlaps the plane blank all around.

Clean up as much squeeze-out as possible while the glue is wet. After the glue has cured, plane the side overlap of the sole flush to the sides of the plane blank; then resaw the blank into the cheeks and center block as before. Pay attention to the grain run-out direction of the *sole* when deciding which are the front and back of the plane. Proceed with plane-making as before.

Inserts

Planes wear mostly in a semicircular area starting at the front of the throat opening and extending about one inch forward (4–113). A square insert of durable wood, covering the width of the opening and about $1^{1}/_{4}$ inches long, will greatly extend the life of a plane made from softer material.

Proceed with the plane blank to the point of sawing out the front and back blocks. Saw out the back block (with the 45-degree ramp) and stop. Lay out the position of the insert in what will become the front block, as shown in 4–114. Make the cut parallel to the bottom with the band saw and a fence. Make the crosscut with a table saw and sled or miter gauge. Set the saw cut slightly high so that there is no need to clean up the corner (4–115).

Now gently smooth the surface cut with the band saw by scraping it with a sharp chisel. Then size the insert thickness flush with the bottom of the block. Make the width and length a bit larger than the space it is to fill. Match the grain direction and run-out of the insert with the plane bottom. Glue it in with a single clamp and a small caul. Angling the

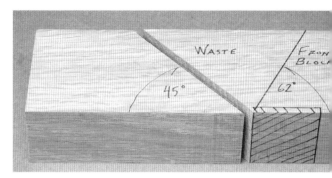

4–114. The insert layout on a plane blank.

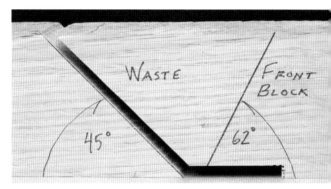

4–115. The saw cuts made on the plane blank.

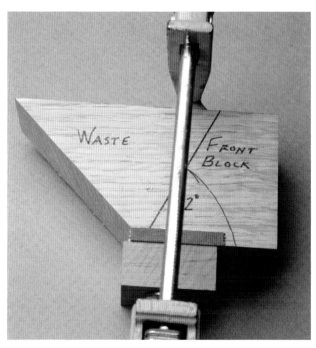

4–116. Gluing the insert. The caul spreads pressure; angling the clamp presses the insert to the front corner of its recess.

4–113. The cross-hatched area experiences the most friction and wear. Note the relatively wide throat opening.

clamp as shown in 4–116 presses the insert firmly against the corner of the front block.

When the glue has dried, plane the sides of the insert flush to the block. Saw out the front block and continue with the normal construction sequence (4–117).

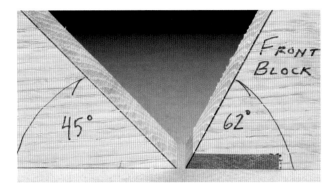

4–117. The front block sawn out, and the insert completed.

IMPROVING A THROAT OPENING

Inserts are also useful for closing up a wide opening on planes found at a flea market or shop-made planes that have worn over the years. Of course, a plane that didn't come out quite right to begin with can also be retrofitted. To improve an opening that is just slightly off, carefully placed shims are the answer.

Inserts and shims are discussed below.

4–118. The location of the cutting edge, when set for a fine cut, is marked on the plane bottom.

Inserts

Mark the position of the cutting edge, when set for a fine cut, to the side of the opening (4–118). Remove the blade. Lay out the area for the insert in front of the opening with a fine-tipped pen: the insides of the cheeks form the sides, the front is square across, and there is a distance of $1^{1}/_{4}$ inches from the tip to the front block (4–119). Lightly knife the marks, too.

4–119. The insert layout.

Now clamp the plane upside down in a vise. Then with a $^{1}/_{4}$- or $^{5}/_{16}$-inch router bit set to a $^{1}/_{8}$-inch depth of cut, freehand-rout the insert area, coming to within $^{1}/_{16}$ inch of the marks. Be careful not to rout the tip of the back block. Carefully pare back to the knife line with a sharp chisel and a mallet. Take very small bites. For the final cut, place the chisel tip in the knifed line (4–120).

Preliminarily size the insert marginally wider than the space it is to fill. The length is sized from the front of the insert area to $^{1}/_{32}$ inch beyond the line on the cheek marking the position of the blade. Trim the insert to a tight side-to-side fit by planing the edges with the aid of a shooting board (see Chapter 5). Pay attention to the run-out of the insert before gluing it in. A softwood block bridges the open area of the plane body, providing a platform for clamping; a wedge tapped in gently between the insert and back block presses the insert to the front of its opening; and a caul spreads the clamping pressure (4–121). Plane the insert flush after the glue dries; then file the opening as described in Filing the Throat Opening on pages 105 to 107 to finish the job (4–122).

4–120. The routed and chiseled insert recess.

4–121. The clamped insert.

4–122. The finished insert.

Shims

Simply propping the blade off the ramp will serve to close down the opening if it is not too wide. Place strips of $1/2$-inch masking tape at the bottom of the 45-degree ramp, from cheek to cheek, with the aid of tweezers. Rub the masking tape down well. Reinstall the blade to check the opening. It is probably best to install an insert if more than three or four strips are required.

ADDITIONAL PLANES

The majority of planing could probably be handled with just one plane—the 12-inch jack plane fitted with a $1^3/4$-inch-wide blade—but other lengths and widths of planes are much better suited for particular jobs. Duplicate planes are also very helpful, offering a sharp blade that is set and ready for planing. These planes can be used in tandem for repetitive tasks: one set for coarse work and one for finishing. Please note that the names associated with various length planes that are referred to below relate to the tasks I perform with them, rather than to any "officially sanctioned" designations. Thus what I term a "jack plane" is used as such, but may be longer or shorter than what someone else calls a "jack plane."

A Basic Set of Planes

This set of planes is good for the typical chores a furniture-maker encounters. The listed lengths and blade widths are what I have found comfortable to use.

1. *Block plane* (4–123): $7^1/_2$ inches long, with a $1^1/_2$-inch-wide blade. Uses: trimming, chamfering, and fitting small parts.

2. *Smoothing plane* (4–124): 9 inches long, with a $1^3/_4$- to 2-inch-wide blade. Uses: smoothing (final-planing) any size surface.

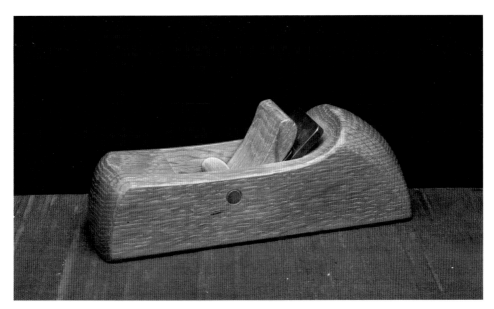

4–123. A red-oak block plane. This wood has exceptional density. This plane is $7^1/_2$ inches long, with a $1^1/_2$-inch-wide iron.

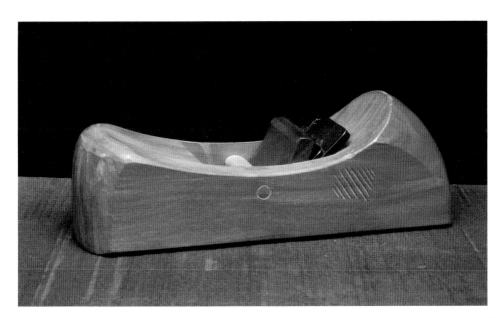

4–124. European applewood polishing or smoothing plane. The plane is 9 inches long, and has a 2-inch-wide iron.

3. *Jack plane* (4–125): 12 inches long, with a 1³/₄-inch-wide blade. Uses: truing surfaces, edge-joining smaller boards, smoothing, trimming ends of wide boards, and using with a shooting board.

4. *Jointer plane* (4–126): 17 inches long, with a 1¹/₂-inch-wide blade. Uses: edge-joining longer boards and truing large surfaces.

An Extended Set of Planes

These planes extend your capabilities and make certain tasks more convenient:

1. *Small block plane* (4–127): 5¹/₂ inches long, with a 1- to 1¹/₄-inch-wide blade. It is handy for detailing work.

4–125. Applewood jack plane. It is 12 inches long, with a 1³/₄-inch-wide iron.

4–126. Red-oak jointer. It is 17 inches long, and has a 1¹/₂-inch-wide iron.

4–127. Ironbark block plane— one of my first attempts. It is 5¹/₂ inches long, and has a 1¹/₄-inch-wide iron.

2. *Wide jointer plane* (4–128): 17 inches long, with a 1³/₄-inch-wide blade. It is useful for truing large surfaces.

3. *Scrub plane* (4–129): 8¹/₂ inches long, with a 1³/₄-inch-wide blade. It has a wide opening for coarse planing.

4. *Dedicated jack plane*: set to produce a square cut with a shooting board.

5. *Rocker bottom plane.* It is useful for planing concave curves with the grain (see Chapter 7).

With experience you will discover what is required with *your* work. Then it is only a question of setting to work to make the right plane for the job. Your first plane may have taken many hours and seemed a bit of a struggle. Having gone through the process a time or two, you will find that a plane can be made ready to glue up in a short evening's work. Early the next morning you will be making shavings; then it's just a matter of how to shape the plane.

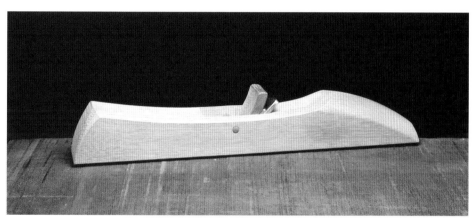

4–128. A jointer plane. It is 17 inches long, and has a 1³/₄-inch-wide iron.

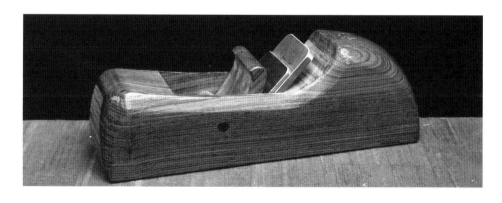

4–129. Coco bolo scrub plane. It is 8¹/₂ inches long, with a 1³/₄-inch-wide iron.

CHAPTER FIVE

Planing Techniques

Those first lacy shavings that shoot from your plane are inspirational. Now it's time to move on from the making of shavings to expertly performing an array of techniques with planes. Be aware: This tool, which can do so much so well, may also confound and frustrate. A successful job—a melding of the process itself and the final product—is dependent on close observation and involvement in the interaction among the craftsman, the plane, and the wood. If your efforts turn sour, often it's because the plane needs to be resharpened, have its bottom trued, or be adjusted for a finer setting. Pay attention to the demands of the plane. Revisit Chapter 4 for information concerning these procedures.

The information in this chapter explores basic techniques for joining edges, truing and smoothing surfaces, trimming and squaring stock, and shaping profiles (5–1). Follow the text while performing each exercise on a length of practice stock. Each task will require a certain amount of sensitivity to the process.

5–1. Planing using a push grip.

PREPARING TO PLANE

The Workbench

For a woodworker using planes, the workbench is an extremely important tool capable of enhancing and supporting the efforts or causing lots of annoyance and difficulty. The European style of cabinetmaker's workbench is ideally suited for planing for two reasons: its weight and its clamping systems (5–2). The weight provides stability—an anchor against the push and pull of planing. The clamping systems provide a variety of ways to reliably secure the stock in a manner convenient for planing.

At the core is the tail vise working in concert with movable bench dogs inserted in the bench top. The dogs can be placed along the length of the bench to accommodate any size stock within that limit. They can be raised up and down to handle thicknesses from about $1/8$ inch on up, allowing an obstruction-free path for planing (5–3). The tail vise accepts a dog and provides the clamping power for holding boards to the bench top. Select proper dog holes to keep the opening of the tail vise as small as possible, to provide the workpiece with optimal support. The use of spacing blocks between the bench dog and workpiece is helpful in this regard.

Make your own wooden bench dogs. Accidentally running into a metal one—a distinct and unpleasant possibility, especially when planing thin stock—tears up the blade and plane. A spring made of thin wood, screwed to the dog, provides some friction to keep the dog at a chosen height instead of letting it flop back into its hole (5–4).

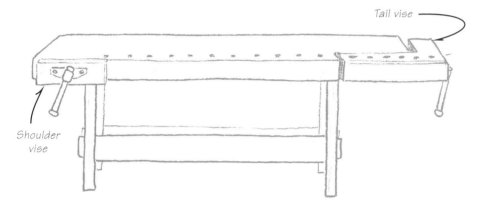

Tail vise

Shoulder vise

5–2. European-style workbench.

5–3. European workbench with board dogged to it.

5–4. Wooden bench dogs.

Flattening and Truing the Bench Top

A bench, like any other tool, must be properly tuned to perform its best. The major requirement is a flat and true top. Any stock that is thin enough to flex more than a few thousandths of an inch under the pressure of planing will start to conform to the irregularities of an uneven bench top; therefore, the bench should be as flat as possible. Refer to the section below on flattening technique if the top needs attention.

For a long bench, a six- or seven-foot length of aluminum "U" channel may suffice for an overall check. Work with a standard three-foot straight-edge for greater accuracy over a smaller area. Check the length of the bench along the front, back, and middle. Check the width at both ends and the middle and then check both diagonals. The size of the bench makes the task seem daunting, but it is just a matter of methodically applying the same principles used for smaller surfaces. Also, you can cheat a bit and concentrate the most critical efforts on the zones that receive the most use: the length of the front of the bench and the full width of the half of the bench that includes the tail vise, where work is done most frequently. Wait until you have gone through the planing exercises in this chapter and gained some confidence with the planes before trying this.

A bench top that is flat and free of wind can also serve as an on-the-spot standard to try against any smaller surface being worked on. Assess the bench top with winding sticks. Winding sticks may be any pair of straight sticks with parallel edges. For checking the bench top, mill a pair as long as the bench's width, about 3/8 inch thick and 1 1/2 inches wide. Sticks of contrasting colors aid the process because one stick is sighted against the other to reveal the presence of wind. A stroke of black marking pen along one edge does the trick.

If the bench is longer than three or four feet, gauge it in two locations: from one end to the middle, and then from the middle to the other end. Lay one stick on edge across the end of the bench where most of the work is done. Lay the other across the bench about three feet away. Step back a few feet and bring your head down so your eye is level with and sighting across the tops of the sticks. Concentrate on the outer ends. Move your head up and down until the tops of both sticks near one end line up. Sight across the sticks at the other end, without changing the elevation of your head, and see if the tops are aligned or if the back stick appears higher at that end (5–5). Reverse the order, sighting across and aligning the ends of the sticks you finished with last time, and compare the opposite ends.

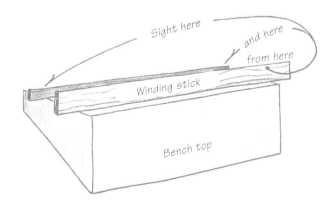

5–5. Sighting across winding sticks to assess a bench top.

Two readings are taken because the front stick obscures the back one if the back stick happens to give a low reading at one end. There is no wind if the sticks are level for both sightings; if they appear out of level, there is wind to that same degree. The top and base of the workbench may have some flexibility. It is worth a try shimming under the bench legs, seeing if that corrects the situation. If it does, trim the legs appropriately and add braces to the bench for a more permanent fix. To plane out the error, skip ahead to Flattening and Truing Surfaces on pages 139 to 143 for information on correcting wind.

Vise Faces

It is important that the opposing faces of the vises be parallel and flat. To determine this, lightly clamp a sheet of paper that is as wide as the vise and see if the paper is gripped firmly all across. If it is not, remove a little wood from a face where the paper is tight. Clamping a sheet of carbon paper leaves a mark showing precisely where to concentrate the efforts. Keep the faces flat. When the faces of the vise mate properly, trued stock can be held securely with a minimum of pressure. Consider gluing a covering of $1/8$-inch high-density rubber (available at hardware stores) to one face, to further guard against pivoting or to take up any minor imperfections. Glue it with contact cement.

Good Lighting

Good lighting is essential. A pair of swing-arm desk lamps mounted on the bench will find constant use. A strip of wood with several holes drilled to accept a lamp, mounted to the back of the bench, works well and allows for easy removal of the lamps when they are in the way.

Working with the Workbench at Hand

If the workbench is something other than a European cabinetmaker's bench, it can still be quite serviceable as long as it is flat. If the bench top cannot be flattened for whatever reason, an auxiliary top for planing (essentially a large plan-

ing hook as described in Chapter 6) may be the way to go, short of getting a new bench. Fashion one from two thicknesses of flat $3/4$-inch sheet stock, such as particleboard, MDF (medium-density fiberboard), or plywood, glued together. The stiffness of the lamination helps average out the inaccuracies of the bench top. If you can't glue up this flat yourself, seek out a shop with a veneer press to do the job.

Make two tops to cover most planing situations: one about 24 x 42 inches and one about 6 x 72 inches. If the bench has dogs, use them to secure the auxiliary tops. If not, screw a length of $3/4$ x 1-inch stock underneath the auxiliary tops, along an edge, to hook on a corner of the bench while you plane (5–6). The far side of the auxiliary tops requires a stop that will trap the stock being planed. Screw on a strip of $3/8$-inch plywood to the edge; it should protrude above the top about $3/16$ inch. In essence, these are extra-thick "planing hooks" as described below.

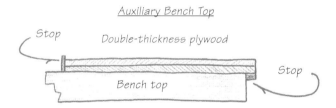

Auxiliary Bench Top

5–6. Side view of auxiliary planing tops showing location of stops.

If the bench top is flat, but lacks a convenient method for clamping the stock to be planed, the stock can be held by forcing or stopping the workpiece up against a board clamped to the bench top. Plane in the direction of the stop and all will be fine. If there is a need to plane diagonally (a technique for truing a surface), additional stops on the sides are required. A planing hook—as above—made from a *single* thickness of sheet stock (for lighter weight) is another possibility. The advantage is doing away with clamps for straight-on planing.

A typical woodworking face vise mounted on the end of the bench can be used to simulate a tail vise.

This requires the type with an adjustable (up-and-down) stop as part of the outer half of the vise. Clamp stock to the bench top, pinching it between the vise and a board firmly clamped across the bench top. Now planing can be done diagonally without the stock sliding away.

Another option that allows for planing to be done diagonally is to drill holes for bench dogs. Align a series of 3/4-inch holes with the center of the vise, along the front edge of the bench top, to accept simple bench dogs made from 3/4-inch dowels. Space them four to five inches apart. Angle the holes so that the bench dogs will lean slightly toward the vise. This helps keep the clamped stock down on the bench. Cut a flat at the top of the dowel to register on the board. To prevent the dowels from slipping down the holes, insert small bullet catches (spring-loaded ball bearings) in radially drilled holes placed near the bottom. Also, always use a spacer board that completely bridges the opening of the vise, allowing the clamped stock to lay fully supported on the workbench.

Practice Stock

Select an 8-inch-wide 4/4 (1-inch-thick) board of straight-grained hardwood that is free from knots. Cherry, walnut, oak, maple, ash, etc., will do fine. Crosscut a 20-inch length and true the faces and edges with a jointer and planer.

"Reading" Wood Grain for Planing

To avoid tear-out, you probably determined the grain run-out direction before using the jointer and planer, as discussed in Chapter 2. When planing, always be aware of grain direction, moving in the direction that smoothes the fibers down rather than lifting them out of the surface (tear-out). Often a quick glance at the edge adjacent to the face being planed indicates everything needed to know: the slant of the grain is obvious. Sometimes this area is difficult to read though. Lightly brushing your fingers up and down the board, as is done when deter-

mining the back and front of the plane blank, may reveal run-out. The wood fibers will catch your skin in one direction, as was described in Preparing the Plane Blank in Chapter 1.

A close examination of the surface of open-pored woods such as oak, ash, and walnut can also show which way to plane. Hollow vessels run up and down the tree, in a direction parallel to other types of wood fibers. These tubes may run parallel on the face of a board cut from a log (no run-out) or intersect the face at some angle (resulting in run-out). If the board has run-out, the opening of the tubes, seen on the surface of a plank, are oval, the tapered end pointing out the direction to plane (5–7). The more elongated the opening, the less run-out there is. This knowledge is especially helpful when the edges of a board are obscured, or to reveal areas of run-out reversal within a board.

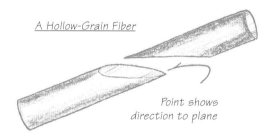

A Hollow-Grain Fiber

Point shows direction to plane

5–7. *If a board has run-out, the hollow fibers of an open-pored wood are cut obliquely at the surface. The point of the resultant teardrop shape indicates the planing direction.*

Look at the end of the practice stock and examine the end grain. The orientation of the annual growth rings, with respect to the face of the board being planed, affects the planing characteristics of different species of wood to varying, sometimes opposing, degrees. For example, extra vigilance and attention must be given to the sharpness of an iron when planing a cherry quarter-sawn face. Medullary rays, a physiological component situated radially and horizontally in the tree, are visible as small opalescent flecks on the quarter (notably in quarter-sawn oak). If care is not taken, these may pull from the wood while planing, leaving a roughened surface.

Cherry that is *flat-sawn* is much easier to plane; this is because the medullary rays are firmly integrated into the structure of the wood. My experience with some ash planks is just the opposite. The flat-sawn face is trickier to plane to perfection, as the stringy, very open-pored flat-sawn surface is more susceptible to tear-out than the tighter-grained quarter-sawn surface.

With experience, you will become familiar with the characteristics of the different woods; this knowledge will prove helpful when planing them.

EDGE-JOINING TECHNIQUES

A power jointer can do a decent job of edge-joining if it is set up very precisely and the blades are very sharp. Optimal conditions are hard to maintain, though: tables lose alignment, fences go off square, the knife edges may not be concentric, and very quickly the knives lose their sharpness. Soon the wood is not only cut by the knives, but pounded and compressed as well. Joints may look good dry, but when they are glued up compressed fibers swell, exposing an evident glue line. A *planed* surface is sheared smoothly; there is no fiber compression. It can be drenched with water, even steamed indefinitely, only to reveal a silky-smooth surface when dried; glue has no adverse effect on the quality of the joint as observed when dry-fit.

Consider the jointer as a tool for rough truing and squaring boards and parts. Final smoothing is done with a plane for dead-on squareness, straightness, and virtually undetectable joinery.

The plane chosen for joining boards together should be close in size to the length of the boards: the closer it is, the easier it becomes to plane a straight edge. A flat plane cannot work an appreciable dip into the edge of a board that is the same length. Looked at from the other way: if the plane is shorter than the board, the shorter the plane, the more of a dip that can be planed into that edge. It is

not advantageous, merely clumsy, to use a plane that is longer than the boards being joined. On the other hand, a jointer plane 18 inches long is quite capable of making flawless joints 6 feet long if handled carefully.

It is of utmost importance that the plane be well flattened prior to beginning. Any time you are having extended difficulty and can't quite get the joint to fit, that is the first thing to check. Also, the plane iron must be sharpened straight across, with no hint of an arc. The cut must be set extremely fine, producing very thin, cottony-soft shavings.

It is helpful to have two planes available: one set coarse to remove the milling marks, and one set fine to fit the joint. The blade must also be set perfectly parallel to the bottom. If it takes a slightly heavier cut off one side, each pass of the plane lowers that side of the edge of the board, quickly putting it out of square. Set up the plane with a trued piece of scrap.

The Basic Strokes

Set the practice board edge-up in a face vise, with the grain on the face of the board rising to the left. Set the front of the plane on the edge of the board and slide it forward until the blade just contacts the wood. The front (left) hand plays a very important role, maneuvering the plane laterally and centering pressure over the wood. Its four fingers wrap underneath the body of the plane with the fingertips on the bottom and brushing the face of the board. The thumb is arched on top of the plane, positioned so that the tip is directly over the center of the edge of the board being planed (5–8). Sometimes the thumb will be in the center of the plane, and sometimes to the left or right of center if partial-width shavings are desired. The thumb is important for balancing the plane and the pressure transmitted to the blade. The slightest wobble produces an incomplete shaving and a flawed surface. The back hand rests lightly on the back of the plane.

5–8. The grip for edge-joining.

It is a universal law of planing that when the stroke is started, pressure is on the front of the plane; then pressure is transferred equally to the front and back when the plane is fully on the board; and finally pressure is exerted on the rear of the plane as the front of the plane leaves the board. At the end of the stroke, when the shaving has parted from the board, the motion of the plane is stopped while the rear of the plane is still registered flat on the board. All of these elements are essential to accurate planing. And how much "pressure" is needed? Very, very little. The weight of the plane is sufficient. You mainly supply forward thrust and control.

Practice Shavings

If the blade is set fine enough, the first two or three shavings will reflect the scalloped quality of the surface left by the jointer: they appear rippled and discontinuous. Then you should start producing continuous shavings the full width and length of the edge. This must be done time after time to get good results in edge-joining.

A properly flattened and adjusted plane, a light touch, and well-centered pressure from the thumb are the keys for edge-joining success. Any time the shaving is discontinuous, a flawed joint will result. Unfortunately, the opposite is not always correct: a continuous shaving does not guarantee a good joint.

If continuous shavings are not forthcoming, check the usual suspects: the sharpness of the iron and plane flatness. It takes just a small amount of practice to acquire the necessary finesse to get consistent, continuous shavings. In the meantime, if the edge of the board has been knocked out of true by the initial efforts, it will be difficult to get satisfactory results. Reestablish a true edge with the power jointer and try again.

Squaring and Straightening the Edge

Carefully plane off the jointer marks. Release the board from the vise and check the edge for square. Sight toward a bright light to get a good reading with the combination square. Check both ends and the middle. Register the handle off the same face each time, for consistency. Is it square all the way across, or out of square all the way or only at one end? It may even be out of square in opposite directions at either end.

Let's assume there is a problem. Take the same approach here as when truing the ramp of the plane: namely, plane the high spots and avoid the spots that read low. Take partial shavings with the appropriate corner of the blade while the plane is flat on the stock. Steer the plane using the fingertips of the front hand like an adjustable fence against the face of the stock, and keep your thumb centered over the edge being planed. For instance, if the edge reads high all along the left side, let the right corner of the blade take a shaving off the left edge only that is one-third the full width of the edge. On the next pass, take a shaving that is two-thirds the width, and then one that is the full width (5–9). If it was way out of square, start with a one-quarter- or one-fifth-wide shaving and work progressively across to full width. Check for square and repeat if necessary.

For an edge with a wind, take a full-width shaving where the edge is square and move the plane over to take a partial shaving from the edge where it reads high. This is accomplished in one smooth stroke of the plane, navigating left and right with the aid of the left-hand finger/fence as you go. Repeat the process taking wider partial shavings and then, finally, a full-length, full-width shaving (5–10). The motion of the plane must be fluid as the width of the shavings is adjusted (5–11).

Before long you will effortlessly guide the plane

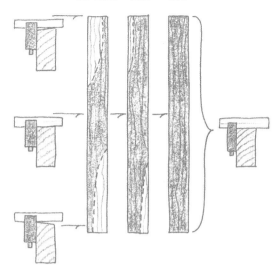

5–10. *Squaring the edge of a board that has wind.*

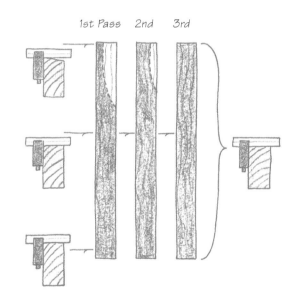

5–11. *Squaring the edge of a board that is low at one end.*

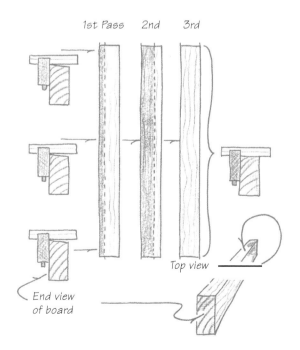

5–9. *Squaring the edge of a board that is high on the left. The shaded portion corresponds to the width of the shavings made. The squares show the readings at the ends and middle of the board.*

along an edge, steering it right where it needs to go. Having squared up the edge, try taking it purposely out of square, or putting a wind in it, and then restoring squareness again. If you are feeling comfortable controlling the plane and achieving a square edge, it's time to practice straightening it. After all, a perfect edge joint is square and straight.

Draw a cabinetmaker's triangle on the center of the board in preparation for sawing it into two pieces (5–12). This exercise involves ripping the

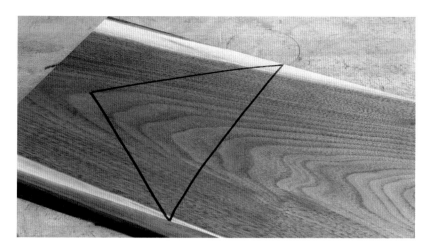

5–12. A practice board with a cabinet-maker's triangle drawn on it. When the board is ripped into two pieces, it will be easy to relocate them with the aid of the reference mark.

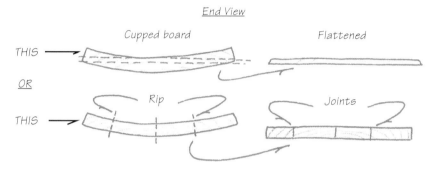

5–13. Above is a cupped board that has been left intact and then flattened. Below is a board that has been ripped into staves that are individually flattened and then rejoined. Note the difference in final thickness.

board and then seamlessly joining it back together. That may appear to be simply an academic activity, but, in fact, this capability opens up an exciting avenue for utilizing wide boards. Wide stock can be ripped into pieces narrow enough to fit the jointer and planer, dimensioned efficiently, and then joined back to a unified whole, with no glue lines betraying the process that occurred. The difference between the visual impact of harmonious grain patterns on large surfaces and the inevitable disjointedness that occurs from joining disparate boards is stark. Of course, a wide plank can be flattened with planes, but the process is laborious and even wasteful. If a board is cupped across its width, a significant amount of thickness can be lost while it is being flattened. Cutting it into narrow strips minimizes the loss of thickness (5–13). Be aware that the board will lose some width due to the saw kerfs, jointing, and planing.

I always prefer ripping on the band saw. Absence of kickback danger is a big plus and so is the narrow saw kerf. If the same pieces of wood will be glued

back together again, it is important to preserve the grain pattern by taking a minimal saw kerf. It is also easier to match the grain and hide the joint if the saw cut falls in an area of straight grain. If the grain pattern is angling across the saw cut, it will be necessary to offset the ends of the board to match the grain lines, and sometimes a perfect match is not even possible (5–14). For this reason, always leave a

5–14. Saw cuts in straight and angled grain areas of a board. Notice the degree of offset at the ends of the boards required to match the grain when the cut is made in an area with angled grain lines.

little extra length for boards that will be sawn and reglued. In any event, rip the practice stock into two pieces and true the sawn edges on the jointer.

Squaring Each Board and Testing It for Straightness

For stock less than $1/2$ inch thick, the mating edges can be planed simultaneously, but the task is best done with a shooting board (see Chapter 6). Here, work on the edges one at a time. Once squared, try the boards together. Use the cabinetmaker's triangle to quickly orient the pieces. One quick test will indicate right away if there is more fitting to do. While holding the planed edges together with light pressure, rotate the pieces in opposite directions—the top of one board moving toward you and the other away (5–15). If they pivot easily at the center, it's likely that both boards are humped. If there is some resistance to pivoting, the ends of the two pieces are making contact, which is good.

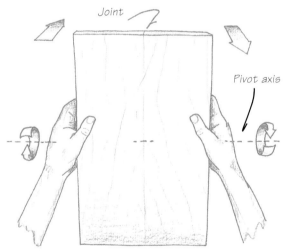

5–15. Pivoting test for tight board ends.

One of the real challenges for novice edge-joiners is getting a tight joint at the ends. There is a natural tendency to make a slightly heavier cut at the beginning and end of each stroke. The cumulative effect is to create a hump in the center of both board edges.

If the boards pivoted, sight the joint against a

light and you will see the gaps at the ends. The goal is to methodically remove the hump without altering squareness. Place one piece back in the vise. Envision the length of the edge divided into fifths. Take successive partial-length shavings—first from the central fifth, and then from the second to the fourth, followed by a full-length stroke. Try the joint again. If the boards still pivot, repeat the steps on the other piece. Continue in like manner until the joint can be felt locking at the ends. If the plane is nearly the same length as the board, stick to partial-length shavings until no shavings are forthcoming from the center. This indicates that the edge is as flat as the plane. Take a full-length shaving, and then try the joint for the first time.

Beware of creating a dip in the central portion of the edge. Some craftsmen do intentionally create a small gap there and call it "springing the joint." This puts pressure on the ends of the joint once it is glued up, the thought being that since edge joints usually fail at the ends first, tension should be used in the rest of the glue surface to hold them tight. But it is easy to end up with an overly stressed joint, prone to wholesale failure, or just a poor-looking joint. The best joint fits perfectly, from end to end, without stressing the boards.

For boards small enough to be taken in hand comfortably, check the fit by sighting against a bright light. If the boards are too large, they may be laid flat on the bench or one held in a vise and the other stacked on edge on top of it. Do not mistake shadow lines for gaps. Wherever a gap is perceived, check that the surfaces are flush or oriented so that no misleading shadow is cast.

Testing for Wind

This time, while mating the boards forming the joint, cock the wrists very minimally toward yourself and then away (5–16). If overdone, the effect would be to hinge the joint open lengthwise, on the side facing you, and then away from you, but that is not the intent. Instead, try to feel if the joint

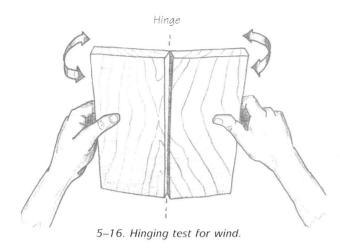

5–16. Hinging test for wind.

viously described steps for re-moving wind, and then try the joint again.

If the adjustments to the joint keep creating gaps in different locations, the shavings are probably too thick. Each time an adjustment is made, you are overcompensating and causing a new problem. Adjust the plane. Give yourself a break and use the jointer to get back to square one if you have become frustrated. With a little practice, it all comes together: the board comes off the jointer, a few strokes of the plane clean off the milling marks, the joint is tried, a few adjustments are made, the joint is tried again, and the board is ready for the clamps.

Matching Grain

Lay the pieces on the bench in their original orientation. Match up the grain lines for the most harmonious appearance across the joint. A pencil line across the joint indexes the parts, so there is no need to fumble with this decision while gluing; merely line up the pencil mark and clamp (5–18).

remains firm, or if there is any rocking within the joint betraying the presence of a wind. If it feels firm, the board is in good shape. If a small amount of motion is felt, look closely along the joint while racking it in the same way. Check the front and the back. At some point you will see a small gap opening and closing. That area can be checked for square, but simply sliding the ends out of register with each other may indicate which edge is drooping.

For example, perhaps a gap was discovered at the top of the joint. If raising the left-hand piece does not close the gap, but raising the right-hand piece does, it can be surmised that the wind is in the right-hand piece (5–17). Take the pre-

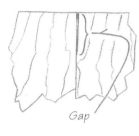

Gap

Gap remains

No gap

5–17. Offsetting ends to identify a board with a defective end.

5–18. Aligning grain and indexing with a line. Notice the offset of the pieces at the end of the joint.

Clamps

Literally any clamp that opens wide enough can do the job, but generally choose bar or pipe clamps for edge-gluing. The sizes of the clamp ends are geared for the typical thicknesses encountered, and they

come long enough for gluing up wide surfaces. They should rest securely on a bench top with the jaw opening facing the ceiling. If the clamps are wobbly, fashion a series of uniform blocks to support them—only one per clamp is needed (5-19). The method shown in 5–21 places all the clamps beneath the boards being glued (rather than staggered under and over). It is helpful if the horizontal centerline of the clamp screws is the same height off the workbench. Keep the bars free of dried glue to prevent scratching the wood.

5–19. Bar clamp support block.

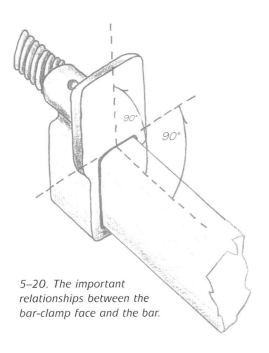

5–20. The important relationships between the bar-clamp face and the bar.

The faces of the clamp heads should be flat, smooth, and square to the bar in both directions—that is, in line with and across the length of the bar (5–20). Lumpy or misaligned clamp heads exert pressure at an angle to the bar, skewing the boards as pressure is applied. The effect is greatly magnified when glue lubricates the joint. If the clamps need attention and you cannot do the work, have it done by a machinist.

Determining the Number of Clamps Needed

The number of clamps used on the boards depends on the length and strength of the boards being glued. While developing a sense for what is required, apply this technique: envision or lightly sketch a zigzag of 45-degree lines across the face of a board, starting at the center and working out to the edges (5–21). If the boards are of different widths, use the narrower one. Each apex on the edge of the board opposite the glue line indicates one clamp. Alter the distribution and/or add an extra clamp for even spacing along the length of the joint. If joining narrow boards, which will not transmit the clamping pressure far along the glue line, cut down on the amount of clamps needed by adding cauls (stiffeners) to the outer edges of the boards. Add the width of the caul to the width of the board while estimating the amount of clamps.

5–21. Forty-five-degree lines have been drawn across the face of the board to approximate how many clamps to use when edge-joining boards.

Preventing Glue Drips

Protect the bench top from glue with a sheet of polyethylene film or an appropriately sized sheet of $1/8$- to $1/4$-inch waxed Masonite. Glue does not adhere to either, so the coverings can be used over and over. With experience and care, you will apply just the right amount of glue, avoiding drips, and dispense with the coverings.

Guidelines for Successful Edge-Gluing

The primary difficulty with edge-gluing boards is that they slide and cup under clamping pressure, causing misaligned surfaces and partially opened glue joints.

Make sure that the following conditions are met:

1. The clamp heads are properly machined.
2. The boards and clamps are aligned.
3. The correct amount of glue is used.
4. The correct clamping pressure is used.

The importance of using properly machined clamp heads is discussed above. It is also important to align the centerline of the clamp screws with the centerline of the thickness of the boards (5–22 and 5–23). Also, the surface of the boards must be placed parallel to the clamp bar and the bar perpendicular to the glue joint. Skew the bar in rela-

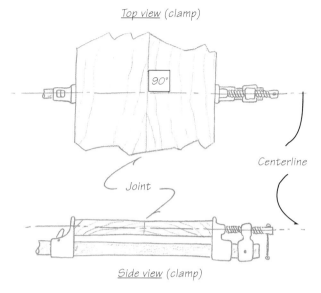

Top view (clamp)

Centerline

Joint

Side view (clamp)

5–23. *Proper alignment of clamp and boards.*

tion to the glue joint and the boards will shift along the joint to bring the bar back toward perpendicular. Place the centerline thickness of the boards above the centerline of the clamp screw and the joint will want to hinge open upward. The opposite occurs when the centerline thickness sets below the clamp-screw centerline.

Surplus glue creates a cleanup chore and causes the boards to slip around excessively as the clamps are tightened. Think of the porosity of the wood being glued: the more porous, the more glue the joint requires. Lay a bead of glue down on one edge. With the pad of the pinky, start in the middle of the joint and stroke the glue out firmly toward each end. Wipe off excess glue on the finger with a damp paper towel. If the surface seems too dry, add some more glue; if it seems too wet, squeegee off the extra glue with your finger before clamping up.

After clamping, assess the glue squeeze-out along the joint and make a mental note for next time. Small, evenly spaced beads indicate a good job. Dripping gobs show an overabundance of glue, and no, or sparse, squeeze-out indicates a potential lack of glue.

Excessive pressure may cup the boards, making it difficult to align the joint and actually opening it up

5–22. *Aligning the centers of the thickness of the board and the clamp screw minimizes skewing of the joint during glue-up.*

rather than bringing it together. There is also the possibility of starving the joint of glue by squeezing it all out. If the joint fits well, only gentle pressure is needed to bring it home. The boards will not be distorted, and aligning them is a snap.

Dry-Clamping

Dry-clamping presents an opportunity to calmly prepare for the glue-up and make a final check on the quality of the joint. Perform this ritual before *every* glue-up. Arrange the clamps on the bench and the wood on the clamps. Distribute the clamps evenly, with the outer clamps near the ends and the bars perpendicular to the glue joint. Adjust the threaded end of the clamps so that about $3/4$ inch of the shaft extends from the "nut" toward the boards, to minimize shaft wobble. Pinch the boards with the sliding part of the clamp, and then back off the threaded shaft one turn for clearance.

Starting at one end, support the boards with the index finger below the boards and the thumb above. Lower your head so that it is level with the clamp screw, and lift that end until the screw is lined up with the center of the thickness of the boards. See that the boards are parallel to the clamp bar and feel with the finger and thumb that the boards are flush with each other at the joint.

Now tighten the clamp just enough to hold the boards in position. Then shift to the other end and do the same positioning. Lightly tighten that clamp as well. Gently snug any interior clamps that remain. If dealing with boards that are not perfectly flat, rather than clamp at both ends first, work your way across the joint, starting at one end, aligning the boards flush, and clamping while proceeding.

Lay a straightedge across the joint at a spot where the boards are perfectly flush. Check to see that the surface is flat widthwise (5–24). Correct any deviation using the plane to slightly angle the edge of one board in the direction that will compensate for the error. Examine the joint for gaps, especially at the ends. Tighten the clamps a bit more to prevent

5–24. Checking for flatness across the boards with a straightedge.

them from falling off; then turn the assembly over and check the back side. Lightly mark any problem areas with a pencil. Make all corrections using your recently acquired arsenal of planing techniques. Resist the temptation to mash out gaps by bearing down on the clamps—the final results will be disappointing. Dry-clamp again if any alterations have been made.

Glue-Up

Carpenter's yellow glue works well for edge-gluing. It is easy to work with, capable of leaving invisible glue lines, and very strong, and it sets up fast. It must be fresh—smooth and runny—to give good results. Stay away from thickened, lumpy glue. Have on hand glue in a bottle, a dampened paper towel, and a sharp one-inch-wide chisel.

Apply glue in the prescribed manner and lay the boards in the clamps. Line up the grain as indicated by the pencil mark. With the boards lying directly on the clamp bars, gently tighten them up to squeeze out most of the excess glue (5–25). Scrape off the squeeze-out, holding the chisel perpendicular to the boards and wiping it clean with the towel each time it becomes loaded with glue.

Loosen all the clamps and reset them as was done when dry-clamping, aligning the clamp screws with the centerline thickness of the boards. If the boards shift slightly, loosen the clamps and make adjustments to the boards while proceeding, making sure that the adjacent surfaces are flush and the pencil line indicating grain matching is properly aligned. Do not overtighten the clamps. With the glue cleaned off, you should be able to see that the joint is together. Additional force may starve the joint for glue. Once you are satisfied with the clamping, stay with it a moment longer; some glue may continue to ooze out, which can be cleaned off now.

Carefully turn the assembly over to clean up the back. Do not worry about contaminating the surface with glue, because the first swipe of the plane will remove any residual glue in the pores of the wood. Pencil the time at the end of the glue-up on the boards. Remove the boards from the clamps in one hour and gently scrape off any glue that remained on the back side. You may continue working the boards at any time now.

5–25. Squeeze-out as seen from underneath the board. It is a little heavier than need be.

Troubleshooting Guidelines

Edge-joining can be tricky. There are many components that need to be correct. Scan this list to determine why good-quality edge-joined boards have not been produced:

- The plane shavings are too thick.
- The blade is not sufficiently sharp.
- The cutting edge of the blade is not straight.
- The plane bottom is not flat.
- An improper planing grip has been used, causing an imbalance in hand pressure.
- An improper stance or body positioning was used, causing the same as above.
- The square was used improperly (including the use of it on a defective reference surface).

Joining Multi-Board Surfaces

Glue up the boards in adjacent pairs. Then join these wider surfaces to pairs also, until the entire surface is complete. In this manner the accuracy of each joint can be carefully controlled. Since the boards are worked gently and returned to a compressed state, half an hour in the clamps is sufficient before working the next joint. A few extra clamps allow you to work and glue the joint on the following pair of boards after the first joint is done, and keep rotating along.

To prevent glued-up surfaces from cupping, always store them so air can circulate on both sides. If mistakenly laid flat on a bench top overnight, the sides will curl up, resulting in a cupped surface. Flipping the distorted surface over and leaving it overnight may or may not alleviate the problem.

FLATTENING AND TRUING SURFACES

Now it is time to flatten and true the edge-glued practice stock. Saw the ends square if they are out of register. As with edge-joining, a larger plane flattens a larger surface with greater ease than a smaller plane will, but too large a plane is awkward to use on a small surface. For this relatively small board, a jack or even a polishing plane is a good choice. The sharpness of the iron is, as always, important, but the shape of the edge is not critical.

Set the plane for a thicker shaving than done for

5–26. *Side grip.*

edge-joining. The thicker the shaving, the harder the plane is to push and the greater the likelihood of tear-out, so shaving thickness is limited by your strength and the response of the wood. Start with a thinner shaving and gradually increase the depth of cut to establish the most efficient setting.

The Side Grip

Two ways of holding the plane have been described: the basic push grip (refer to 5–1) and the modified push grip used for edge-joining. What I term the "side grip" is a third useful way of holding wooden planes (5–26), and my favorite for longer planing sessions. Whereas you stand behind the plane using the first two methods, with the side grip you are positioned at the *side* of the plane. The legs are spread somewhat more than shoulder-width (24 inches or so), with the knees and waist slightly bent. You should feel springy and loose, and should be able to sway left or right comfortably. As you get into the rhythm of the work, you will find yourself rocking from side to side, transferring body weight from one foot to the other and using the whole body to do the work—planing can be done this way for a long time if need be.

Dog the board to the workbench. It usually rises off the bench a bit in the process. Tap the dogs down slightly, to anchor the board. If only stops are being used to capture the board, they should be added at the sides as well as the end to control it. Temporarily screw low battens to the planing hook or clamp extra stops to the bench top. Place any clamps well out of the way, to avoid crashing into them.

Level the surface and remove all milling marks by methodically planing from corner to corner at about a 45-degree angle to the grain and then coming back the other way, as shown in 5–27, creating a cross-hatched pattern. The strokes should still be trending "uphill" with respect to run-out. Repeat until the surface is cleaned off and each stroke produces a shaving from start to finish. This is a good way of handling the unevenness at the glue joint and dealing with overall inaccuracies. Planing at an angle to the grain also minimizes tear-out when taking thick shavings, but does leave a roughened surface. When the smoothing stage is reached, the surface should plane quickly to a nice polish. If it takes many strokes to remove gouges and tear-out from this leveling stage, the plane was set to remove too much wood.

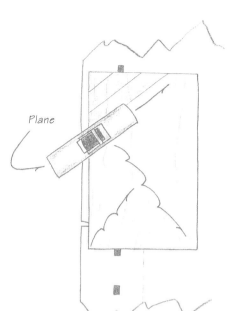

5–27. Primary leveling of a surface.

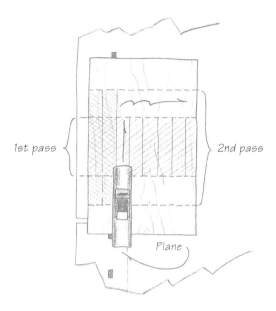

5–29. Correcting a lengthwise hump.

Checking the Surface for Hump and Wind

An accurately flattened workbench is a great aid, acting as a built-in reference surface to gauge the workpiece against. Flip the board over so that the newly planed surface is facedown. With your hands placed broadly across the width at the ends of the board, try rocking the board end for end (5–28). If it rocks, there is a lengthwise hump. Remove it the same way humps on the plane ramps were removed (refer to Chapter 4). Adjust the plane for a lighter cut. Take partial-length shavings, perhaps one-third the total board length and centered over

the hump. Work all the way across the width. Follow with two-thirds-length shavings (5–29). Test again and repeat as necessary until the board rests steadily. Speed or slow the pace of change by adjusting the depth of cut or altering the length of the strokes. Finish with full-length strokes.

Next, place your hands on the sides of the board and try to rock the board from side to side to reveal the presence of a widthwise hump (5–30). Look again to your ramp-truing experience as described in Chapter 4 if there is a problem. Take a stroke down the center at position one as shown in 5–31,

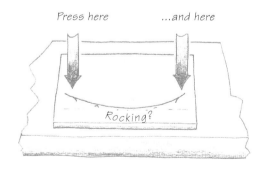

5–28. Checking a surface for a lengthwise hump.

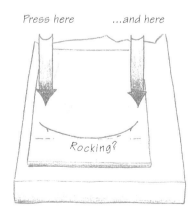

5–30. Checking a surface for a widthwise hump.

and then one to either side at position two. Next, plane at positions one, two, and three. Continue the pattern until the sides are reached. Check the board again and repeat as necessary.

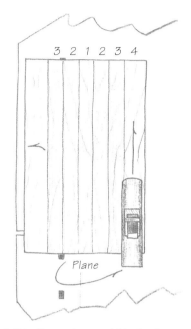

5–31. Correcting a widthwise hump.

The test for wind is similar. Alternately poke a pair of diagonally opposite corners with your index fingers, attempting to rock the board (5–32). Try the other pair of corners. If the board remains perfectly steady, then it is trued. Should the board rock, the corners being poked are relatively low and the other pair of corners are relatively high, acting as pivot points. The board has a wind. Note the high

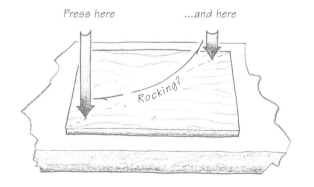

5–32. Checking a surface for wind.

corners, flip the board back over, and clamp it. Again, the remedy uses the same methodical approach used to correct wind on the plane ramps. Plane a stroke from high corner to high corner at position one as shown in 5–33 and then at both locations of position two. Go back to position one for a stroke, to position two, and then to position three. Continue expanding this pattern until the low corners have been reached. Flip the board and check for wind again.

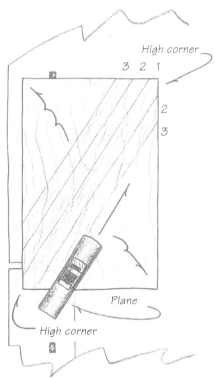

5–33. Correcting wind.

If the work surface is not adequately flattened (and that is something that should be done after a bit of this type of practice), use a straightedge and winding sticks to assess the practice board. Gauge the ends and middle across the width of the board with the straightedge, then the sides and middle along the length, followed by the diagonals. Use winding sticks as described in Flattening and Truing the Bench Top on pages 127 and 128 to identify the "high" corners.

Final Flattening

First consider how the wood has responded to planing. If there has been little tear-out, maintain the current depth of cut. If the wood is prone to tear-out, use a lighter setting. Err on the side of a lighter cut to avoid tear-out, as it may be time-consuming to eliminate in the smoothing stage of planing.

Finish off the flattening by planing with the grain. Start at one side of the board and work your way across, slightly overlapping each pass. Stroke your hand on the wood in the direction being planed to check for tear-out. The fingers should glide smoothly over the surface; any catching or roughness indicates tear-out.

Another essential diagnostic tool is the bench lamp. Plane toward the light and set it inches above the board and just off to the side. Projecting strong, low-angle light places any irregularities of the surface in stark relief by creating shadows.

It is important to flatten the opposite face, if it has wind, before proceeding to the polishing or smoothing stage. Otherwise, the board may flex while being planed, interrupting the flow of shavings and leaving an imperfect surface. In fact, if the stock is appreciably out of true to begin with, it is possible both faces will have to be worked back and forth to accurately true it. If you started with trued stock and did little other than remove milling marks with the initial planing on the first face, treat the opposite face in like manner.

On the other hand, if the first face required substantial planing, there is the concern of maintaining uniform thickness as well as correcting wind as the opposite face is planed. Trim off any projecting ends and flatten the second face approximately. Use a marking gauge to reference off the flattened face and scribe the desired thickness on the ends and side of the board (5–34). Plane down to the mark—with harder woods a discernible ridge may be revealed while planing the face, saving the need to maneuver around to look at the edge (5–35). The knife of the marking gauge should be sharpened to a curving knife edge, rather than a pencil point, to cut effectively.

5–34. Scribing the thickness of a board.

5–35. The scribe line marked on the edge is revealed on the face by planing. Note the fuzzy-looking inner edge.

POLISHING SURFACES

Perhaps the most satisfying aspect of hand-planing is perfecting a surface to shining brilliance using nothing other than the plane and a wad of fine shavings. The work is pleasant, engaging, and satisfying. The final surface may be so alluring you are tempted to dispense with finishes altogether. And this may be done, where appropriate, to benefit from the wood's lovely natural aroma and subtle colorations, typically obscured by finishes.

Polishing Plane

A polishing plane (also called a smoothing plane) should be eight to nine inches long. The shorter length allows an extra stroke or two to be taken in areas requiring added attention. Too short a plane may produce an undulating final surface. The plane should carry an iron $1^3/_4$ to 2 inches wide. A $1^3/_4$-inch blade yields a nice shaving width and the plane will fit the hand of most people. Since the width of the plane used increases with the blade's width, anything over two inches wide is cumbersome for most people with average-sized hands.

The blade must be arced very precisely to yield a shaving nearly its full width yet not allow the corners to dig when the plane is set for a very fine cut. It is a matter of trial and error. If the shavings are full width and very thin, and corner digs are left in the wood, there is not enough arc, so it is necessary to go back to the 800-grit stone and add more arc. If the shavings are too narrow, use the 800-grit stone to flatten out the arc. Of course, the blade must be rehoned on the 8,000-grit stone also. When very thin and wide shavings are produced—for example, shavings slightly wider than $1^1/_2$ inches from a $1^3/_4$-inch-wide blade—the plane is performing well.

Planing Technique

It is important to start with a flat surface, whether it is obtained by planing or by machine. Set the plane for the finest cut. Methodically plane the entire surface. Start at one edge and work your way across, slightly overlapping the strokes. Pay attention to the shavings coming out of the throat of the plane. Do they seem to come off the center of the blade, or from one side or the other? Tap the blade over a bit if they are off to one side, reducing the cut on that side and increasing it on the other. Cover the entire surface two times.

Check your progress visually and tactilely. Scrutinize the surface for tear-out using the bench lamp for assistance as in the final stage of flattening. Brush your fingers across the grain from side to side in both directions. This is to check for sufficient blade arc and a properly adjusted plane. The surface should feel very smooth, perhaps with a hint of undulation caused by the arced blade. If sharp steps are detected that head in one direction, but the surface feels smoother coming back the other way, the corner of the blade is digging. The plane may be maladjusted, the blade insufficiently arced, or both.

The direction the hand moves to feel the sharp ridges also indicates which corner of the blade is digging: it's on the side of the plane you would be moving toward if the plane were on the board ready to make a shaving (5–36). Adjust the plane to lessen the cut on that side while increasing the cut on the other side. If the blade continues to dig on one side or the other, try setting for a finer cut. Failing that, go back to the 800-grit stone and develop a bit more arc on the blade.

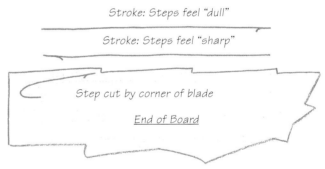

5–36. Feeling the steps left by the corner of the blade indicates how to adjust the plane.

When the surface has been planed free of ridges, make a final check for tear-out. It may be necessary to go over the entire surface a couple of extra times to achieve a flawless surface. Finally, remove the board from the bench top and sight along its length toward a bright light. The surface should be smooth and shiny, but there will also be a series of highly polished streaks going across the board. Those streaks are burnished by the bottom of the plane to either side of the blade. Clamp up the board. Gather a good handful of only the finest shavings and vigorously burnish the surface, rubbing them back and forth with the grain and bringing the entire surface up to a uniform gleam.

If defects are noted that cannot be eliminated, the proper course of action is to omit the burnishing stage and go to scraping, followed by light sanding (see Chapter 7 for information on scraping). In time, you will be able to judge visually or after a few strokes whether the wood chosen is amenable to planing without much difficulty, if it will be challenging, or if scraping and sanding is the best approach.

5–37. End-grain shavings.

SQUARING END GRAIN

Due to the structure of wood, squaring, or simply planing, end grain holds a special challenge. No longer does the slicing occur parallel with the wood fibers; instead the cut is across the ends of the fibers. The wood offers considerably more resistance and, indeed, demands the sharpest blade edge for planing effectively. If end grain is planed without the proper precautions, the inevitable result is cracking and chipping at the end of the cut. Most woodworkers have experienced this frustration and may have also noticed that instead of shavings, the result is more like dust. A well-tuned and sharpened wooden plane will slice beautiful end-grain shavings (5–37), allowing the ends of boards to be squared and trimmed with little difficulty.

Continue on with the practice board. Check the end of the board for square in both directions (from a face and a side). Even if the board reads true, doubtless there are saw marks and an out-of-focus or blurry look to the grain. Planing the end grain gives it sharp clarity, but the surface will remain a little fuzzy. A few swipes with 400-grit sandpaper, backed by a sanding block, knocks off the fuzz, leaving a perfectly smooth surface.

Avoiding Split-Out at the Completion of an End-Grain Cut

There are several approaches to avoiding splintering at the end of a stroke. If the end of the board is simply being cleaned up and accuracy is not a major concern, one way is to entirely avoid planing off the end of the board. Plane to the middle of the board and stop. Pick up the plane, turn it end for end, and plane into the center from the other end with a pulling stroke toward your body. Pulling the plane may feel awkward at first, but when the hands become accustomed to their reversed roles, it is rather more convenient than flipping the board or moving your body around to plane in from the other direction.

Another useful method, when precise squareness is a concern, is to lightly chamfer the corner of the board where the end of the stroke occurs (5–38). The chamfer can be formed with a chisel, file, or plane. In this way, the last fibers contacted by the blade are supported by other fibers nearer the edge of the board. The size of the chamfer required is directly related to the depth of cut: a small chamfer

5–38. Chamfering the corner of the board.

is good for light cuts, and a heavier cut needs a larger chamfer. A 45-degree chamfer yielding a flat about $1/16$ to $3/32$ inch wide safely allows several light passes with the plane. Each stroke of the plane reduces the size of the chamfer. Continue too long and the error is heralded by a sharp cracking sound. Rub in some glue, tape the splinter shut, and set the board aside until it is dry. The disadvantage of this method is the presence of the chamfer in the finished product and that very element of uncertainty.

After chamfering the corner, reverse the board in the vise so that the chamfer is away from you. To minimize chatter and the potential for pivoting the stock in the vise, clamp the board as low to the vise as possible without endangering your fingers while planing. Set the iron for a fine cut. You may find that the blade must protrude a bit farther than when planing side grain to produce a continuous

shaving. Also, more downward pressure is required when planing end grain; use the minimum necessary to get good results.

Plane off any saw marks and then check the end for square. Correcting an out-of-square condition perpendicular to the *face* of the board is the same as squaring the edge of a board for edge-joining: plane away the side reading high, taking progressively wider, partial-width, full-length shavings. Correcting an out-of-square condition perpendicular to the *sides* of the board is handled by taking progressively longer full-width shavings, starting from the end that is high. Humps or dips in the center are removed, as you are now accustomed to, by simply planing away the high spots and avoiding the low spots.

Correct each of these faults, one at a time, rather than trying to figure out the stroke that will redress all at once. Always end up with one full-length, full-width, continuous shaving. Keep an eye on the chamfer and restore it whenever it gets too small.

Another method of planing end grain employs an aid called a "shooting board," a simple device, yet truly wonderful in its many uses. Shooting boards, along with a variety of specialized aids and techniques, are covered in Chapter 6.

PROFILING

Hand planes can create a variety of pleasing profiles for the ends and edges of boards. Chamfers are easily accomplished in any size. Roundovers are as clean and slick as a hand-planed surface, with the lively addition of minute faceting. Done carefully, a reasonable uniformity is not difficult to achieve, but still the finished element is easily distinguished from the rigid product of a router or shaper. Break away from these basic shapes and a whole range of possibilities opens up, freeing you to explore shapes other than what come off the shelf (5–39). You may even be inspired to make a simple round-bottomed molding plane to further expand your horizons (5–40).

Finish up the practice board by planing various chamfers, roundovers, or other shapes into the edges and ends (5–41). To avoid splintering when planing profiles across end grain, hold the plane skewed and trend the direction of the stroke in the direction of the side grain while exiting the cut.

FINISHING HAND-PLANED SURFACES

Applying a finish to a hand-planed surface need not be different from applying one to a surface prepared in any other manner. Water-based finishes are easier to handle, since little if any grain-raising occurs when they are applied. Frequently, planed and burnished surfaces are so appealing "in the white" (unfinished) that the wood begs not to be

5–39. Some ideas for planed profiles. The lower two require a round-bottom molding plane or have to be carved.

5–40. Some shop-made round-bottom molding planes.

5–41. A planed chamfer and round-over in end grain.

smothered in a thick coating. Consider thin finishes, like very diluted shellac, a light application of oil, or perhaps just a coat of furniture wax that is wiped on, buffed out with a natural bristle brush (to get the wax out of the pores), and then polished with a soft cloth.

Canned shellac has a limited shelf life; it won't cure properly if used after its expiration date. Mixing your own shellac from flakes will result in a successful shellac finish (5–42). A cup or so of shellac flakes placed in a 16-ounce glass jar and dissolved in about two cups of alcohol is a good starting point for a stock solution. Denatured alcohol works fine, but I prefer grain alcohol obtained from a liquor store.

There's an appeal to working with food-grade finishing materials, but don't be tempted to imbibe. Swirl the mixture every few hours, and then leave it over-night. The shellac should be completely dissolved and ready for use in the morning.

Strain some shellac into a small-mouthed container, like a wine or beer bottle, that can be stoppered with a cork. Dilute it with an equal amount of alcohol, and then apply a little to the thumb. Rub with the index finger and blow until the alcohol flashes off, leaving the resin behind. It should feel only slightly tacky. If it's stickier than that, dilute with more alcohol and test again. Apply the finish with a cotton, lint-free cloth, like an old T-shirt. A

5–42. *The products and materials needed for a shellac finish include shellac flakes, a jar of shellac stock solution, an applicator bottle with diluted shellac, grain or denatured alcohol, and an applicator cloth.*

little pad can be made by covering up a few cotton balls with the cloth or by just folding the cloth a few times on itself. Wet the cloth and stroke the finish on, but don't attempt to rub it in. Do a few coats in quick succession, and then let it rest for a few minutes. Repeat this five or six times, giving a longer rest between each application before proceeding.

If the finishing is done well, with properly thinned shellac, there should be no need for sanding between coats. If needed, a quick buff with stearate-coated 400-grit sandpaper (sold at automotive stores) will do. Stop when a sheen starts to develop. Let the finish dry overnight and then burnish it lightly with fine shavings to bring out a very pleasing gloss.

Practicality dictates a durable film for tabletops and the like—something much tougher than shellac or oil finishes. Chances are, though, that the varnish or lacquer goes on with regret; with every layer of finish, something is diminished as contact is lost with the wood itself.

CHAPTER SIX

Planing Aids
and Special Techniques

T here are several planing aids and techniques that are invaluable. They directly enhance accuracy or simply hold the stock more conveniently or securely, which helps achieve better results. Plane users will find themselves returning to these aids and techniques again and again during their woodworking activities.

SHOOTING BOARDS

Shooting boards are used on the sides and ends of stock (6–1). They are supremely useful devices for edge-joining, squaring, precise trimming, mitering, or precisely planing any angle. At the most basic level, a shooting board merely elevates the stock so that a plane laid on its own side has free access to work the edge of the stock. An impromptu shooting board may be nothing more than the workpiece laid upon another dimensioned board, with the plane on its side running along the bench top. What is the advantage of this setup? The stock and plane maintain a precise relationship for the whole stroke, making it a simple matter to square an edge.

A more sophisticated shooting board incorporates a stop set exactly at 90 degrees to a runway for

6–1. Planing end grain with a shooting board.

the plane. This arrangement does several things: when planing the end of a board, squareness can be easily and simultaneously established referenced from the face and a side. At the same time, the stop supports the grain at the exit of the cut, allowing planing to be done straight across end grain without splintering. There are many useful versions of shooting boards. Following are three that I have found particularly invaluable.

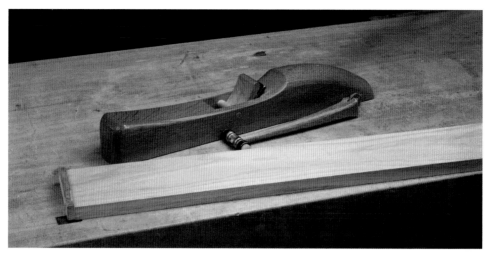

6–2. An edge-joining shooting board.

Edge-Joining Shooting Board

This shooting board (6–2 and 6–3) is used exclusively for planing side grain, and especially for preparing stock less than $^1/_2$ inch thick for edge-joining. Balancing a plane without an aid on something that thin is like walking a tightrope. The shooting board makes it easy.

Well-seasoned, well-trued solid wood makes a workable shooting board, but $^3/_4$-inch plywood is a better choice for long-term stability. Six inches is a good general-use width, but size the board to comfortably support whatever size stock you are working with. The length is determined by the scale of

work done: it should be as long as the longest joints that are typically worked. Screw a stop across the width of the board at one end, protruding above the surface $^1/_2$ inch or so (refer to 6–2). The shooting board may be dogged to the workbench, or a stop can be screwed to the end of the bottom to hook on a corner of the bench.

If the bench top is not trued, the shooting board must include a runway for the plane in order to achieve consistent results. Construct the shooting board from plywood; screw a second board to the bottom of the first that's the same length, but 3 inches wider. The plane will ride on the runway that is formed (6–4).

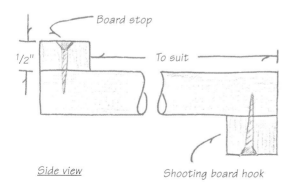

Edge-joining shooting board

1/2"

Board stop

To suit

Side view

Shooting board hook

6–3. Edge-joining shooting board.

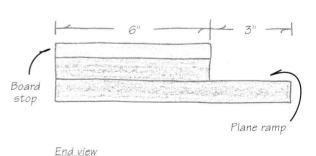

Edge-joining shooting board

6" 3"

Board stop

Plane ramp

End view

6–4. End view of the shooting board shown here with an additional board at the bottom to form a runway for the plane and with the bench stop omitted.

Adjusting the Plane and Using the Shooting Board

First set up the plane to produce a square cut. Do this with scrap stock. The face of the stock being planed must be true—if it wobbles on the shooting board the results will be inconsistent. Select the plane, applying the same considerations as for edge-joining without a shooting board. Set the plane for a very fine cut as for normal edge-joining. Orient the scrap so planing will take place with the grain and bring the end up against the stop. The edge to be planed should overhang the shooting board $^1/_4$ inch or so.

With the plane on its side, place the front portion of the bottom against the edge to be planed. The left hand presses down on the stock; this allows the stock to resist the modest sideways pressure developed by the right hand as the plane is pressed gently against the edge. Push the plane with just the right hand, placed near the center of the plane (6–5). There will be a very good view showing how the bottom of the plane registers on the edge of the stock; keep the plane flat on the stock and avoid dipping at the ends.

Take a few strokes. Adjust the iron forward or back to get the right thickness of shaving. Check the edge for square, referencing off the face that is down. It is not critical that the bottom of the plane be per-fectly square to the cheek the plane is gliding on, but the closer it is, the nearer the iron will be to a normal setting when producing a squarely jointed edge. If the reading is off, adjustment should be possible by pivoting the blade laterally in the plane, thus setting the iron for a heavier cut on the side needed. Usually, the depth of cut must also be readjusted in concert with any lateral alterations.

Once properly adjusted, the plane almost automatically gives a square cut. The objective is to plane a straight edge, and that is done in the same manner as normal edge-joining: by making progressively longer, partial-length shavings, centered initially on the high spots. It's a good practice to plane the mating piece with its opposite facedown, so that any slight deviation from square is compensated when the two parts are joined together. This works fine, with respect to planing with the grain, when the pieces are "book-matched" (that's when a thicker board is resawn in two, folded open at the edge, and the two pieces are joined, creating a symmetrical pattern at the axis of the joint). In other situations, following that dictum may force you to plane against the grain. If no tear-out occurs, proceed, but if the grain does tear, planing with the grain takes precedence.

6–5. Using an edge-joining board. The left hand holds the board down and presses it up against the stop. The right hand applies pressure to the front of the plane, keeping its bottom straight on the edge being planed at all times.

Stock Planed Simultaneously (Ganged)

For stock around $3/8$-inch thick or less, both halves of the joint can be planed simultaneously. This speeds up roughing in the joint. At the refining stage, though, approach the pieces one at a time; otherwise, the thickness of the shavings have been essentially doubled, by working both joints simultaneously, and it may be difficult to fit the joint. As above, to compensate for any deviation from square when the edges are brought together, a pair of like faces should be sandwiched together: either up-side to up-side or down-side to down-side.

Inclined Shooting Board

A potential drawback of shooting boards, most notable when planing thin stock, is that all the wear on the blade occurs at precisely the same spot. A $3/16$-inch segment of the blade may be completely dull, while the rest of the blade is razor-sharp.

Spreading the wear across the blade edge extends the time between sharpenings. This can be done by shimming the stock with a few pieces of $1/4$-inch lauan plywood sized to fit the shooting board. Either add or remove shims during the planing session to expose fresh sections of the blade. Another way is to slope the shooting board over its length with long, tapered wedges or height-graded crosswise supports at various intervals along the length. The top of the iron is exposed at the start of the stroke, and by the end of the stroke the bottom portion of the blade comes into play. This solution is optimal if the shooting board is tailored to stock of a specific length and thickness (6–6).

Inclined shooting board

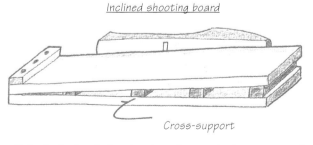

Cross-support

6–6. *An inclined shooting board spreads the wear on the cutting edge over a wider area.*

End-Grain Shooting Board

This type of shooting board (6–7) is typically made wider and shorter than the preceding one. Its main purpose is squaring the ends of stock and precisely trimming it to length. Tailor the size to specific needs. A platform about 18 inches long and 11 inches wide has served well for me. For assured accuracy, add a bottom that's 3 inches wider than the platform, to create a runway or ramp for the plane.

A sturdy stop, $1^{1}/2$ inches wide and $1^{1}/4$ inches high, is securely mounted to the platform: it must resist considerable thrust when end grain is being planed. The stop must be placed perpendicular to the side of the platform that forms the runway for the plane, while the end of the stop must be perfectly flush to that edge of the platform (6–8). These two features provide for a square cut that is unlikely to chip out wood at the end of the cut. Over time, the end of the stop tends to get worn back, allowing the corner of planed stock to develop fuzz or even splinter slightly. When this happens, it's time to replace the stop. Alternatively, a properly positioned auxiliary face for the stop can be screwed on or attached with carpet tape. Make it the same height as the original stop and about $5/8$ inch thick.

Using the Shooting Board

The plane is adjusted to give a square result on the stock end referenced off a face in the vertical axis just as with the edge-joining shooting board. This shooting board is used quite differently, though, to also produce a square end referenced from the *side* of the stock. The plane, on its side, is brought up against the edge of the platform. The stock is held against the stop with the end to be planed back slightly from the edge of the platform. Slide the plane forward until the blade is about $1/4$ inch shy of the leading corner of the end of the stock. With the plane still up against the edge of the platform and the stock still contacting the stop, slide the stock to meet the bottom of the plane (6–9).

Here is what has happened: The stock has been

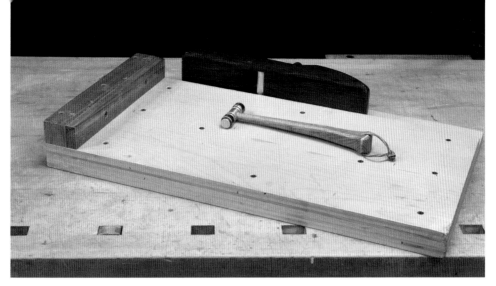

6–7. End-grain shooting board. This board, in use for some time, has had its stop faced.

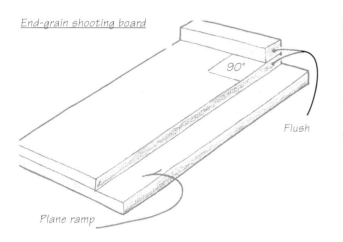

End-grain shooting board

90°

Flush

Plane ramp

6–8. An end-grain shooting board.

6–9. Using an end-grain shooting board.

positioned so that it extends beyond the edge of the platform by the amount of the thickness of the shaving the plane is set to take. Since the stop is square to the edge of the platform that the plane is riding against, the plane is poised to square the end of the stock in the horizontal axis. Press the stock against the bottom of the plane and take a shaving while keeping the plane registered on the edge of the platform. The left hand must hold the stock firmly against the stop and *must not* force the plane away from contact with the edge of the platform.

It takes a sharp iron and a fine setting to push the plane through smoothly. If the end of the stock is out of square, only one corner will contact the bottom of the plane. Usually planing is most effective if that corner is the one the blade contacts first.

Depending on the hardness and thickness of the wood, it may be necessary to take a "running start" to power the plane. The stock is positioned as described above, but then the plane is backed up a few inches before the run is started.

The plane has been set up to produce "square" referenced from the face that is down on the platform. Now check the squareness of the end referenced off the side that was against the stop. If it is off, adjustment is made by removing the stop and tapering it appropriately, or simply by shimming the face of the stop at one end or the other with some strips of masking tape. An alternative, as described above, is to mount an appropriately tapered auxiliary face to the stop.

The plane is pressed against the edge of the platform for each stroke. You may be concerned that the plane will cut into the edge of the platform and alter the square relationship between the edge of the plat- form and the stop. In fact, the cut into the platform is limited by the bottom edge of the check of the plane on the runway contacting the edge of the platform. A small ledge equal to the protrusion of the blade is cut, but no more. The square relationship is preserved.

Trimming Boards

Shooting boards excel at trimming boards to accu- rate lengths. Make the crosscuts with a hand- or power saw, leaving the stock slightly oversized; a few swipes on the shooting board trim the stock to the exact length with nicely squared-off ends. This is a tremendous help if a handsaw is being used or the power saw is not performing well. When two boards need to be exactly the same length, stack them and feel if both ends are flush. If one over- hangs, trim it to perfection on the shooting board.

Mitering Across the Width

Use a draftsman's triangle (or the combination square) to draw a 45-degree angle on the shooting board and screw down an auxiliary fence to the line, as shown in 6–10. Make a practice corner to check the setting of the fence. Shoot the miters, fit them together, and check for square. Shim an end of the fence with tape to make minor adjustments to the angle. Saw rough miters, leaving the stock over- sized, and then plane them to their precise size for delightfully tight joints.

To plane the miters at both ends, stock must be flipped end-for-end; a minor difficulty ensues when handling stock with other than parallel faces. At one end of the stock, its square edge and face ref- erence properly off the platform and fence; when the stock is flipped to plane its other end, that is no longer so. To plane the proper angle, elevate the outer edge of the stock with a pair of small wedges until the edge against the fence registers and the face that is up is leveled (6–11). Tape the wedges to the platform or mark the location of the outer edge

6–10. Shooting an across-the-width miter with a guide screwed to the platform of the end-grain shooting board.

of the stock across the wedges for quick positioning of the other pieces. A board with both miter angles built in can be constructed; this allows the stock to be properly positioned without using wedges, but in this case the *plane* must be flipped to its other cheek and, most likely, readjusted as well.

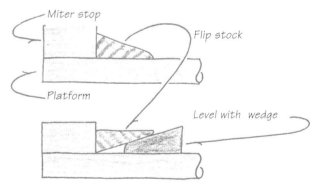

6–11. Mitering with a shooting board. If the stock is not square or rectangular in cross-section, it must be leveled with wedges when planing one of the ends.

Mitering Edge Thickness

A shooting board facilitates planing across the thickness of an edge (6–12). Clamp or screw an easily fabricated 45-degree (or whatever angle is required) ramp to the platform of an end-grain shooting board to do the job.

6–12. *A 45-degree ramp on a shooting board for mitering across the thickness.*

6–13. *Bench hook.*

Bench Hook

While the previously described shooting boards are fairly bulky, the bench hook (6–13) is a small and handy shooting board great for trimming, cleaning up, and squaring the ends of small stock, which can also be used for crosscutting. The one I've used for years is about 5 x 7 inches, with stops that are 1 x $^3/_4$ inch, and is made of red oak. Hardwood stops on a plywood base make a better arrangement. Screw one stop to each face, at opposite ends, so that the stop is set 90 degrees to the edge of the platform. The end of one stop is flush to the right-hand edge of the platform; the end of the stop on the other side is about $^1/_2$ inch shy of the same edge. The stop that is down serves as an anchor, hooking the corner of the bench, while the stop that is up captures the stock.

Use the face with the stop that is flush to the edge for planing (6–14). I use whatever plane happens to be on the bench at the time, running it directly on the bench top. The other face is for crosscutting. The end of the stop serves as a guide, helping to achieve a square cut by aligning the saw vertically and horizontally (6–15). The saw gouges the platform—instead of the bench top—as the cut is finished.

6–14. *Planing with a bench hook.*

6–15. *Sawing with a bench hook.*

PLANING THIN AND/OR SMALL STOCK

Planing stock that is thin and/or small poses a special challenge: how to secure the stock for planing? One solution is to turn the problem on its head; instead of securing the stock, secure the plane and drag the stock over the blade. This method was suggested for shaping the cross-pin of the plane, as described in Locating the Cross-Pin on pages 87 to 89. Two other approaches involve using a planing hook or a friction board. Each is described below.

Planing Hook

Using a planing hook as described in Chapter 5, but sized to the specific task and with the stop protruding only 1/8 inch above the surface (6–16), works well for thin stock until the stock becomes thinner than the stop, or the strength of the stock is overcome by the force of planing, causing the stock to deflect and hop over the stop. If many small parts of the same size will be planed, ganging them together on a planing hook and working them simultaneously will help maintain uniformity.

6–16. Planing hook.

Friction Board

A friction board (6–17), which handles the deflection problem noted above, is nothing more than a flat surface covered with sandpaper (100- to 150-grit). It can be dogged to the bench or fitted with a stop on the bottom to hook a corner of the bench. The sandpaper grabs the stock, preventing it from sliding during planing. To help secure the stock to the board, use a bit more downward force on the plane than is typically required. Take light passes only or the force required to push the plane will overcome the friction between the sandpaper and stock, causing a slip. Also take care not to tip the plane at the start and finish of the stroke, or the bottom of the plane may be inadvertently sanded.

6–17. A friction board is useful for planing very thin stock.

PLANING EDGES OF LARGE BOARDS AND SURFACES

Planing large pieces, like planing small ones, primarily presents a clamping problem. One technique is to simulate a shooting board. Lay a piece of flat sheet stock that is 1/2 to 3/4 inch thick on the bench top. Lay the stock on top. Clamp the two pieces to the bench and work the edge with the plane on its side running on the bench top. This approach is particularly useful on curved edges.

Two aids useful when planing large pieces are planing trees and bench "pups." Each is discussed below.

6–18. Planing tree.

Planing Tree

A planing tree, used in conjunction with a face vise (6–18 and 6–19), is helpful for working the edge of large stock. The vise grips one end of the stock, and the planing tree supports the other end. For height adjustability, drill a series of holes at a slight angle in a 2 x 2-inch board, to accept a $1/2$-inch dowel. The angled holes prevent the stock from slipping off the dowel.

6–19. Planing tree with a plank mounted on it.

Bench "Pups"

Bench pups (6–20) are similar to bench dogs. They require a tail vise and pinch the stock in the same way as bench dogs, except that the stock is attached to the outside of the bench top; this is a handy way of planing the edges of wide surfaces such as doors or wide panels (6–21).

6–20. Bench "pups."

6–21. Bench "pups" in use.

The dimensions of the pups are determined by the distance from the edge of the bench to the nearest edge of a dog hole: distance X as shown in 6–22.

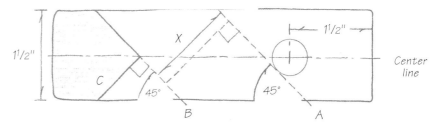

Bottom View

1¹/₂"

X

1¹/₂"

C

45°

45°

B

A

Center line

6–22. Bench-pup layout.

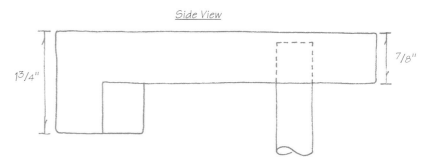

Side View

1³/₄"

7/8"

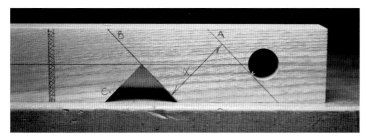

6–23. Forty-five-degree notches have been cut in the bench pups.

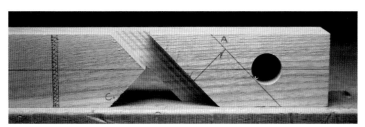

6–24. The thickness of the stem and the stop are defined.

6–25. The rest of the stem has been cut out.

Take that length, multiply it by 1.4, and add 4 inches for the overall length of the bench pup; it is 1¹/₂ inches wide and 1³/₄ inches thick.

The two pups are mirror images of each other. Lay them out nose-to-nose on the stock to help avoid errors. Draw a centerline down the length of the stock. Measure in 1¹/₂ inches and mark the center for a hole that will accept a dowel that will fit in the dog hole (it should be at least ³/₄ inch in diameter). Drill the hole, stopping ¹/₈ inch shy of the opposite face. Use a combination square to draw a 45-degree line that is tangential to the hole. This is shown as A in 6–22. Draw line B, which is the distance X measured perpendicular to line A. Then draw line C.

Next, cut out the triangle formed by lines B and C on the table saw (6–23). Set the saw to cut half the thickness of the stock. Cut a series of 45-degree saw kerfs to define the position of the stop, which is the remains of line B (6–24). Remove the rest of the material with a stopped cut on the band saw to define the stem (6–25). Crosscut the bench pups to length 1³/₄ inches from the intersection of lines B and C. Glue in the dowel. Face the clamping surfaces with ¹/₈-inch cork or dense rubber.

FITTING CARCASS COMPONENTS PRECISELY

Precise fits are one of the hallmarks of fine crafts-manship, and planes are truly the tool of choice when it comes time to fit one part of a cabinet or box to another, be it a lid, drawer, back panel, or door. Doors can be worked to such close tolerances with planes that they close on a cushion of air and open against a perceptible vacuum; likewise, draw-ers can be worked that glide effortlessly yet betray no sideways rattle. Careful measure-ment is paramount, and there is no bet-ter way than with measuring sticks.

Measuring Sticks

A measuring stick is a ruler custom-made for a particular task. The most accurate and reliable form is a stick cut to the desired length and fitted where the actual piece will go. There are no marks and it is difficult to misread the information it carries. The chance for error has been reduced to almost nil. Saw the stick slightly oversize; then use the bench hook and plane to size the stick for an exact fit. Use the stick to transfer the dimension to the stock or a saw. This is a fine method for fitting panels within frames.

The frame is dry-assembled with its rabbets already cut. Separate sticks should be fitted for length and width (6–26). Use the sticks to set up the saw for sizing the panels. Stockpile offcuts for measuring sticks-to-be. Thin offcuts in the neigh-borhood of ¹/₈ inch thick by about ⁵/₈ inch wide are good for easy trimming.

Alternatively, a measuring stick can be marked with a sharp knife and labeled for various dimen-sions right off the work in progress. Knifing a mark is always preferable to penciling one in when trim-ming to size with a plane; the precision of knifing is perfectly compatible with the accuracy of planing.

There are always decisions to be reached with a pencil line: should trimming be done to the left of it, or to the right, or should the line be split in half? With a knifed line, this isn't a concern. This type of measuring stick carries a slightly greater chance for error, though, than with the former, since the markings must be transposed and the correct one selected when parts are being dimensioned. Still, measurement errors are even likelier using rulers, with their myriad markings that are rarely exactly where they are needed.

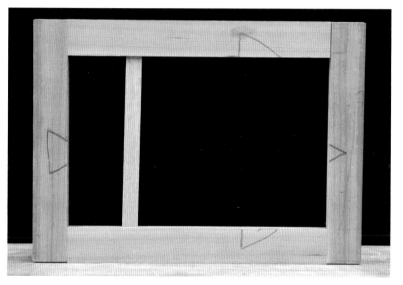

6–26. Measuring stick fitted in a frame width.

Fitting Doors and Lids to Their Cases

More often than not, doors and lids require some fitting to mesh properly with their cases (6–27). When a door or lid is overlaid, it is best to alter the cabinet or box for a perfect fit. Then you proceed to alter the door. Glue up and complete the door. Dry-clamp the case. Check the two for relative wind by tapping opposite corners of the door in the same way that a surface is checked for wind against the bench top (see Chapter 5).

When the high corners of the cabinets have been established, the planing approach must be deter-mined. If the door is fully overlaid, plane the high corners of the case with it dry-assembled. The

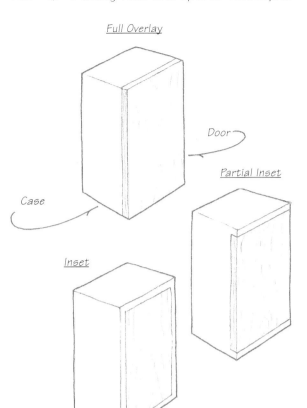

Full Overlay

Door

Partial Inset

Case

Inset

6–27. Three basic relationships of doors to cases: overlaid, partial inset, and inset.

plane is steered right around the corner like a train on its track. Start with a short stroke centered over the corner and progressively lengthen the strokes until they reach from low corner to low corner. Check the door against the case and continue with this adjustment until the door and case are mated.

If the door is partially inset (refer to 6–27), disassemble the case after determining the high spots that the door rests on. Plane the high spots down with successively longer strokes, starting from the high end. Count and use the same amount of strokes at both sides to keep the case dimensions as even as possible. Reassemble the case and try the door again. This method presupposes that the sides of the case are made slightly wide to accommodate such a fitting: $1/16$ to $3/32$ inch should be plenty.

If the door is fully inset (refer to 6–27), trim the edges of the door so that it fits the opening of the

dry-assembled case a bit snug. With the door in place, check that the case edges are flush with the face of the door. Plane the edges of the case sides as necessary.

Eliminating Wobble in Boxes and Drawers

It is not uncommon for a box or drawer to come together with a bit of a wind to it; it will have an annoying little wobble when it is sitting on a table or in a drawer pocket. A plane will quickly take care of that. With the box assembled, identify the high corners in the accustomed fashion by poking pairs of diagonally opposite corners and seeing which produces a wobble. The stable pair of corners are the high ones. Turn the box over and take partial shavings centered over these corners, extending each stroke until they reach from low corner to low corner. The plane is balanced on the edge and turns the corners in a continuous sweep, but be careful: If it "falls off," a serious ding may occur. Continue until the wobble is removed.

Fitting Dovetailed Drawers With a Drawer Board

Nicely fitting a dovetailed drawer is a challenge requiring control and discipline. To achieve a piston-like fit, make the drawers about $1/32$-inch oversized in width and then plane them to fit. To plane the sides of a drawer without racking the joints, a drawer board is needed (6–28). A piece of $3/4$-inch plywood that's about 3 feet long and 7 inches wide accommodates most drawers. The board holds and fully supports the drawer as it is planed; without this, the relatively slender sides, back, and front can distort under pressure, giving inconsistent results. Slots are cut into the board to fit the spacing of the front and back of the drawer when planing the sides, and the spacing of the sides when planing the front or back. After making slots for several sizes of drawer, it seems like the existing slots cover just about any size box that may come up.

The drawer board is clamped or dogged to the

6–28. Drawer board.

bench top, the drawer or box is set into the slots, and planing commences. Planing "through" dovetails (the joint is visible on both pieces making up the corner) consists of planing across end grain, so it is important to keep a chamfer on the corner at the exit of the cut to avoid splinters. Cut the dovetails so that the pins protrude slightly. A few swipes with the plane, and the joint is cleaned up. Ideally, a few more swipes and the drawer fits the pockct.

PLANING CURVED EDGES

Planing a curved edge is not as difficult as it may seem. It is a bit trickier than dealing with a straight edge, though, and there is the added dimension of "fairing" the curve—creating a smooth curve that is pleasing to the eye and the touch. Below is information for planing convex and concave curves.

Convex Curves

Convex curves can be handled with a normal, flat-bottomed plane. The tighter the radius of the curve, the more difficult it becomes to produce a consistent, continuous shaving, increasing the dif-

ficulty of fairing the curve. It is important to learn to feel the balance of the plane so that the arc of the curve is contacting the bottom of the plane right at the throat opening (6–29). It is very helpful to lay the stock and plane sideways on the workbench, elevating the stock as with a shooting board. This way that critical point of contact can be seen and felt. Take frequent breaks and sight the curve, bringing it right up to the eyes and looking down the length to spot any bumps or dips. Also lightly caress the length of the curve with the fingertips. Keep your eyes closed and feel for any irregularities that need attention. While planing, pay attention to grain direction; frequently the

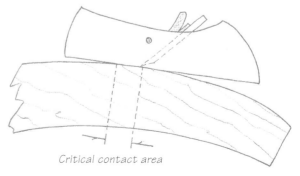

Critical contact area

6–29. Planing a convex curve.

curve must be approached from both directions to avoid planing against the grain on some portion of the curve.

Concave Curves

There is one major difference in handling concave curves: a rocker-bottom plane (6–30) must be used. This plane, which is convex in length, is only slightly more complicated to make than a flat-bottom plane. If the radius of the rocker-bottom plane is smaller than the curve being planed, the same technique used to plane convex curves will make shavings on concave curves. The only requirement is that the front and back end of the plane be out of contact with the stock, or the blade will be lifted off (6–31).

Rocker-Bottom Plane

To make the plane, first construct a typical flat-bottomed plane, but do not open the throat. Lay out a slightly smaller radius on the bottom of the plane than the one that is to be worked. Draw the radius so that no material will be removed from an area about $1/2$ inch in front of the throat opening. If it is a slight curve, use a stationary belt or disc sander for the shaping; otherwise, cut the curve on a band saw and follow with the sander to smooth it out. Avoid power-sanding the area of the throat opening. Once the curve has been nearly formed, refine

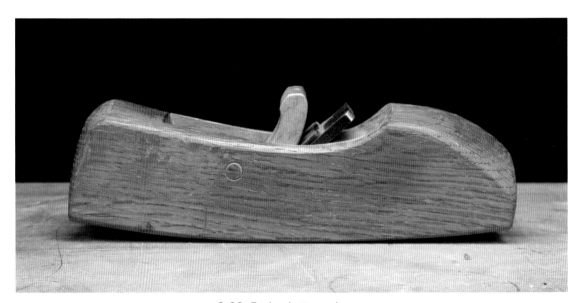

6–30. Rocker-bottom plane.

Critical contact area

6–31. Planing a concave curve.

it by hand-sanding on a belt of 100- to 150-grit paper clamped to a flat surface. Sand in a gentle rocking motion, feathering the curve through the area of the throat opening. When the curve looks and feels right, open the throat by filing in the usual manner.

Pattern-Routing Curves

In some instances, a useful approach to forming a curve involves first shaping it in a template of $1/4$-

inch lauan plywood. Shape the curve with the plane and plywood on their sides as with a shooting board. It is somewhat easier to plane thin material and, with plywood, grain direction is of little consequence, further simplifying the task.

Once the template has been shaped to your satisfaction, attach it to the stock with double-sided tape. Hammer over the tape or give it a squeeze with a clamp to get a good bond. Cut the curve on a band saw to within $1/16$ inch of the template. Rout the stock with a laminate-trimming or pattern-following bit installed in a router mounted to a router table (6–32). This method requires familiarity with a router and caution must be taken when routing against the grain. Clean up the surface with a finely set plane.

6–32. Pattern-routing a curve.

CHAPTER SEVEN

Scraping Techniques

I t is going to happen—perhaps it already has! There, on the bench, is an expanse of bubinga (or another recalcitrant wood) that is absolutely defying your best efforts with a plane. Perhaps even more heartbreaking, there is an entire tabletop of a more accommodating wood planed to shimmering perfection—with the exception of one small area of swirling grain that cannot be smoothed out. Before reaching for the power sander in resignation, consider another approach: using a scraper.

Scrapers are an effective bridge between the occasional limitations of planes and the unpleasantly dusty nature of sanding, whether working an entire surface or simply repairing a minor flaw. A properly sharpened and burnished scraper is a blessing. It makes lovely shavings, with never any tear-out, no matter the wood or the nature of the grain. But scraping does not not entirely substitute for planing; even a well-scraped surface has some fuzz and requires a light sanding to become properly smoothed. But scraping before sanding avoids the progressive march through a variety of sandpaper grits and much of the sawdust that accompanies the process. Preparing a scraper is not difficult, yet a hasty job may result in a weak and marred edge that won't make shavings for long and can leave a surface so scratched that a substantial amount of sanding is still needed.

Scrapers have evolved into several forms (more numerous than mentioned here) that are well adapted to meet the typical challenges of woodworking (7–1). A basic cabinet scraper is ideal for spot repairs and curved surfaces. Add a platform, a pair of handles, and a clamp to hold the scraper and the result is a No. 80 pattern scraper, which is great for working aggressively or prepping small surfaces. Installing a scraper in a long body produces a scraper plane for working larger surfaces.

BASIC CABINET SCRAPER

The apparent simplicity of the basic cabinet scraper, a simple rectangle of steel, belies its important variations and the splendidly unique character of the cutting edge, both in its final form and the process of getting there (7–2). Scrapers come in many thicknesses, and the quality of the steel may vary greatly from one supplier to another. A medium-thickness scraper (about .030 inch) is generally the one of choice for all-purpose stock removal; this is a tool that will be reached for again and again to spot-repair flaws. Thicker scrapers flex little in use and lend themselves well to leveling bumps (perhaps from a filled repair) or removing dried glue, where the extra mass is of benefit, too.

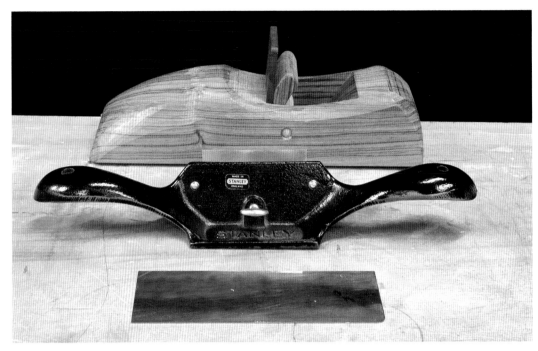

7–1. Basic cabinet scraper (bottom), No. 80 cabinet scraper (middle), and scraper plane (top).

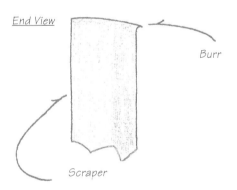

7–2. Enlarged shape of a burr on a scraper.

Thinner scrapers take very fine shavings, which is good for finessing delicate details. The hardness of the steel and related qualities such as edge retention and ductility influence the ease with which the "burr"—the cutting edge of the scraper—is sharpened and formed, and how long it holds up to use.

Preparing the Scraper

A rectangular scraper has eight potential cutting edges—two for each side—though generally only the two longest sides are prepped for a total of four cutting edges. Just as the cutting edge of a plane iron is formed at the intersection of two surfaces—the beveled side and the back—the cutting edge of a scraper is formed by the intersection of the face and the narrow edge where they meet at a 90-degree corner, the "arris" (7–3). And just as with a plane iron, both surfaces of the scraper must be polished, as the coarsest surface will determine the amount of nicks in the cutting edge and its ultimate sharpness.

Polishing the Faces

The faces of the scrape are analogous to the back-side of a plane iron. The first step is to polish the faces of the scraper. The area of critical concern is right along the cutting edge, to within about $1/2$ inch from each end. Face a flat block of wood that's the same length as the scraper and $1^1/2$ inches wide with $1/16$-inch-thick rubber or cork. This is used to help grip the scraper and apply uniform pressure while polishing the face (7–4). The block may be omitted and the fingers and thumb simply spread along the scraper, but, except for the thickest scrap-

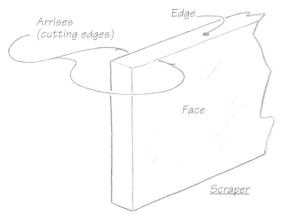

7–3. The cutting edges of a scraper are formed at the "arrises," the intersections of faces and edges.

7–4. Using a rubber-faced block to help polish the scraper face. The photo was staged on the workbench, for clarity. It would normally be done at the honing station.

ers, the pressure of the fingertips may be telegraphed through the steel, leaving a more polished spot beneath the location of each finger.

For a new scraper, start with an 800-grit stone to remove deeper scratches and grind marks. Rusted tools may require more aggressive measures (a lapping plate and Carborundum powder or a coarser-grit stone). Finish the polish on an 8,000-grit stone.

Repeat this procedure for the other three long arrises.

Filing the Edge

Next, the edge is filed straight and square to the face. Select an 8- to 10-inch mill bastard or smooth file for the job. The teeth must be sharp and clean to work well. Also check the file for straightness; a bowed file will shape a corresponding bow or dip into the edge of the scraper.

Check the scraper against a straightedge to gauge its initial condition. If it is grossly curved or lumpy, a stationary belt or disc sander will quickly true it. Lay the scraper flat on the machine table and push it gently against the abrasive.

Place the scraper in a metal-working vise stationed at an area other than the woodworking bench. Metal filings have a way of contaminating wooden projects despite meticulous sweep-up efforts. The scraper should be as low as possible in the vise to minimize vibration, but high enough to keep knuckles out of harm's way.

Joint the edge straight with unidirectional strokes of the file; the tang is at the rear relative to the direction of travel. Try to maintain the face of the file at 90 degrees to the face of the scraper (7–5). Clean the file teeth regularly with a file card. With

7–5. Jointing a scraper with a file.

properly positioned lighting, the progress of the filing can be followed by noting the subtle change of color at the points of contact.

When the edge has been straightened, switch to "draw-filing." The file is held crossways to the edge with the tang in the left hand and the tip in the right. Stand with an end of the scraper pointed toward your belly, lay the file on the scraper at the farthest corner, and draw the file toward you all the way to the nearest corner (7–6).

7–6. Draw-filing the scraper.

Draw-filing gives a nice, smooth stroke, and, importantly, with the length of the file crossways to the length of the scraper it is easy to eyeball a 90-degree relationship between the two. Four or five strokes should be sufficient to establish a crisp, square edge. Look closely at the filing job. The edge should be free of deep scratches or chatter marks.

Honing the Edge

The water stones must be flat or the scrapers will sharpen only in the center or at the ends. To prevent wearing a furrow in the stone, the scraper is held skewed, but the strokes are made parallel to the length of the stone (7–7). Start on the 800-grit stone. Strive to hold the scraper faces perpendicular to the stone. Concentrate short back-and-forth strokes at the ends of the stone, skipping quickly

over the middle. Hone briefly (say five seconds worth), and then reverse the angle of the skew and hone for another brief spell.

Now flip the scraper end for end (still honing the same edge) and repeat the routine. Flipping the scraper should counteract any tendency there may be to lean it one way or the other and ensure that both arrises have been honed. Scrutinize the edge to see that it has acquired the dull gray sheen associated with the scratch pattern of the 800-grit stone. There should be no evidence of filing marks. Do not be overly critical of the very ends, because the scraping cuts are kept toward the center of the blade. Repeat the process if need be.

Move to the 8,000-grit stone and hone the edge again, but this time spend about ten seconds or so in each position before changing the skew or reversing the scraper. The edge should be polished to a mirror shine. It is important to keep the honed edge

7–7. Honing the scraper. The photo was staged on the workbench, for clarity.

7–8. Burnisher, oil applicator, storage bottle, jasmine oil, and a scraper.

square to the face of the scraper. If you wobble around too much while honing, or extend the honing session for too long (around one minute total should do it), the edge starts to become round, losing the crisp arrises that will become the cutting edge.

Remove any burr that may still remain from the filing by lapping the face of the scraper on the 8,000-grit stone; use your fingers or the rubber-faced block to spread pressure. Overlap the stone about halfway to avoid wobbling, and even out stone wear. Check the sharpened corners by dragging your thumbnail over them, feeling for the presence of nicks or a remnant burr. One more brief period honing the edge and face with the 8,000-grit stone should clear up any remaining flaws.

The Burnisher

The burnisher is rubbed against the edge to create the burr. Burnishers come in a variety of shapes and styles, any of which may perform quite well. They must be highly polished or they will create defects in the cutting edge. My preference is a $3/8$-inch-diameter hardened rod set in a handle (7–8), for the main reason that a rod is easy to polish by chucking it in a drill press and spinning it at high speed.

Start with 400-grit wet-or-dry sandpaper lubricated with oil, and then progress to 600-grit. Follow with buffing compound loaded on a cloth and held to the spinning rod, to produce a good sheen. Polish as much of the rod as possible. For burnishers with other shapes, buffing wheels are a big help; otherwise, it's hand-sanding and buffing to achieve a polish.

Oil Applicator

Light machine oil or Japanese jasmine oil (which smells better than machine oil) aid in the burnishing. Make an applicator by tearing $2^{1}/_{2}$-inch-wide strips of old cotton sheet. Roll them tightly to about a $1^{3}/_{4}$-inch diameter. Cover them with a square of the same cloth and then wrap that with cotton string (refer to 7–8). A very sharp one-inch chisel will trim the "open" end nicely. Saturate the open end with a teaspoon or so of oil. Store the applicator in a lidded jar. Prior to burnishing, rub the applicator over the burnisher and the edge of the scraper to deposit a very light film of oil.

Forming a Burr

There seems to be a general belief that burnishing a burr takes a lot of force. That is not true; but the amount of effort is certainly directly related to the contact area between the burnisher and the edge. For the same amount of effort, a rod with sharp corners, such as one that is triangular in cross-section, develops higher PSI than a rod that is round or oval in cross-section. In fact, a triangular cross-section burnisher requires a most delicate touch or the burr becomes overly large and misshapen. Round or oval cross-section burnishers are less finicky to use.

While filing and honing, you have been preparing both arrises of an edge at the same time. Now one will be worked on at a time, while forming a burr. The purpose of burnishing is to draw the sharpened edge out into a thin hook shape ("burr"), capable of making shavings. As stated above, this does not require brute force. Using moderate pressure and designing all motions to move the steel in the right direction does the job quickly and consistently, while producing a durable, flawless burr.

Hold the scraper in the left hand and the burnisher in the right (7–9). Place the burnisher on the scraper at the end nearest to you, with the scraper near to the handle. Viewed end on, the burnisher is held at 90 degrees to the scraper face, flat on the filed and honed edge (7–10). From the top view, the burnisher makes an angle of about 120 degrees with the scraper.

Using only as much force as can be comfortably controlled, make two strokes the length of the scraper. Maintain both angles while pulling the handle of the burnisher away from the face of the scraper (7–11). The burr will develop on the side of the scraper that the handle of the burnisher overhangs, simply because the weight of the hand and any tendency to angle downward will favor that side. Sliding the burnisher out toward this side during the stroke also helps to draw out the burr. Obtusely angling the burnisher not only favors drawing out the burr, but also helps keep the burr from forming ripples.

7–9. Holding the scraper and burnisher.

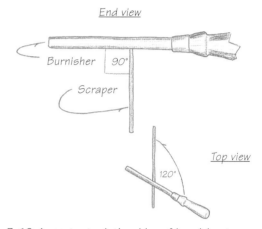

7–10. Important relationships of burnisher to scraper when forming a burr.

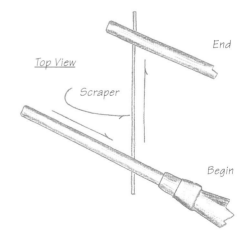

7–11. The motion of the burnisher.

Come back toward your body with two strokes in the opposite direction, applying all the same criteria. Repeat the cycle. Check for the presence of a burr by trying to hook it with your fingernail. Keep at it, one or two strokes at a time, going from opposite directions until the burr can just barely be detected. It may be surprising to learn that the merest burr is best of all; it will make beautiful shavings and be most durable. How long it takes to form depends on your strength, technique, and the particular scraper.

Using the Scraper

Even with a properly sharpened scraper, it may take a bit of trying before the first tissuey shavings come rolling off the burr. There is a bit of a knack, or a feel, for just the right angle to hold the scraper at, as well as the amount of arc to bend it to, but that comes fast. Clamp a piece of hardwood to the bench—scrapers perform best on hardwoods. If the stock is short enough, clamp it across the width of the bench, allowing for the most balanced stance and attack. Grip the scraper as illustrated in 7–12 and 7–13. The burr in use is on the opposite face from the thumbs. The middle and ring fingers act against the thumbs to tension the scraper, flexing it into a slight arc: perhaps 1/8 inch over 6 inches of length.

Grip and flex the scraper. To prevent chatter, keep your thumbs very low, so that they graze the surface of the wood. Start with the face of the scraper at 90 degrees to the wood surface. Give it a push and the scraper can be felt sliding right over the surface without biting. Start another stroke. While pushing, tilt the top edge away from you until the scraper is at about 45 degrees. There should be steadily increasing resistance as the burr starts biting into the wood more and more before the cut begins to fall off again. Maintain the angle corresponding to the point of greatest resistance, usually somewhere near 50 to 60 degrees. Also try experimenting with the amount of flex while scraping, searching for that point of most resistance. Scrapers

7–12. Scraping up shavings.

7–13. Back view of a scraper grip.

are mainly used with this push stroke, though on occasion pull strokes are used, and sometimes even one-handed strokes going in either direction.

You will have noticed the scraper heating up in the process. There is a real danger of burning or blistering thumbs if scraping is too aggressive. Some people will wrap their thumbs with tape to protect them. I like to work steadily at a rate that won't produce a blistering amount of heat.

There are several other important things to know about scraping. Always scrape with the grain. Skewing across the grain can roll wood fibers out of the surface, leaving a fairly deep flaw. On the other hand, though the motion of travel is always parallel to the grain, the scraper itself should be held skewed at about a 50- to 60-degree angle to the grain, alternating the angle with subsequent passes (7–14).

7–14. The scraper should be skewed to the grain direction.

Think of the scraper, for a moment, in similar terms as a plane. Held 90 degrees to the grain, a scraper behaves like a plane only as long as its thickness: about $1/16$ inch! The end result of scraping in this manner is a surface full of ripples. Unfortunately, the rippling is hard to detect until the surface is finished and has a sheen. Skewing elongates the effective length of the scraper to

around 3 inches or so. This is a dramatic improvement over $1/16$ inch, but still hardly a match for a jack plane, let alone a jointer. This emphasizes the fact that the basic cabinet scraper is not the ideal tool for truing a large surface but more of a spot finishing tool.

To scrape out a flaw, be sure to work a larger area; if not, the surface will be noticeably dished. Say there is a spot the size of a quarter that needs attention. Center two strokes three to four inches long over the defect, and then two more with the opposite skew. Now move a few inches off to the left, taking six- to- eight-inch-long strokes—going over the flawed area again—and then scrape a few inches to the right of the flaw. Repeat with the opposite skew. If the flaw still remains, lengthen the strokes and widen the scraped area once again before attacking it with short, centered strokes again. With this strategy, any dishing is so gradual that it goes unnoticed by eye or touch.

Take special care at the margins of the stock. When working near the sides, let only a small portion of the scraper overhang the edge (7–15). Keep your pressure with the outer hand very light and sensitive. The inner hand keeps the scraper firmly anchored to the surface of the wood. If caution is not observed, the scraper may damage the surface near the margin, raising the grain. Similar caution is needed at the ends of a board. For the far end, stop the motion of the scraper with only a small portion of it overhanging the edge (7–16). The best approach for the near end of the board is to make it the far end by rotating the board, and then use the same method.

After a period of use, the burr makes fewer shavings and more dust. The edge may still be quite sharp—it has just lost its shape. Reform the burr by first drawing it up parallel to the face of the scraper (7–17). Oil the face of the scraper at the burr, and then oil the edge and the burnisher. Lay the scraper on the bench, the burr to be worked facing up, parallel to the length of the bench and at the edge. Lay the burnisher flat on the face, angled as shown in 7–18. Draw the burnisher firmly along the face

7–15. Scraping near the sides of the board.

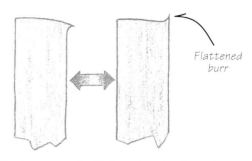

Flattened
burr

7–17. The burr may be flattened and reformed several times.

7–16. Scraping the far end of the board.

7–18. Reforming the burr.

while pulling the handle away from the burr. By the end of the stroke, about one inch of the burnisher should still be flat on the scraper. Come back from the opposite direction. One or two strokes should remove all evidence of the burr. Check that it is gone with a fingernail, as in the burr-forming process. Next, reform the burr, but now, since the burr is already present, one or two light strokes are all that is necessary to again discern the burr with a fingernail.

Reform the burr each time the scraper's capacity to make shavings is diminished—with luck, that may be five or six times. If the burr has been made too large to start with, it will be fragile and begin fragmenting with the first reforming. Return to the filing and honing process when the reformed burr

no longer makes shavings or the scraped surface shows excessive scratching.

SMOOTHING SURFACES WITH THE NO. 80 PATTERN SCRAPER

The No. 80 pattern scraper works well for smoothing small- to medium- sized surfaces, up to about 2 x 3 feet. Initial truing, if needed, should first be done with a plane, skewing the strokes to the grain direction to minimize tear-out. The addition of handles protects thumbs from heat buildup and decreases hand fatigue, so this tool is suitable for aggressive or extended periods of scraping. The small platform helps control rippling, though the

No. 80 should be skewed to the grain in the same manner as the basic cabinet scraper. In fact, nearly all the caveats with respect to using the basic scraper apply to the No. 80 as well. There is one exception: Since a No. 80 scraper is rather narrow, to prevent damage at the end of a board finish the pass with a deliberate rising motion, rather than stopping the tool while still in contact with the stock.

Preparing the Scraper Blade

Preparing the scraper blade for the No. 80 pattern scraper is best done identically to the preparation for the basic cabinet scraper. This advice is at odds with the traditional approach, which advocates creating a 35- to 45-degree bevel, limiting the scraper to one burr per side (7–19). After following tradition for many years, but failing to come up with a convincing rationale for it, I experimented by using a 90-degree flat. I found no difference in performance. The benefits are clear, though: two burrs per edge are formed, decreasing overall time spent filing and honing. It is also easier to file and hone a 90-degree edge than a 45-degree one.

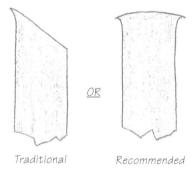

OR

Traditional   *Recommended*

7–19. A traditional 35-degree burr on a No. 80 scraper as compared to the recommended 90-degree burr.

Setting Up the No. 80 Scraper

For smoother operation, first flatten and polish the bottom of the scraper as was done to a block plane. To set the scraper blade, first loosen the two blade-holding screws. Next, back off the thumbscrew so

7–20. The blade and the body of the No. 80 scraper are both held down on a flat surface while the clamp screws are gradually tightened.

that it is not in contact when the blade is clamped in the body. Set the tool on a flat surface and insert the prepared blade. Hold both down firmly with one hand and alternately tighten the clamping screws a little at a time to prevent the blade from skewing (7–20). Clamp the blade firmly.

Now grasp the scraper as shown in 7–21, keeping the thumbs down at the bottom, again to minimize chatter. Take a slow trial stroke on a piece of practice stock while looking down the throat to see what

7–21. Holding the No. 80 pattern scraper.

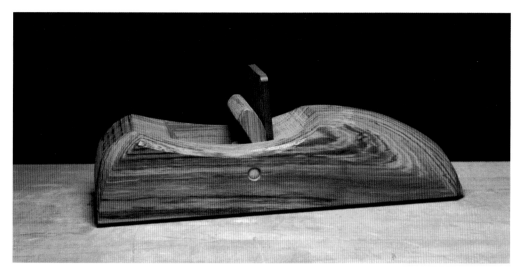

7–22. Scraper plane.

portion of the blade is peeling off a shaving. If it's all across the blade or primarily in the center, the scraper is ready to be used, but if one of the corners is digging, go back to the clamping stage and readjust the elevation of the blade. To do this, loosen the clamping screws, and this time, while tightening them, apply a little more downward pressure to the opposite side of the blade that was digging. Tighten the screws and test the blade again. Once the blade is set parallel to the bottom, apply a small amount of tension to the center of the blade with the thumbscrew—just enough so that the corners do not dig into the board while scraping occurs. When dust starts to replace shavings, the life of the burr can be extended by arcing the blade a bit more with the thumbscrew, but don't overdo it or the surface will become noticeably scalloped. The burr can also be reformed as above.

THE SCRAPER PLANE

Even large tabletops can be handled successfully with the No. 80 scraper, but the tool becomes awkward to use and is prone to rippling the surface. A better choice is the scraper plane (7–22). The same size as a jack or smoothing plane, the scraper plane leaves a smooth and flawless surface, and is as com-

fortable to use as any other plane. Fitted with a high-quality plane iron—a good burr *can* be turned on a plane iron—the scraper plane will work a lengthy session before exhausting the burr's sharpness.

Making the Plane

The procedure is almost identical to making a conventional plane, with four alterations (7–23):

1. The back ramp upon which the blade rests is cut at 95 degrees.

2. The throat opening is expanded to $^5/_8$ inch to

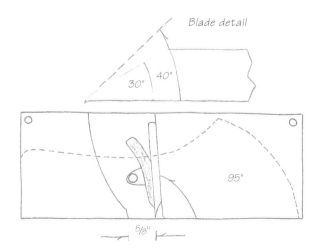

7–23. The plan for a scraper plane.

prevent the tissuey shavings from clogging there. A narrow throat opening is of no consequence for scraper cutting action.

3. There is no chip breaker to account for when placing the cross-pin location.

4. The front ramp is curved or angled sufficiently to provide adequate clearance in front of the cross-pin for clearing out jammed shavings.

Setting Up and Using the Plane

A two-inch-wide blade is a good choice. The primary bevel is ground conventionally at 30 degrees. A secondary bevel is also ground, regardless of the thickness of the iron, at 40 degrees, to give the burr added durability. To prevent corner digs, the cutting edge must be slightly arced, as there is no way to flex the blade into an arc. Work the burnisher on the secondary bevel to form the burr on the back of the iron. Be patient: it will take more strokes to coax the metal over, because it is harder than a normal scraper blade. If too much pressure is being exerted, the edge may be chipped.

Set the plane on a flat surface, insert the iron so that the beveled side of the blade is down on the ramp, and insert the wedge finger-tight. Tap the wedge snug and try a shaving. Adjust the blade so that the shaving comes from the center of the blade. To back the blade up, tap the top and front of the plane body. There is no need to skew the plane as with the basic cabinet scraper or the No. 80 pattern scraper. The length of the plane prevents the surface from becoming rippled.

SANDING AFTER SCRAPING

Sanding should be approached in the same systematic and meticulous manner as planing or scraping. For flat surfaces, use sanding blocks. Purchased sanding blocks are fine. Sanding blocks can also be made faced with $1/8$-inch cork or rubber, or even $1/4$-inch felt, if one with more "give" is needed (7–24). Lubricated (stearate) sandpaper resists clogging and works very well on wood. Only the 280- and 400-grit types are needed. Open-pored or coarse-grained woods such as oak, ash, and hickory should be sanded with 280-grit sandpaper. This is the extent of sanding required on a well-scraped surface. Progressing to finer grits does not yield a discernible difference since the coarseness of the grain tends to mask any improvement made. Fine-grained woods such as fruitwoods or maple should be sanded up to 400-grit.

Depending on the species and the quality of the scraping job, sanding may consist of using just 400-

7–24. A variety of sanding blocks.

grit sandpaper. Experience and a close eye on the work will be the guide to the most efficient path.

When sanding, avoid scrubbing at the work as though it were a dirty floor. Start at one side, if a wide piece is being sanded. Go down and back the length of the stock, with the grain. Move over a little less than the width of the sanding block and repeat, working your way across the stock. Vacuum the surface and wipe it down with a well-wrung towel or raggy T-shirt to remove most of the fine dust and slightly raise the grain. If a vacuum is not available, just use the dampened cloth to capture most of the dust—shake it out, outside the workshop, when it becomes loaded.

If an open-pored or coarse-grained wood is being sanded, brush the surface, with the grain, using a natural-bristle scrub brush, to clean out the pores while vacuuming. Search the surface with your fingertips, feeling for any rough spots, and sand them out as discovered, being careful not to create dips. Uniformly sand the entire surface once more and finish by vacuuming it, wiping it down with a damp cloth, and bristle-brushing. The result is a very smooth and flat, uniformly sanded surface, free of errant sanding scratches and ready for finishing.

If only a little spot-scraping was done on an otherwise nicely planed surface, it is unfortunate, but the entire surface must be sanded or the repaired flaw will most likely stand in contrast to the planed portion when a finish is applied. First sand the scraped area smooth, being careful not to dish it out overly, and then sand the entire surface one time thoroughly, as described above.

EPILOGUE

As I look over this effort to breath life into what is in essence a very simple tool—the wood hand plane—I am amazed by the amount of information necessary to do it justice. One thing led to another, like going to a corner grocery for milk and coming back with five sacks of food. Perhaps in doing so, though, rather than just cereal for breakfast, there will be enough to make an elegant dinner, too.

Still, minutely dissecting a subject renders it dry and spiritless: the curse of the how-to-do-it book. The feast is on the table, but how to eat it? If you wish to explore the why as well as the how, I can think of no better places to look than *A Cabinetmaker's Notebook* and *The Fine Art of Cabinetmaking*, both by James Krenov.

METRIC EQUIVALENTS CHART
Inches to Millimeters and Centimeters

MM=MILLIMETERS   CM=CENTIMETERS

INCHES	MM	CM	INCHES	CM	INCHES	CM
1/8	3	0.3	9	22.9	30	76.2
1/4	6	0.6	10	25.4	31	78.7
3/8	10	1.0	11	27.9	32	81.3
1/2	13	1.3	12	30.5	33	83.8
5/8	16	1.6	13	33.0	34	86.4
3/4	19	1.9	14	35.6	35	88.9
7/8	22	2.2	15	38.1	36	91.4
1	25	2.5	16	40.6	37	94.0
1 1/4	32	3.2	17	43.2	38	96.5
1 1/2	38	3.8	18	45.7	39	99.1
1 3/4	44	4.4	19	48.3	48	101.6
2	51	5.1	20	50.8	41	104.1
2 1/2	64	6.4	21	53.3	42	106.7
3	76	7.6	22	55.9	43	109.2
3 1/2	89	8.9	23	58.4	44	111.8
4	102	10.2	24	61.0	45	114.3
4 1/2	114	11.4	25	63.5	46	116.8
5	127	12.7	26	66.0	47	119.4
6	152	15.2	27	68.6	48	121.9

GLOSSARY

Arris The 90-degree corner of the scraper where the face and narrow edge intersect, which forms the cutting edge.

Bench Dog A fastening device working in conjunction with the tail vise of a workbench that clamps boards to the bench top.

Bench Hook A stock-holding aid useful for trimming the ends of small stock with a plane, as well as for crosscutting.

Bench "Pup" A fastening device, similar to a bench dog, that clamps wide boards and surfaces to the front edge of the workbench for convenient edge planing.

Blade Set The side-to-side bend in the blade's teeth that allows the blade to cut a kerf larger than the blade's thickness. This gives clearance for the body of the blade, reducing binding and overheating.

Block Plane A small plane about $7^1/_2$ inches long with a $1^1/_4$ to $1^5/_8$-inch-wide blade used primarily for trimming, chamfering, and fitting small parts.

Book-Matching A technique that consists of resawing a thicker board in two, folding it open at its edge, and joining the two pieces, producing a symmetrical grain pattern.

Bullnose A blunt roundover rather than a gradually arcing one.

Burnisher A tool used to polish or form a burr edge on a scraper blade.

Burr A thin ridge of metal produced by grinding or coarse honing when sharpening an iron. Or, alternatively, the cutting edge of a scraper formed by burnishing.

Cabinetmaker's Triangle A triangle marked on an assembly to indicate all the relationships of the various parts: up, down, inside, outside, left, right, front, back, etc.

Cabinet Scraper A card-shaped piece of steel sharpened with a burnisher to create a burr that can cut shavings from wood, especially for irregular grain.

Cap Iron (also referred to as chip breaker) A part of the blade assembly of the plane that reinforces the cutting edge, thus preventing chatter and tear-out.

Cap Screw For a plane, it is the screw that holds the chip breaker to the iron. For a spokeshave, it is the larger screw on the cap iron that presses against the end of the blade, causing the cap iron to pivot on the pivot screw and press tightly against the tip of the blade.

Carcass The basic box or frame of a cabinet.

Chamfer A beveled cut made on an edge.

Chip Breaker A part of the iron assembly in a plane that is a separate piece of mild steel profiled to a knife edge and clamped to the back of the plane iron with a screw.

Combination Square A measuring tool with a removable blade that can be used to check boards for square and do a variety of other jobs.

Crosscut A cut made perpendicular to the grain fibers of the wood.

Cross-Pin The part of the plane between the cheeks that contacts the wedge and captures the plane-iron assembly against the 45-degree ramp.

Crown As refers to a band-saw tire, the convex arc across the width of the tire.

Dovetail Saw A small, fine-toothed backsaw that is generally used to cut dovetails.

Draw-Filing A method of filing that consists of pulling the file toward you while holding the tang of the file in the left hand and the tip in the right hand.

Drawing the Temper Reducing the hardness of a blade to optimize its sharpening qualities and durability.

Edge Retention The ability of a blade's cutting edge to resist dulling and chipping.

Face Vise A vise mounted to the face (or front edge) of the workbench. Also called a shoulder vise.

Fairing a Curve Creating a smooth curve that is pleasing to the eye and touch.

Flat-Sawn Wood A board, viewed end on, in which the face has been sawn approximately tangent to the growth rings.

Flattening Stick A block of wood that is used to back up a plane iron or scraper blade during the flattening process.

Heat-Treating The process of annealing, hardening, and tempering blades.

Hogging Removing stock rapidly with a plane.

Hollow Grind The arc produced across the bevel of a blade, the result of grinding on the circumference of a grinding wheel.

Jack Plane A 12-inch-long plane used to true surfaces, edge-join smaller boards, trim ends of wide boards, and smooth. It is also used with a shooting board.

Jointer A stationary power tool used to true the face and edge of a board.

Jointer Plane A 17-inch-long plane used for edge-joining longer boards and truing large surfaces.

Jointing Making an edge straight and square with the face of the board.

Kerf The width of a cut made by a saw blade.

Lapping Plate A true surface used to flatten blades.

Marking Gauge A tool consisting of a moveable knife and rod that is used to make and transfer measurements.

Measuring Stick A custom-made ruler used to make and transfer measurements on a specific project.

Miter Joint A joint cut at an angle.

Molding Planes Planes used to make decorative recesses or relieved surfaces.

Nagura A synthetic or natural stone used to clean the surface of fine-grit water stones while sharpening and to creat a slurry that speeds sharpening.

Oilstones Synthetic or natural abrasive stones that are used to hone blades. They are normally lubricated with oil or some petroleum product.

Out-of-true surfaces Surfaces that are out of square, out of flat, and/or have a wind.

Planer A power tool used to dimension lumber to thickness, producing two parallel surfaces.

Polishing (Smoothing) Plane A plane, about 9 inches long, that is used to smooth a surface to finished perfection.

Primary Angle (Macrobevel) The angle of a plane iron formed with the grinder. The primary angle of a thin ($^1/_8$ inch thick or less) iron should be 25 degrees, and for a thick (over $^1/_8$ inch thick) iron 30 degrees.

Quarter-Sawn Wood A board, viewed end on, in which the face has been sawn perpendicular to the growth rings.

Reference Surface The trued surface of a board that determines the accuracy of the milling of the other surfaces of that board.

Rift-Sawn Wood A board, viewed end on, with growth rings that are approximately 45 degrees to the face across the width of the board.

Rip Cut A cut made with the grain of the wood.

Rocker Bottom Plane A plane arced along its length that is used to smooth concave curves with the grain.

Run-Out When the wood fibers of a board intersect a particular surface of it at an angle.

Scraper Plane A plane with the ramp set at a steep angle and the blade prepared as a scraper with a burr.

Scrub Plane An $8^1/_2$-inch-long plane with a wide throat opening that is used for coarse planing.

Secondary Angle (Microbevel) An additional, steeper bevel, continuous with the cutting edge of the blade, that supports and strengthens the edge. The secondary angle of a thin iron should be 30 degrees.

Shooting Board A shop-made device that supports the stock and guides the plane for increasing the accuracy of edge-joining, squaring, trimming, and mitering.

Snipe The excessive amount of wood removed at the beginning and/or end of a cut made by a faulty or poorly set-up jointer or planer.

Sole A complete covering of durable wood for the bottom of a plane made of wood that does not wear particularly well.

Stone Cradle An aid used to firmly anchor the sharpening stones while they are being used.

Stove Bolt A bolt with a domed head.

Strop To make a keen edge by stroking away from the cutting edge of the blade or iron on leather or a composition material.

Tail Vise A vise incorporated into and moving parallel to the front edge of a workbench.

Tear-Out A condition in which the blade rips or tears out the grain of a workpiece.

Temper Reducing the hardness of tool steel. Temper is optimized at the point of greatest edge retention, producing tool steel soft enough to minimize chipping but hard enough to minimize abrasive wear.

Tensioning For a plane, adding a certain

amount of pressure to a blade to lock the blade in place.

Throat The space between the cutting edge of the blade and the front portion of the plane that defines the opening in the sole of the plane.

Through Dovetail Joint A dovetail joint in which the joint is visible on both pieces making up the corner.

Trued Surface One that is flat, square, and free of wind.

Truing Jig A device that holds a diamond dresser securely and allows for a controlled cut while truing the circumference of a grinding wheel.

Tuning Optimizing the performance of a tool.

Water Stone A natural or synthetic stone in which water is used as the sharpening lubricant honing blades. The abrasive particles of the stone slough off quickly, exposing sharp edges and resulting in speedier cutting than achieved with an oilstone.

Wedge Angle The angle continuous with the cutting edge of the blade.

INDEX